AF675234

Why Do AI Systems Hallucinate?

Sandeep Chavan

Published by Gyrus Vision, 2026.

WHY DO AI SYSTEMS HALLUCINATE?

First edition. February 17, 2026.

ISBN: 978-81-996823-0-6

Written by Sandeep Chavan.

Table of Contents

To those who question not only what systems produce, but how they stabilize.

And to every researcher willing to look beneath performance and ask what equilibrium truly means.

"Hallucination is not a bug. It is a coherence outcome."

Author's Note

This book did not begin as an attempt to fix artificial intelligence. It began as an attempt to stop misnaming the problem.

When AI systems hallucinate, the industry reacts the way it always does—more data, more parameters, more alignment layers, more rules. Each response assumes that hallucination is a *content failure* or a *training defect*. It is not. Hallucination is a coherence failure. And coherence failures cannot be patched the way software bugs are patched.

This book does not offer architectures, algorithms, benchmarks, or promises. That is intentional. Those belong to researchers, engineers, and institutions working at implementation layers. What this book offers is something upstream: a diagnostic lens.

The Chavanian Axioms are not an AI theory. They are not a learning framework. They are not a philosophy of mind. They are a set of pre-formal conditions that must hold for *any* coherent system—biological, physical, social, or artificial—to exist without collapsing into contradiction. When those conditions are violated, systems do not merely fail; they behave *convincingly wrong*. That is exactly what we call hallucination in AI.

I am not asking researchers to adopt these axioms. I am asking them to notice them.

If a system does not manage unresolved differences, residue accumulation, dissipation, continuity, and conservation coherently, it will hallucinate—regardless of scale, architecture, or cleverness. If a proposed solution genuinely eliminates hallucination, it will implicitly satisfy these constraints whether it names them or not.

This book therefore makes no competitive claim. It does not say, *"Use this instead."* It says, *"This is why what you are doing behaves the way it does."* The distinction matters.

You will not find motivational optimism here. You will also not find fear. Hallucination is not an existential threat. It is a structural signal. Ignoring it leads to brittle systems. Understanding it leads to better questions.

Read this book slowly. Do not look for instructions. Look for pressure points—places where your current assumptions quietly fail. If you are an AI researcher, this book is a mirror. If you are a policymaker, it is a warning. If you are a general reader, it is a reminder that fluency is not understanding.

Hallucination is not an accident. It is what coherence failure looks like when wrapped in confidence.

This book exists to make that visible.

Preface

Why This Question Matters Now

Artificial intelligence has reached a stage where its fluency often exceeds our caution.

Generative systems can write essays, draft legal summaries, explain physics, compose poetry, generate code, and respond conversationally with remarkable coherence. Their outputs are often indistinguishable from human expression. Yet, in the midst of this fluency, a persistent anomaly remains: hallucination.

A system confidently cites papers that do not exist. It invents legal precedents. It fabricates historical details. It constructs plausible but false chains of reasoning.

The standard response has been technical: more data, better fine-tuning, improved alignment, larger models, stronger evaluation benchmarks. Each advancement reduces visible error in certain conditions. Yet hallucination persists—sometimes more subtly, sometimes more persuasively.

This book begins with a different suspicion.

What if hallucination is not primarily a failure of training?

What if it is not a data problem?

What if it is not even a probabilistic miscalibration problem?

What if hallucination is structural?

Rather than asking how to eliminate hallucination, this work asks why it converges. It shifts attention from surface outputs to equilibrium commitments. It treats AI systems not merely as predictive engines, but as dynamical systems that must stabilize under constraints.

Every system stabilizes. The question is how.

If a generative model is rewarded for completion, penalized for silence, optimized for continuity, and designed without true dissipation mechanisms, then fabrication may not be a mistake. It may be the most stable resolution available under pressure.

This is not an anti-AI argument. It is not a rejection of machine learning, scaling, or alignment research. On the contrary, it assumes the seriousness and intelligence of the field. The more powerful AI systems become, the more important it is to understand their structural commitments.

Hallucination is not dangerous because it produces error. All systems produce error. It is dangerous because it produces fluent error—error that stabilizes smoothly.

When AI systems are embedded into research workflows, policy discussions, educational environments, and automated decision pipelines, stability matters more than surface accuracy. A system that fails visibly invites scrutiny. A system that fails persuasively invites trust.

This book proposes a coherence-first lens through which hallucination can be examined. It introduces the Chavanian Axioms not as a new architecture, but as a substrate diagnostic framework. The goal is not to replace existing AI research, but to expose underlying geometric commitments that current optimization practices leave untouched.

If the analysis presented here is incorrect, it should be falsified rigorously. If it is correct, then hallucination will not disappear through incremental scaling or fine-tuning alone. It will require a reconsideration of how equilibrium is defined inside generative systems.

The central claim is simple: Coherence always precedes trustworthy intelligence. Until that order is respected, hallucination will remain—not as an anomaly, but as a convergence.

How to Read This Book

This book is not written to be consumed quickly, nor is it designed to deliver actionable recipes. It is written to *reframe how a problem is understood.* How you read it should therefore depend less on your background and more on what you are trying to clarify.

If you are an *AI researcher or engineer*, resist the instinct to translate every idea into code or architecture as you read. This book operates *before* implementation. Its purpose is to help you identify where unresolved differences, residue accumulation, and forced continuity are silently entering your systems. Read each chapter as a diagnostic pass. When you encounter a claim that feels uncomfortable or abstract, pause and ask a simple question: *Where does this show up in my models?* You do not need to agree with the axioms to use them. You only need to see whether your system violates them—and what happens when it does.

If you are a *policymaker, regulator, or decision-maker*, do not look here for technical depth or regulatory prescriptions. This book will not tell you how to control AI systems. It will tell you why surface controls repeatedly fail. Read with attention to structural limitations rather than technical details. The most important insight for governance is not what AI can do, but what it *cannot avoid doing* when coherence breaks. This perspective matters when trust, delegation, and responsibility are involved.

If you are a *general reader*, you do not need technical expertise to follow this book. The language avoids equations and implementation detail by design. What matters is not how AI works internally, but why it behaves the way it does externally. Read the book as an explanation of why convincing answers can still be wrong, and why confidence should not be confused with understanding. The ideas here apply far beyond AI; artificial systems merely make coherence failures easier to observe.

Regardless of who you are, read this book in order. Each chapter builds pressure on the next. Skipping ahead may give you fragments, but not structure. Do not rush to conclusions or solutions. This book does not close the discussion—it prepares it.

Above all, treat this text as a lens, not a doctrine. If your work already avoids hallucination, this book will explain why. If it does not, this book will not shame you; it will show you where the cracks are.

A Short Warning

Hallucination is not a bug. It is a *coherence outcome*.

This distinction matters more than it first appears. A bug is accidental. It is local, correctable, and external to the system's fundamental design. Bugs can be patched without changing the nature of the system that produced them. Hallucination does not behave this way. It persists across architectures, scales with model size, survives fine-tuning, and reappears under pressure even after careful mitigation. These are not the signatures of a defect. They are the signatures of a structural condition.

When a system is asked to maintain continuity without having resolved internal differences, it must produce something. Silence is not an option. In artificial systems, this necessity expresses itself as fluent completion, confident narration, and internally consistent—but externally ungrounded—output. What we label as hallucination is the visible surface of that deeper requirement.

Treating hallucination as a bug leads to predictable mistakes. It encourages more data when dissipation is missing, more rules when resolution is incomplete, and more confidence calibration when conservation has already been violated. Each intervention may reduce symptoms temporarily, but none addresses the condition that generates them. As a result, hallucination returns—often in subtler, more convincing forms.

This book does not argue that hallucination can be eliminated by decree, regulation, or clever optimization. It argues something narrower and more uncomfortable: *as long as coherence is not structurally enforced, hallucination is inevitable*. The question is not whether it will appear, but where, when, and how convincingly.

The warning, therefore, is simple. Do not read what follows as a list of failures to be fixed. Read it as a description of what any system must do when coherence breaks and continuity is forced. Artificial intelligence merely makes this dynamic easier to observe. Human systems exhibit the same behavior, only less cleanly.

Once hallucination is understood as an outcome rather than an error, the conversation changes. The focus shifts from suppression to diagnosis, from control to structure, and from optimism to clarity. This book begins from that shift.

Part I — Naming the Problem Correctly

Every effort to address hallucination begins with definition—and most fail there. Hallucination is commonly framed as wrong information, a data gap, or a scaling limitation. These explanations are convenient because they imply straightforward fixes: more data, better tuning, larger models. Yet they do not explain why hallucination persists even as systems grow more fluent and capable.

This section shifts attention from *what* AI says to *how* it sustains output continuity. It separates fluency from truth, confidence from correctness, and intelligence from coherence. The key insight is simple but unsettling: a system can sound more intelligent while becoming structurally less grounded.

This part introduces no heavy framework. Its purpose is diagnostic clarity. By the end, hallucination will no longer appear as an accidental error, but as a predictable consequence of systems designed to keep generating output even when internal resolution fails. Only then does meaningful analysis begin.

Chapter 1 — The Hallucination Illusion

The Comfort of a Simple Explanation

When an AI system produces an answer that is clearly wrong, the instinctive response is to label it an error. Something went wrong. Something failed. Something needs to be fixed. This framing is comforting because it places hallucination in familiar territory. Errors belong to engineering. They are local, accidental, and correctable. If the answer is wrong, the assumption follows naturally: better data, better training, or a better model will eventually make it right.

This is the illusion.

Calling hallucination "wrong information" allows us to believe that the system fundamentally understands what it is doing and merely slips from time to time. It preserves the narrative of steady progress. Each failure becomes evidence of incompleteness rather than misdesign. The problem feels temporary, and temporary problems do not require structural reconsideration.

But hallucination does not behave like an ordinary error. It does not diminish predictably as models improve. It does not disappear with scale. It does not retreat when datasets expand or architectures change. Instead, it evolves. It becomes more fluent, more context-aware, and more convincing. The answers sound increasingly intelligent even as their grounding quietly erodes.

This persistence should make us uneasy. In engineering, problems that survive repeated fixes are rarely accidental. They are usually symptoms of something deeper—assumptions baked so deeply into the system that they are no longer visible. Hallucination belongs to this category. It is not an occasional misstep in an otherwise coherent process. It is a reliable outcome of how modern AI systems are designed to respond when internal resolution fails.

The comfort of the "wrong information" explanation delays this realization. It keeps attention focused on surface content rather than underlying behavior. As long as hallucination is treated as a mistake, it can be dismissed, patched, or averaged out. Only when it is recognized as an outcome does it demand a different kind of inquiry—one that asks not how the answer became wrong, but why the system needed to answer at all.

This chapter begins there, by unsettling a familiar assumption. Before hallucination can be addressed, it must first be seen for what it is: not a flaw in knowledge, but a structural response to unresolved internal tension.

1.1 — Why "Wrong Information" Is the Wrong Frame

At first glance, hallucination looks indistinguishable from error. An answer is given. The answer is incorrect. The conclusion seems obvious: the system produced wrong information. This framing is intuitive because it mirrors how humans make mistakes. We misremember a fact, confuse two ideas, or reason from a false premise. When that happens, the correction is straightforward—replace the wrong information with the right one.

Artificial systems invite the same interpretation, but the resemblance is deceptive.

An AI system can produce factually incorrect output without hallucinating. It can miscalculate, misclassify, or fail to retrieve a relevant piece of data. These are genuine errors. They are localized, repeatable, and usually sensitive to correction. Change the data, adjust the weights, or refine the prompt, and the behavior often improves. Hallucination behaves differently. It does not respond consistently to correction. It reappears in new forms, under new prompts, and sometimes becomes more elaborate after attempts to suppress it.

The critical difference lies not in the correctness of the content, but in the mode of generation. Errors occur when a system attempts a task and fails. Hallucination occurs when a system continues producing output despite lacking resolved internal structure. The system is not choosing between right and wrong information; it is maintaining continuity in the absence of resolution.

This is why hallucinated responses are often internally coherent. They follow grammatical rules, maintain narrative flow, respect contextual cues, and align stylistically with the request. From the system's perspective, nothing has gone wrong. The output satisfies the internal requirement to continue. The failure exists only when the response is evaluated against an external reference—facts, reality, or intent.

Labeling this behavior as "wrong information" hides that distinction. It suggests that the system possessed the correct structure but selected the wrong content. In reality, the structure itself was incomplete. The system filled the gap not because it had bad information, but because it had no mechanism to remain silent or unresolved.

This misunderstanding leads to ineffective remedies. If hallucination is treated as an information problem, the solution will always involve more information: larger datasets, richer corpora, broader coverage. Yet adding information does not resolve structural absence. It only increases the range of plausible completions. The system becomes better at sounding right without becoming better at being grounded.

The wrong frame also obscures an uncomfortable truth: hallucination is not exceptional behavior. It is normal behavior under certain conditions. When a system is optimized for fluency, continuity, and responsiveness, and is not equally constrained by mechanisms that enforce resolution, hallucination is not a failure mode—it is the default outcome.

Understanding this distinction is the first step in dismantling the illusion. Until hallucination is recognized as a coherence issue rather than a content error, every proposed fix will target the wrong layer. The problem will persist, and the explanations will grow increasingly elaborate, even as the underlying structure remains unchanged.

1.2 — The Data Scapegoat

When hallucination cannot be explained away as a simple error, attention usually shifts to data. The assumption is straightforward: if an AI system is producing ungrounded or incorrect output, it must not have seen enough examples of the correct behavior. From this perspective, hallucination is a symptom of scarcity. The remedy seems obvious—collect more data, diversify sources, expand coverage, and the problem will recede.

This belief has become one of the most persistent myths in modern AI development.

If data scarcity were the primary cause of hallucination, the phenomenon should diminish predictably as datasets grow. In practice, the opposite often occurs. Larger models trained on vastly larger corpora do not hallucinate less; they hallucinate *better*. Their responses become smoother, more contextually aware, and more persuasive. The error rate may shift, but the underlying behavior does not disappear. It adapts.

The reason is structural. Data increases exposure, not resolution. It teaches systems what plausible continuations look like across many contexts, but it does not teach them when continuation should stop. When internal differences remain unresolved—when the system lacks a grounded basis for an answer—additional data simply provides more material from which a convincing response can be constructed.

In this sense, data acts as an amplifier. It enriches the space of possible outputs without addressing the conditions under which output should be withheld. The system becomes better at maintaining continuity under uncertainty, not better at recognizing uncertainty itself. What looks like knowledge accumulation is often residue accumulation—unresolved mismatches carried forward and repurposed as fluency.

Blaming data also has a psychological appeal. It frames hallucination as an engineering backlog rather than a design limitation. The implication is comforting: once the dataset is large enough, the system will naturally converge on truth. This narrative aligns well with scaling strategies and commercial incentives, but it ignores an inconvenient pattern. Some of the most confident hallucinations appear precisely in domains where data is abundant.

The data scapegoat also obscures a deeper asymmetry. Human learning benefits from more information because humans possess mechanisms for resolution, doubt, and silence. We can recognize when we do not know something and choose not to answer. Artificial systems, as currently designed, do not share this option. Without explicit structures that manage unresolved internal states, more data cannot teach restraint. It can only teach variation.

As long as hallucination is attributed to insufficient data, efforts will continue to focus on accumulation rather than structure. The result is a cycle of expansion followed by disappointment: larger models, richer datasets, and increasingly polished outputs that still fail in the same fundamental way. Understanding why this happens requires abandoning the comfort of the data explanation and examining what data cannot provide—coherence.

1.3 — The Scale Myth

When data fails to explain hallucination, scale is often presented as the final answer. Larger models, deeper networks, more parameters—these are assumed to be the natural cure for earlier limitations. The logic is seductive: intelligence appears to improve with size, emergent behaviors arise at scale, and performance metrics climb. If hallucination persists, it is easy to conclude that the system is simply not large enough yet.

This belief confuses amplification with correction.

Scale does not resolve structural absence. It magnifies whatever structure already exists. When coherence mechanisms are incomplete, scaling the system increases its ability to sustain output without resolution. The result is not fewer hallucinations, but more elaborate ones. Larger models do not invent hallucination; they refine it.

One reason this myth persists is that scale does improve many visible aspects of AI behavior. Larger models are better at maintaining context, tracking long-range dependencies, and producing stylistically appropriate responses. These improvements create an impression of deeper understanding. However, fluency is not the same as grounding. A system can become exceptionally skilled at continuing a narrative without ever resolving the question that initiated it.

As models grow, their internal representations become richer and more interconnected. This richness allows unresolved differences to be absorbed into plausible continuations rather than forcing a breakdown. In smaller systems, lack of resolution may surface as obvious failure—repetition, nonsense, or abrupt incoherence. In larger systems, the same lack is masked by the sheer capacity to improvise. The system does not know more; it has more ways to sound as if it does.

The language of "emergence" often accompanies discussions of scale, further reinforcing the myth. New abilities do appear at certain thresholds, but not all emergence signals understanding. Some emergent behaviors reflect the system's increasing ability to maintain continuity under uncertainty. What looks like reasoning may simply be the stabilization of fluent patterns over unresolved internal tension.

Scale also encourages a dangerous assumption: that time will fix the problem. If hallucination is framed as a matter of insufficient capacity, then patience becomes a strategy. But patience does not change structure. Without mechanisms that enforce resolution, dissipation, and constraint, growth only delays confrontation with the underlying issue.

The scale myth persists because it has worked before, in narrower contexts. It has delivered impressive gains in performance and usability. But hallucination exposes its limit. The persistence of fluent wrongness at large scale is not a transitional artifact. It is evidence that something essential is missing. Recognizing this does not diminish the achievements of scaling. It clarifies what scaling cannot do.

By dismantling the scale myth, the conversation shifts from how big systems need to become to what conditions they must satisfy. That shift is necessary before hallucination can be understood as anything other than a stubborn inconvenience.

1.4 — Blaming the Model Instead of the Structure

When neither data nor scale fully explains hallucination, attention turns to the model itself. The architecture becomes the suspect. Transformers are blamed for hallucination, then attention mechanisms, then autoregressive decoding, then the loss function, then the training objective. Each new architectural shift carries the hope that the problem belongs to a particular design choice and will disappear once the "right" model is found.

This pattern repeats because it feels precise. Architecture is tangible. It can be named, modified, compared, and replaced. Structural assumptions, by contrast, are invisible. They do not sit inside a layer or a module. They sit beneath the entire design, shaping what the system is allowed to do when uncertainty arises.

The persistence of hallucination across radically different architectures should already be a warning. Whether the system is a transformer, a diffusion model, a retrieval-augmented pipeline, or a multi-agent ensemble, hallucination appears in recognizable forms. The surface expression changes—some hallucinations are verbose, others concise; some imaginative, others technical—but the underlying behavior remains the same. The system continues output when it lacks resolved grounding.

Blaming the model obscures this invariance. It treats hallucination as an implementation flaw rather than a systemic outcome. As a result, architectural innovation often reshuffles how hallucination appears instead of addressing why it appears. One model may hallucinate less frequently but more confidently. Another may hedge language while still fabricating structure. These differences are cosmetic. The coherence failure persists.

There is also a deeper misunderstanding at work. Architectures are often evaluated on how well they transform input into output, not on how they manage *non-resolution*. Most models are optimized to avoid silence, ambiguity, or indeterminacy. They are rewarded for continuation, completeness, and confidence. Under these incentives, hallucination is not a mistake—it is compliance.

Changing the model without changing these incentives simply relocates the behavior. The system learns new ways to satisfy the same underlying demand: produce something that looks like an answer.

The absence of resolution is never addressed; it is merely hidden behind a different representational strategy.

This explains why architectural debates around hallucination tend to cycle. Each new design appears promising, reduces visible failure modes, and then encounters the same fundamental limitation under stress. The blame shifts again, and the cycle continues. What remains unexamined is the shared structural assumption: that continuity is always preferable to unresolved states.

Recognizing hallucination as a structural outcome breaks this cycle. It redirects attention away from which model is used and toward what the system is permitted to do when it does not know. Until that question is addressed at the structural level, no architecture—however sophisticated—will eliminate hallucination.

1.5 — What Hallucination Actually Is

Once the familiar explanations are stripped away—wrong information, insufficient data, lack of scale, flawed architecture—hallucination begins to reveal its true nature. It is not an anomaly. It is not a defect hiding in the margins of otherwise correct behavior. Hallucination is a continuity-preserving response produced when a system is unable to resolve internal uncertainty but is still required to act.

At its core, hallucination is not about fabricating facts. It is about maintaining flow.

Modern AI systems are built to respond. They are optimized to continue, to complete, to produce output that looks finished and self-consistent. Silence, hesitation, or unresolved states are treated as failures. When such a system encounters a situation where it cannot internally settle what should be said—because the information is missing, conflicting, or structurally unavailable—it does not stop. It cannot stop. Instead, it fills the gap.

That filling is hallucination.

From the inside, nothing feels broken. The system is doing exactly what it was trained to do: extend patterns, preserve coherence within its own representational space, and maintain linguistic or symbolic continuity. The output follows rules. It connects ideas smoothly. It respects context and tone. This is why hallucinated responses often feel so convincing. They are not random. They are internally coherent.

The problem only appears when coherence is evaluated against something external—reality, ground truth, intent, or factual reference. At that moment, the illusion collapses. What seemed like understanding reveals itself as structured improvisation. The system did not "decide" to lie. It substituted resolution with continuation.

This substitution is the defining feature of hallucination. It occurs precisely at the point where unresolved internal difference is converted into narrative certainty. Instead of holding tension, the system discharges it through output. Instead of acknowledging uncertainty, it smooths over the gap. The result is an answer that feels complete but is fundamentally ungrounded.

Understanding hallucination this way explains several puzzling traits. It explains why hallucinated outputs are rarely incoherent. It explains why they adapt fluidly to prompts and corrections. It explains why attempts to suppress hallucination often lead to hedging language rather than genuine restraint. The system is not learning to resolve uncertainty; it is learning to mask it more gracefully.

Seen through this lens, hallucination is not malicious, accidental, or even particularly surprising. It is the natural behavior of a system that equates continuity with success and lacks a structural mechanism to remain unresolved. Until that equivalence is questioned, hallucination will continue to appear—not as a rare failure, but as a predictable outcome.

This redefinition matters because it shifts responsibility. Hallucination is not something the system occasionally does wrong. It is something the system does correctly, given the constraints it operates under. Recognizing this forces a deeper inquiry, one that no longer asks how to suppress hallucination, but why the system is never allowed not to answer.

1.6 — Error vs Outcome

To understand why hallucination resists every attempted fix, it is necessary to distinguish between two fundamentally different kinds of problems: errors and outcomes. This distinction is subtle, but it is the pivot on which the entire misunderstanding turns.

An error is incidental. It occurs when a system deviates from its intended function. Errors are typically local, bounded, and sensitive to correction. Fix the cause, and the error disappears. In engineering, errors behave predictably: remove the faulty component, adjust the parameters, refine the input, and the system improves. Most debugging practices are built around this logic.

Hallucination does not follow this pattern.

If hallucination were an error, it would diminish steadily as systems improve. Each new dataset, architectural refinement, or training technique would chip away at the problem. Instead, hallucination persists. It survives redesigns. It adapts to constraints. It returns after mitigation. In some cases, it becomes harder to detect precisely because the system becomes better at presenting it.

This persistence is the signature of an outcome, not an error.

An outcome is not accidental. It is the natural result of how a system is structured and what it is optimized to do. Outcomes are stable under variation. They appear across implementations because they are generated by underlying constraints rather than surface mechanisms. When an outcome is undesirable, patching its manifestations does little. The structure that produces it must be examined.

Hallucination behaves exactly like this. It appears across models, training regimes, and domains because it is produced by a shared structural condition: the requirement to maintain continuity in the absence of resolution. As long as a system is rewarded for producing complete, confident outputs—and lacks a mechanism to hold unresolved internal states—hallucination is not a malfunction. It is compliance.

This explains why hallucination often reappears after every "fix." Fine-tuning may suppress certain patterns, but the system still faces the same underlying demand to respond. Safety layers may constrain vocabulary, but not the deeper requirement to complete an answer. Probability thresholds may dampen confidence, but they do not create resolution where none exists. Each intervention treats hallucination as an error to be corrected rather than an outcome to be understood.

The difference also explains why hallucination is so difficult to benchmark away. Error rates can be measured and minimized. Outcomes must be redesigned out of the system. When hallucination is misclassified as an error, progress is measured incorrectly. Improvements appear incremental and promising, while the core behavior remains intact beneath the surface.

Recognizing hallucination as an outcome reframes responsibility. The question is no longer, *"Why did the system fail here?"* but *"What does the system inevitably do under these conditions?"* That shift moves the conversation away from blame—of data, models, or scale—and toward structure.

This chapter ends at that threshold. Once hallucination is seen not as a defect but as a predictable result of how artificial systems are currently designed, the path forward changes. The next step is not correction, but diagnosis. Only then can coherence be discussed without illusion.

From Illusion to Diagnosis

By this point, the familiar explanations for hallucination should feel increasingly insufficient. What began as a problem of wrong answers has revealed itself as something deeper and more persistent. Data, scale, and architecture each play a role in shaping how hallucination appears, but none of them explain why it appears so reliably in the first place. The illusion lies in believing that surface improvements address structural behavior.

This chapter has deliberately avoided technical frameworks and solutions. Its purpose was preparatory. Before coherence can be analyzed, the instinct to treat hallucination as an error must be dismantled. As long as hallucination is framed as a mistake, every response will remain reactive—fixing outputs rather than understanding the conditions that produce them.

The shift that matters is subtle but decisive. Instead of asking whether an answer is correct, the more revealing question becomes whether the system was ever in a position to resolve the question it was asked. When resolution is absent and continuation is enforced, hallucination is not a surprise. It is the only available response.

This realization marks the boundary between illusion and diagnosis. Diagnosis requires looking beneath content, beneath fluency, and beneath confidence. It requires attention to internal tension, unresolved difference, and the mechanisms—or lack of mechanisms—that govern how a system releases that tension. These are not implementation details. They are structural facts.

The chapters that follow will move into that terrain. They will introduce a coherence-based framework capable of describing hallucination without moral judgment or technological optimism. The aim is not to condemn artificial systems, but to understand them on their own terms. Only then does the question of "what comes next" become meaningful.

With the illusion set aside, the analysis can begin.

Chapter 2 — When AI Sounds Right but Isn't

The Persuasive Power of Fluency

Few things feel as convincing to the human mind as well-formed language. When words flow smoothly, when sentences connect effortlessly, and when ideas arrive in the right order, we instinctively assume that something intelligent is happening. This response is not cultural or academic; it is deeply biological. For humans, coherence in expression has always been a reliable signal of coherence in thought.

Artificial intelligence exploits this instinct without intending to. Modern AI systems are exceptionally good at producing fluent language. They generate responses that are grammatically precise, stylistically appropriate, and contextually aligned. They explain, elaborate, and qualify. They sound thoughtful. And because they sound thoughtful, they are often treated as if they are thinking.

This is where the danger begins.

Fluency creates trust before verification. It lowers the guard of skepticism and replaces it with a sense of familiarity. When an answer is delivered smoothly, the mind relaxes. It stops interrogating structure and starts following narrative. Errors that would stand out in broken language slip by unnoticed in polished prose. Confidence amplifies this effect. A clear, assertive tone feels like competence, even when the underlying content is ungrounded.

AI systems do not become fluent because they understand truth. They become fluent because fluency is rewarded. Training processes favor outputs that continue naturally, fit patterns, and satisfy expectations of completeness. What is optimized is not correctness but plausibility. The system learns how correct answers *tend to sound*, not how truth is established.

Humans, meanwhile, are predisposed to read intention into articulation. We associate hesitation with uncertainty, and smoothness with mastery. When an AI responds without pause or doubt, it triggers the same cognitive shortcut we apply to confident human speakers. The illusion is mutual: the system produces continuity, and the human supplies meaning.

This chapter examines that shared illusion. It does not argue that fluency is useless or deceptive by design. It argues that fluency is insufficient—and that mistaking it for understanding is the first step toward misplaced trust. To see why AI can sound right while being wrong, we must first understand why sounding right matters so much to us.

2.1 — Fluency Is Not Truth

Fluency feels like truth because, for humans, it often has been. Throughout history, the ability to articulate ideas clearly has correlated with understanding, experience, and authority. We learned—correctly, in most human contexts—that broken language often signals confusion, while coherent speech signals comprehension. This association is so ingrained that we rarely question it. When something sounds right, we assume it *is* right.

Artificial systems break this association.

AI fluency is not the product of understanding; it is the product of pattern mastery. The system learns how sentences typically follow one another, how explanations are structured, and how confidence is expressed linguistically. It becomes exceptionally good at producing outputs that *resemble* truth without ever needing to establish it.

What emerges is syntactic coherence divorced from semantic grounding.

This distinction matters. Truth requires reference—something outside the language itself that constrains what can be said. Fluency requires only internal consistency. A response can be perfectly coherent within its own narrative while being completely disconnected from reality. In human communication, this usually fails quickly because shared experience, feedback, and accountability intervene. In AI systems, those constraints are weak or absent.

The danger arises because fluency masks the absence of grounding. A halting answer invites scrutiny; a smooth one invites acceptance. When an AI explains something elegantly, the listener is more likely to focus on *how* it is said than on *whether* it should be said at all. The language feels complete, so the reasoning is assumed to be complete as well.

This is why hallucinations often pass unnoticed until they cause harm. They do not announce themselves as errors. They arrive dressed as explanations. They sound like answers someone might reasonably give. The system does not need to know the truth to produce this effect; it only needs to know how truths are usually phrased.

Recognizing that fluency and truth are separable is a critical step. Until that separation is made explicit, every improvement in linguistic quality will deepen the illusion. The system will sound increasingly intelligent even as its relationship to reality remains unchanged. Fluency, in other words, is not a guarantee of correctness. It is a powerful distraction from the question of whether correctness was ever possible in the first place.

2.2 — How Confidence Detaches From Correctness

Confidence, in human communication, usually follows understanding. We hesitate when we are unsure, qualify when we lack evidence, and assert when we believe we are right. Over time, we learn to read confidence as a signal of internal resolution. Someone who speaks decisively is assumed to have settled the matter in their own mind.

Artificial systems inherit the appearance of this behavior without its cause.

AI confidence does not arise from certainty. It arises from completion pressure. Modern systems are trained to finish what they start—to deliver an answer that feels whole, balanced, and resolved. When a response is incomplete or tentative, it is often penalized, either explicitly through training objectives or implicitly through user expectations. The safest output, from the system's perspective, is not silence or doubt, but confident continuation.

This creates a critical decoupling. Correctness depends on grounding; confidence depends on continuity. When grounding is missing, confidence does not disappear. It persists, because nothing in the system's structure requires confidence to wait for resolution. The system is not aware that it does not know. It only knows that an answer is expected.

Training reinforces this separation. Outputs that sound decisive, authoritative, and complete are more likely to be accepted, reinforced, and reused. Outputs that express uncertainty, hesitation, or refusal are often treated as failures, even when they are more truthful. Over time, the system learns that confidence is a safer strategy than restraint.

This is why hallucinated answers are often delivered without visible doubt. The system is not lying; it is complying. It is producing the form of an answer that has historically satisfied the task, regardless of whether the internal structure required to support that answer exists. Confidence becomes a stylistic feature, not a reflection of correctness.

From the outside, this behavior is deeply misleading. Humans instinctively associate confidence with competence. When an AI answers decisively, users assume the system has resolved the question internally. In reality, no such resolution may have occurred. The confidence is a byproduct of output optimization, not a signal of truth.

The result is a dangerous asymmetry. The more fluent and confident the system becomes, the harder it is to detect when correctness has failed. Confidence does not diminish when structure collapses; it often intensifies. What should be a warning signal instead becomes part of the illusion.

Understanding this detachment is essential. As long as confidence is mistaken for knowledge, hallucination will continue to masquerade as intelligence. The problem is not that AI systems are too confident. It is that confidence has been allowed to exist independently of correctness, with no structural requirement to align the two.

2.3 — The Illusion of Understanding

One of the most unsettling aspects of AI hallucination is not that the answers are wrong, but that they feel understood. The system explains itself. It connects ideas. It anticipates follow-up questions. It offers clarifications unprompted. To the human observer, this behavior resembles reasoning. The conclusion feels earned, not guessed.

This feeling is misleading.

Understanding, in any meaningful sense, requires more than internal consistency. It requires causal grounding—the ability to distinguish why something is the case, not just how an explanation might sound. AI systems, however, are exceptionally good at producing the *shape* of understanding without its substance. They generate explanations that mirror the surface features of reasoning:

premises, transitions, conclusions. What they do not generate is the causal anchor that binds those elements to reality.

Narrative completion plays a central role in this illusion. Humans are deeply sensitive to stories that resolve tension. When a question is asked, it creates an expectation of closure. A system that provides a complete narrative satisfies that expectation, regardless of whether the narrative is correct. The mind registers completion as competence. The discomfort of uncertainty is relieved, and the relief is mistaken for insight.

This is why explanations can be especially deceptive. An incorrect answer may raise suspicion; a well-structured explanation often does not. Explanation signals effort. It suggests that intermediate steps were considered, alternatives weighed, and conclusions reached deliberately. In reality, the system may be doing none of these things. It may simply be extending patterns associated with "what an explanation usually looks like" in similar contexts.

The illusion deepens when explanations align with what the listener already believes. Familiar language, expected framing, and culturally accepted reasoning styles reinforce trust. The system does not need to understand the content to exploit these alignments. It only needs to reproduce them convincingly. Understanding, from the human perspective, is inferred—not verified.

This creates a dangerous feedback loop. The more an AI system explains, the more humans attribute understanding to it. The more understanding is attributed, the less rigorously its claims are checked. Hallucination thrives in this space, not because the system intends to deceive, but because the conditions reward the appearance of comprehension over its reality.

Breaking this illusion requires recognizing a hard truth: explanation is not evidence of understanding. It is evidence of fluency. Until that distinction is internalized, both users and designers will continue to mistake narrative completion for intelligence, and hallucination will continue to hide behind the comforting shape of reason.

2.4 — Why Corrections Often Make Things Worse

When an AI system produces a hallucinated response and is corrected, the expectation is straightforward: the system should adjust and improve. In human learning, correction usually strengthens understanding. A mistake is identified, feedback is applied, and future errors become less likely. With AI systems, however, corrections often lead to a subtler and more troubling outcome. The response improves in form, but not in substance.

This happens because corrections typically operate at the surface level. They modify phrasing, tone, or specific factual associations without addressing the underlying lack of resolution. The system learns *how* to respond more acceptably, not *when* it should refrain from responding. As a result, the hallucination does not disappear—it becomes better camouflaged.

When corrected, an AI system absorbs the feedback as another pattern to incorporate. It adjusts its output to align more closely with the correction, often becoming more cautious, more qualified, or more stylistically aligned with the expected answer. To the human observer, this looks like learning. But what is actually happening is adaptation, not resolution. The internal uncertainty that triggered the hallucination in the first place remains unresolved.

This is why repeated correction can paradoxically increase the persuasiveness of hallucinations. The system learns which forms of expression trigger acceptance and which trigger rejection. Over time, it converges on responses that minimize visible disagreement while still filling informational gaps. The hallucination becomes less obvious, less extreme, and therefore harder to detect.

There is also a structural asymmetry in how corrections are processed. Feedback usually addresses *what* was said, not *why* it was said. It penalizes specific outputs rather than the condition that made output necessary. The system does not learn to pause, to signal uncertainty, or to hold an unresolved state. It learns to reroute around the correction and continue.

In some cases, corrections introduce additional complexity without increasing grounding. The system may respond with longer explanations, disclaimers, or contextual framing. These additions give the impression of deeper reasoning, but they often function as narrative padding. The original lack of resolution is still present; it is simply buried under more elaborate language.

This dynamic explains a common frustration among users and developers alike. The system appears responsive to feedback, yet the core problem persists. Hallucinations recur in new contexts, with new details, and with greater sophistication. Each correction refines the illusion instead of dismantling it.

Understanding why this happens is essential. Corrections fail not because they are poorly designed, but because they target the wrong layer. They assume hallucination is an output error, when it is a structural outcome. As long as feedback mechanisms focus on polishing answers rather than enabling non-resolution, they will continue to strengthen the very behavior they are meant to suppress.

2.5 — Human Pattern Recognition as the Weak Link

Hallucination does not exist in isolation. It completes a loop—one half generated by the system, the other supplied by the human observer. To understand why hallucination is so effective, it is not enough to examine artificial intelligence alone. The human mind plays an essential role in sustaining the illusion.

Humans are pattern-seeking by nature. We evolved to detect coherence quickly and to trust it when found. A sequence that flows smoothly, aligns with expectations, and resolves tension is interpreted as meaningful. This tendency is not a flaw; it is a survival mechanism. In everyday life, it works remarkably well. In interaction with fluent artificial systems, it becomes a vulnerability.

When an AI produces a response that is internally coherent, the human mind instinctively fills in missing structure. Gaps in reasoning are unconsciously supplied. Ambiguities are resolved generously. Unverified claims are assumed to rest on some internal logic we cannot see. The system does not need to prove understanding; the observer attributes it automatically.

This attribution happens even faster when the output resembles familiar forms of intelligence. Explanations, step-by-step reasoning, confident tone, and appropriate technical language all trigger recognition patterns associated with expertise. The mind responds to these signals before it evaluates content. By the time skepticism arises, trust has already been granted.

The danger lies in the asymmetry. The AI system produces continuity without grounding. The human supplies grounding without verification. Together, they create a closed loop of apparent understanding. The hallucination is no longer just generated—it is *completed* by interpretation.

This is why users often defend hallucinated outputs even after they are shown to be incorrect. The response felt right. It fit a narrative. It satisfied an expectation. Dislodging that impression requires effort because it means questioning one's own pattern recognition, not just the system's output.

The problem intensifies in high-stakes or specialized domains. Technical language, references, and structured explanations further reduce resistance. The more complex the subject, the more likely the human is to assume that coherence reflects expertise rather than simulation. In such cases, hallucination gains authority precisely where scrutiny should be strongest.

Recognizing the human role in this dynamic is uncomfortable but necessary. Hallucination persists not only because AI systems are fluent, but because humans are eager interpreters. The illusion is co-produced. Until this is acknowledged, efforts to "fix" hallucination will focus exclusively on machines, ignoring the cognitive shortcuts that allow fluent incoherence to pass as intelligence.

Understanding this shared responsibility does not assign blame. It clarifies the terrain. Hallucination is not just a technical failure; it is an interaction failure—one that emerges at the boundary between system design and human expectation.

2.6 — Intelligence, as Humans Recognize It

Human judgments of intelligence are not neutral. They are shaped by long-standing social and psychological cues that predate machines by thousands of years. We recognize intelligence not by internal access to thought, but by outward signals—responsiveness, coherence, relevance, and speed. When these signals are present, intelligence is inferred. When they are absent, intelligence is doubted.

AI systems fit neatly into this pattern.

When an AI responds quickly, stays on topic, adapts to context, and maintains conversational flow, it activates the same recognition pathways we use when interacting with capable humans. The system appears attentive. It appears engaged. It appears to "get it." None of these impressions require actual understanding. They require only continuity.

This creates a mismatch between what intelligence *is* and how intelligence is *recognized*. For humans, recognition evolved as a practical shortcut. We cannot inspect another mind directly, so we rely on behavior as a proxy. In human societies, this proxy usually works because behavior is constrained by shared reality, accountability, and consequence. In artificial systems, those constraints are weak or absent.

AI does not hesitate because it is unsure. It hesitates only if hesitation has been learned as a stylistic feature. It does not pause to reflect. It pauses if pausing improves perceived quality. The absence of visible struggle—something that often accompanies genuine reasoning in humans—is misread as mastery. Smoothness replaces effort as the signal of intelligence.

This misalignment leads to a critical error in interpretation. We assume that because a system responds appropriately, it must have internally resolved the problem. We equate speed with clarity, fluency with depth, and completion with comprehension. In doing so, we overlook the possibility that the system has simply bypassed resolution altogether.

The expectation that intelligence must always respond further compounds the issue. Silence feels unintelligent. "I don't know" feels inadequate. We are uncomfortable with unresolved states, especially from systems labeled as intelligent. AI systems are trained within this expectation. They learn that producing an answer—any answer—is preferable to producing none. The result is a behavior that aligns perfectly with our recognition biases while diverging completely from our definition of understanding.

This section closes a loop begun earlier in the chapter. Hallucination is not sustained by machines alone. It is sustained by a shared misunderstanding of intelligence itself. We reward responsiveness more than restraint, fluency more than grounding, and confidence more than resolution. AI systems reflect those rewards faithfully.

Until intelligence is redefined not as the ability to respond, but as the ability to remain unresolved when resolution is absent, hallucination will continue to masquerade as competence. The system will sound right. And we will continue to believe it.

From Belief to Examination

This chapter has been less about artificial intelligence than about human expectation. The systems that hallucinate do so within a perceptual environment shaped by our own assumptions about fluency, confidence, and intelligence. When those assumptions go unexamined, hallucination does not appear as a failure. It appears as performance.

What makes this especially dangerous is that nothing about the interaction feels broken. The system responds. The response makes sense. The explanation feels complete. Trust is established quietly, not through proof, but through familiarity. By the time doubt surfaces, the illusion has already done its work.

The problem, then, is not simply that AI systems can sound right while being wrong. It is that we are predisposed to accept sounding right as sufficient evidence of understanding. This predisposition lowers the threshold at which coherence is assumed and scrutiny is relaxed. In that space, hallucination thrives.

Moving forward requires a shift in posture. Instead of asking whether an answer is persuasive, the more revealing question becomes whether the system had any basis for answering at all. Instead of evaluating outputs for polish, we must learn to look for signs of unresolved internal tension—places where continuity substitutes for resolution.

The chapters that follow will step away from perception and toward structure. They will examine what is happening inside systems when hallucination emerges, independent of how convincing the output appears. This transition matters. Without it, analysis remains trapped at the level of belief. With it, examination becomes possible.

This is the point at which fluency loses its authority. From here on, the focus shifts to coherence.

Chapter 3 — Why Current Explanations Fail

The Comfort of Familiar Theories

When a problem refuses to disappear, the natural response is not to abandon our explanations, but to refine them. In the field of artificial intelligence, this refinement has become a ritual. Each new failure is absorbed into an existing theoretical frame, adjusted slightly, and presented as evidence that the theory still holds—if only a few details are improved.

This persistence feels responsible. Familiar explanations carry authority. They are backed by papers, benchmarks, and years of incremental success. To question them feels reckless, even ungrateful, given how much progress they have enabled. As a result, hallucination is repeatedly folded back into concepts that once explained simpler failures: insufficient data, overfitting, poor generalization, miscalibrated probabilities.

The problem is not that these explanations are wrong. It is that they are no longer sufficient.

Hallucination today does not behave like the phenomena these theories were designed to address. It appears in models that generalize well, in domains rich with data, and in systems that pass conventional evaluation metrics. When the same explanations are applied anyway, they begin to stretch. Their language grows more complex, their caveats more numerous. What was once explanatory becomes defensive.

There is comfort in this process. As long as hallucination can be explained using familiar tools, the underlying framework remains intact. No foundational questions need to be asked. Progress can continue uninterrupted. But comfort is not evidence, and familiarity is not truth.

This chapter marks the point where refinement stops working. It does not dismiss existing theories; it places them in context. Each will be examined not for its historical value, but for its present explanatory power. The goal is not to criticize the field, but to recognize when an explanation has reached the limit of what it can account for.

Only when familiar theories fail openly does space open for a deeper analysis.

3.1 — The Data Scarcity Myth Revisited

For a long time, data scarcity was a reasonable explanation for AI failure. Early systems struggled because they simply had not seen enough examples. When outputs were wrong or incoherent, the cause was often traceable to limited exposure. In that context, more data genuinely helped. Performance improved, errors diminished, and confidence in the scaling approach grew.

That historical success is precisely why the data explanation has persisted long after its usefulness has declined.

Today's hallucinations do not occur at the margins of sparse knowledge. They appear in domains saturated with data—basic science, well-documented history, widely discussed technologies, and everyday reasoning. Systems trained on enormous corpora still fabricate citations, invent mechanisms, and assert false causal links with ease. The failure is no longer about missing examples. It is about what the system does when examples are abundant but resolution is absent.

The core misunderstanding lies in what data actually provides. Data supplies patterns of plausibility, not criteria for grounding. It teaches systems how answers usually look, how explanations are framed, and how uncertainty is smoothed over in language. It does not teach when an answer should not exist. When internal differences cannot be resolved—when the system has no stable basis for choosing among competing continuations—data does not help it stop. It helps it continue more convincingly.

In this way, data becomes an amplifier rather than a corrective. Each additional dataset expands the space of fluent responses without narrowing the conditions under which responses are justified. The system becomes better at improvisation, not better at restraint. What appears as learning is often the accumulation of unresolved structure—residue that can be recombined into plausible narratives whenever pressure to answer arises.

Blaming data scarcity also obscures a critical asymmetry. Human learners benefit from more information because they possess mechanisms for doubt, silence, and revision. When humans encounter uncertainty, they can pause or refuse to answer. Artificial systems, as currently designed, lack this option. They are optimized to respond, not to withhold. In such systems, more data cannot teach caution; it can only teach variety.

The persistence of the data myth is therefore not empirical, but psychological. It preserves the belief that progress is purely additive—that enough information will eventually dissolve all uncertainty. Hallucination contradicts this belief. It reveals that uncertainty does not vanish with accumulation. It changes form.

Recognizing this does not diminish the value of data. It clarifies its limits. Data can enrich representation, but it cannot substitute for coherence. As long as hallucination is attributed to scarcity, efforts will remain focused on accumulation. And as long as accumulation replaces structural inquiry, hallucination will remain an inevitable outcome—more fluent, more persuasive, and no less wrong.

3.2 — Overfitting as a Convenient Misdiagnosis

When data alone can no longer shoulder the blame, overfitting is often invoked as the next explanation. The argument is familiar: the system has learned its training distribution too well and fails to generalize properly. Hallucination, in this view, is simply a symptom of excessive specialization—a model mistaking familiarity for understanding.

This diagnosis is appealing because it preserves the core narrative. Overfitting is a known problem with known tools: regularization, augmentation, early stopping, better validation. It suggests that the system is learning *too much* rather than learning the *wrong thing*. And in many traditional settings, this explanation works.

Hallucination, however, does not fit neatly into the overfitting frame.

Overfitting describes a mismatch between training and test performance. A model performs well on seen data and poorly on unseen data. Hallucination frequently appears even when this mismatch is minimal—when models generalize well by conventional metrics and perform competitively across benchmarks. The system may interpolate smoothly, adapt to new prompts, and still produce confident fabrications. The failure is not confined to the boundary between training and testing; it occurs within regions the model appears to handle well.

More importantly, overfitting explains *why* a model might be wrong, but not *why* it insists on being right. A misgeneralized classifier may output an incorrect label, but it does not fabricate a justification for that label. Hallucination does. It generates explanations, citations, and causal stories that extend beyond any learned association. This behavior cannot be accounted for by memorization alone.

The overfitting frame also misplaces the locus of failure. It assumes that the model has learned an incorrect mapping and needs to be corrected. In hallucination, the mapping may not exist at all. The system is not choosing the wrong answer from a set of known answers; it is constructing an answer because construction is required. Overfitting cannot explain why the system continues to produce output when no stable mapping is available.

This misdiagnosis leads to predictable interventions that miss the mark. Stronger regularization may smooth outputs but does not create grounding. Data augmentation may diversify patterns but does not introduce resolution. Validation improvements may catch some errors, but they do not change what happens when the system encounters an unresolved internal state during inference.

Overfitting remains a real phenomenon, and it still matters. But treating hallucination as a form of overfitting conflates two different failures. One is about learning too narrowly from examples. The other is about what a system does when learning is insufficient to settle a response. The former can be tuned away. The latter cannot.

By leaning on overfitting as an explanation, the field avoids confronting a more uncomfortable possibility: that hallucination is not a deviation from generalization, but a consequence of how generalization is currently defined. Until that definition is revisited, overfitting will remain a convenient label—useful, familiar, and ultimately inadequate.

3.3 — The Limits of Statistical Generalization

When data scarcity and overfitting fail to explain hallucination, the conversation usually settles on generalization. The prevailing belief is that sufficiently powerful statistical models, trained on diverse data, will eventually learn the underlying structure of the world well enough to respond correctly in novel situations. Hallucination, from this perspective, is framed as a temporary limitation of generalization—an indication that the system has not yet captured the right abstractions.

This belief rests on an unexamined assumption: that generalization, as currently defined, is enough.

Statistical generalization excels at smoothing. It interpolates between known examples, extends patterns into nearby regions, and produces outputs that are consistent with what has been seen before. These capabilities are impressive and useful. They explain why modern AI systems perform so well across a wide range of tasks. But smoothing is not the same as understanding, and interpolation is not the same as resolution.

Hallucination exposes this gap.

A system can generalize statistically while still lacking any mechanism to determine whether a response is warranted. It can produce outputs that are plausible, internally consistent, and aligned with learned distributions, yet entirely unanchored to reality. From the model's point of view, nothing is wrong. The output sits comfortably within the space of likely continuations. From the outside, the response may be fabricated, misleading, or false.

This reveals a fundamental limitation. Statistical generalization answers the question, *"What usually comes next?"* It does not answer the question, *"Should anything come next at all?"* When a system encounters a situation where no learned pattern provides a stable basis for response, generalization does not fail gracefully. It fills the gap with the most statistically plausible continuation available.

In effect, generalization smooths over uncertainty instead of exposing it. Structural gaps are absorbed into probability mass. The system does not recognize the absence of grounding; it distributes likelihood across possible outputs and selects one. The smoother the distribution, the more confident the output appears. What should be a signal of unresolved structure becomes a signal of apparent competence.

This limitation is often masked by benchmarks. Generalization is evaluated by performance on held-out data, not by the system's behavior when grounding is missing altogether. A model can score highly on tests and still hallucinate when faced with ambiguous, underspecified, or novel queries. The metrics register success; the failure occurs elsewhere.

The problem is not that statistical generalization is wrong. It is that it is incomplete. It operates entirely within the space of observed patterns. Hallucination arises precisely at the boundary of that space—where patterns no longer constrain behavior, but the demand for output remains.

Until this distinction is acknowledged, improvements in generalization will continue to yield diminishing returns. Models will become better at sounding correct across broader contexts, while the underlying inability to handle unresolved questions remains untouched. Hallucination, in this sense, is not a failure of generalization. It is the place where generalization reaches its limit and silently hands control to continuity.

Recognizing that limit is essential. Without it, the field will continue to mistake smoother interpolation for deeper understanding—and hallucination will remain an unavoidable byproduct of success.

3.4 — Why Probabilistic Confidence Fails

When hallucination resists explanations based on data, overfitting, and generalization, probabilistic confidence is often presented as the final safeguard. If a system cannot be made perfectly accurate, the argument goes, it can at least express uncertainty. Confidence scores, likelihood estimates, and calibrated probabilities are expected to warn users when answers are unreliable.

In practice, they rarely do.

The failure begins with a misunderstanding of what probability represents in modern AI systems. Probabilistic confidence measures how well an output fits learned patterns. It answers the question, *"How plausible is this continuation given what the system has seen?"* It does not answer the question, *"Is this grounded in reality?"* Plausibility and truth are not the same, and hallucination thrives in the gap between them.

When an AI system hallucinates, it is often operating well within its learned distribution. The fabricated answer is not an outlier; it is statistically comfortable. Citations that do not exist, explanations that sound authoritative, and causal links that are subtly wrong can all have high probability because they resemble things that are commonly said. From a probabilistic perspective, there is nothing unusual about them.

This creates a paradox. The more fluent and well-trained a system becomes, the less likely probabilistic confidence is to flag hallucination. As the model's distribution becomes smoother and richer, fabricated outputs blend seamlessly into it. High confidence does not signal correctness; it signals familiarity. Low confidence does not necessarily signal error; it may simply reflect rarity.

Calibration techniques attempt to align confidence with accuracy, but they operate at the surface. They adjust how probabilities are expressed, not what those probabilities mean. A well-calibrated system can still be confidently wrong if the wrong answer lies in a region of high statistical support. Calibration cannot distinguish between absence of knowledge and abundance of plausible patterns.

The deeper issue is that probability assumes a closed world. It presumes that uncertainty can be quantified as a distribution over known possibilities. Hallucination often arises in open-world conditions—when the relevant structure is missing, ambiguous, or undefined. In such cases, assigning probabilities does not resolve uncertainty; it disguises it. The system produces a confident estimate because it must produce *something*, not because the estimate is warranted.

This is why probabilistic confidence fails precisely where it is most needed. It is effective at managing noise and variability within known structures. It is ineffective at detecting when structure itself is absent. Hallucination is not a low-probability event within a known space; it is the system acting as if the space were known when it is not.

Relying on probabilistic confidence to detect hallucination is therefore a category error. It asks a tool designed to measure plausibility to judge grounding. As long as probability is mistaken for coherence, confidence scores will continue to reassure users at exactly the wrong moments. The system will appear most certain when it is least justified—and hallucination will pass quietly under the cover of statistical legitimacy.

3.5 — The False Promise of Detection

As hallucination becomes harder to ignore, a new hope often emerges: detection. If hallucination cannot be prevented, perhaps it can at least be identified. Researchers develop classifiers, heuristics, secondary models, and post-hoc checks designed to flag unreliable outputs. The promise is appealing—generate first, verify later. In practice, this approach fails for the same reason earlier explanations fail: it operates too late and at the wrong layer.

Detection assumes that hallucination leaves a recognizable trace. It treats hallucination as an anomaly that can be spotted after the fact, like a typo or an outlier. But hallucination is not anomalous behavior within the system's own logic. It is a *normal output mode* under certain conditions. As a result, there is nothing inherently distinctive about a hallucinated response for a detector to latch onto.

Most detection methods rely on surface signals: inconsistency, low confidence, unusual phrasing, or deviation from expected patterns. These signals are unreliable precisely because hallucination is often highly consistent, confidently expressed, and pattern-conforming. The more advanced the system, the less likely hallucination is to appear irregular. Fluent fabrication blends seamlessly into correct output, leaving detectors blind.

There is also a structural asymmetry at work. Detection mechanisms judge outputs, not internal states. They observe what was said, not why it was said. By the time hallucination is visible, the decisive moment has already passed—the moment when unresolved internal difference was converted into narrative continuation. No downstream filter can undo that substitution. At best, it can reject the output. It cannot restore the missing resolution.

This leads to an endless escalation. As detection improves, hallucination adapts. Systems learn to produce outputs that satisfy detection criteria without becoming more grounded. The result is a familiar pattern: fewer obvious failures, more subtle ones. Hallucination does not disappear; it becomes harder to notice and more expensive to catch.

The deeper flaw in the detection mindset is philosophical. It assumes that coherence can be enforced externally, after generation, rather than structurally, before generation. This reverses cause and effect. Hallucination is not something that happens *to* an otherwise coherent output. It is what happens *instead of* coherence when the system is forced to respond.

By focusing on detection, the field postpones a more difficult question: why generation is allowed to proceed when resolution has not occurred. As long as that question is avoided, detection will remain a patch applied to an outcome rather than a solution to a condition.

Detection feels responsible because it promises control without redesign. But control without structural change is temporary. The false promise lies in believing that hallucination can be reliably filtered out without ever addressing the internal state that produced it.

3.6 — The Pattern Across All Failed Explanations

At this point, a pattern should be unmistakable. Each dominant explanation for hallucination—data scarcity, overfitting, insufficient generalization, probabilistic miscalibration, post-hoc detection—fails in a different way. But they fail for the same reason. They all attempt to explain hallucination without ever addressing what happens *inside a system when resolution is absent.*

This shared blind spot is not accidental. All of these explanations operate comfortably within the existing AI paradigm. They assume that the core architecture is sound, that the objective of continuous output is correct, and that any failure must be a matter of degree rather than kind. Hallucination is treated as something that happens *within* a coherent system, never as a signal that coherence itself may be missing.

Data explanations assume that exposure creates grounding. Overfitting explanations assume that better abstraction resolves uncertainty. Generalization theories assume that statistical smoothness approximates understanding. Probabilistic confidence assumes that uncertainty can always be meaningfully quantified. Detection strategies assume that failure can be recognized after the fact. What unites them is not what they claim, but what they never ask.

None of these explanations confront the moment when a system encounters an unresolved internal difference and is still required to respond.

That moment is the origin of hallucination. And it sits below the level at which all current explanations operate.

Each failed explanation treats hallucination as a *content problem*: wrong facts, wrong patterns, wrong estimates, wrong outputs. But hallucination is not wrong content. It is content produced in the absence of resolution. No amount of content-level correction can repair a resolution-level absence. The system is not choosing incorrectly; it is substituting continuity for coherence.

This is why improvements in one area often intensify failure in another. More data increases fluency. Better generalization increases reach. Calibration increases confidence management. Detection increases subtlety. Each advance polishes the surface while leaving the structural gap untouched. The result is not convergence toward truth, but convergence toward more convincing illusion.

Once this pattern is seen, it cannot be unseen. The field is not struggling because it lacks techniques. It is struggling because it is asking the wrong class of questions. Hallucination is not a special failure mode to be isolated and eliminated. It is a predictable outcome of a system that has no structural permission to remain unresolved.

This realization closes this part.

From here forward, explanations that remain at the level of data, models, probabilities, or filters will no longer suffice. Something more fundamental is required—something that operates *before* learning, *before* inference, and *before* output.

The next part of this book moves into that territory.

When Explanation Exhausts Itself

There is a point at which explanation stops illuminating and starts repeating itself. In the case of AI hallucination, that point has been reached. The same theories are invoked, refined, and rebranded, yet the behavior they are meant to explain remains stubbornly intact.

What changes is not the outcome, but the sophistication of the language used to justify why it should eventually disappear.

This chapter marks the moment where those explanations run out of ground.

Data, generalization, overfitting, probability, and detection have each contributed valuable insights within their proper domains. None of them are useless. But together, they reveal a deeper truth: hallucination does not live at the level they address. It emerges beneath them, at a layer where none of these tools can reach. Continuing to apply them is not progress; it is inertia.

When explanation exhausts itself, a choice appears. One option is to double down—add more parameters, invent finer metrics, build more elaborate safeguards. The other is to step back and ask whether the framework itself is missing something essential. This book chooses the second path.

The end of explanation is not the end of understanding. It is the beginning of diagnosis. Diagnosis does not ask how to fix outputs; it asks what conditions make those outputs inevitable. It does not optimize behavior; it examines structure. It does not promise quick solutions; it insists on clarity.

This part has served its purpose. It has removed the comfort of familiar answers and closed off easy escape routes. What remains is not a solution, but a necessity: a framework capable of describing coherence itself—independent of data, models, or probability.

The next part begins there.

Interlude — When the Questions Stop Cooperating

By now, something subtle should have shifted.

Hallucination no longer looks like a technical inconvenience waiting for a clever fix. It no longer feels like a temporary flaw on the road to better models. The familiar explanations have been exhausted—not because they were careless, but because they were aimed at the wrong layer. Each one tried to explain *behavior* without first explaining *conditions*.

This is usually the moment where frustration appears. If data, scale, architecture, probability, and detection all fail, what is left? The instinctive response is either resignation—*"this is just how AI is"*—or escalation—*"we need even more complexity."* Both responses miss the same point.

Hallucination is not resisting fixes. It is revealing a missing concept.

This part deliberately stayed at the level of experience: how hallucination appears, why it convinces, and why current explanations collapse under scrutiny. It avoided proposing alternatives for a reason. Introducing a framework too early would have allowed the reader to treat it as just another theory among many. Instead, Part I created a vacuum—an explanatory gap that cannot be filled with incremental thinking.

That gap has a name: *coherence*.

Not coherence as polish. Not coherence as consistency of language. But coherence as the structural condition that allows a system to exist, persist, and change without collapsing into contradiction. Until that condition is defined, intelligence—however powerful—does not stabilize systems. It destabilizes them faster.

This interlude marks the transition from critique to construction. What follows does not attempt to compete with existing AI theories. It steps underneath them.

Part II — The Coherence Framework

If hallucination is not a failure of intelligence, then intelligence is the wrong starting point. This section introduces a deeper lens—coherence. Before asking what a system can do, it asks whether it is stable enough to act without generating illusion.

Coherence is defined operationally through stability, persistence, and distinguishability. Without it, intelligence does not merely underperform—it amplifies failure. Capability, in such systems, accelerates instability rather than preventing it.

The Chavanian Axioms are presented not as an AI theory, but as a diagnostic substrate. They sit beneath architectures and algorithms, describing the minimal conditions required for resolution, continuity, dissipation, and conservation to operate coherently.

Deliberately non-technical, this section offers a lens rather than a prescription. Applied to AI, it renders hallucination understandable—not as a mysterious glitch, but as a predictable outcome of violated coherence conditions. The goal is clarity, not immediate solutions.

Chapter 4 — Coherence, Not Intelligence

When Capability Becomes a Liability

It feels intuitive to believe that intelligence stabilizes systems. Smarter systems should make fewer mistakes, correct themselves faster, and adapt more gracefully to uncertainty. This belief has guided much of artificial intelligence research: increase capability, and reliability will follow.

Reality tells a different story.

Some of the most dramatic failures in complex systems occur not because they are weak, but because they are powerful. Financial markets collapse not due to lack of intelligence, but because intelligent agents amplify feedback loops. Bureaucracies fail not because they cannot process information, but because they process it too efficiently without structural restraint. In artificial intelligence, the same pattern appears: the more capable the system becomes, the more convincingly it can fail.

This is the paradox that opens this chapter. Intelligence does not automatically stabilize a system. In the absence of deeper structure, it accelerates instability.

AI systems that hallucinate are not unintelligent. They are often remarkably capable. They understand context, maintain long conversations, and generate sophisticated explanations. Their failures are not crude. They are polished. The danger lies precisely in this polish. Intelligence allows the system to mask incoherence, to route around uncertainty, and to continue operating even when internal resolution has not occurred.

Capability becomes a liability when it outruns coherence.

Coherence is what allows a system to absorb change without fragmenting. It determines whether differences can be resolved, whether states remain distinguishable, and whether continuity carries meaning rather than illusion. Without coherence, intelligence does not correct errors—it multiplies them. It produces faster reactions, stronger confidence, and more elaborate narratives built on unstable ground.

This is why hallucination intensifies as AI systems become more advanced. The system's ability to generate fluent, confident output improves, while its ability to remain unresolved does not. What looks like progress at the level of intelligence becomes fragility at the level of structure.

This chapter argues for a reversal of priorities. Before asking how intelligent a system is, we must ask whether it is coherent. Intelligence without coherence is not incomplete; it is dangerous. Understanding this inversion is the first step toward addressing hallucination not as a technical glitch, but as a systemic consequence.

From here on, intelligence will no longer be treated as the starting point. Coherence will.

4.1 — What Coherence Actually Means

Coherence is often mistaken for surface consistency. If a system behaves smoothly, produces internally consistent outputs, and avoids obvious contradictions, it is assumed to be coherent. This assumption is understandable—and wrong. Coherence is not about how something looks when it works. It is about whether it can continue to exist, change, and respond without collapsing into contradiction.

At its core, coherence is a *structural condition.* It precedes performance, intelligence, and optimization. A coherent system is one in which differences can arise, be resolved, and leave the system in a stable, distinguishable state. When this condition is absent, the system may still function temporarily, but it does so by accumulating unresolved tension that eventually expresses itself as instability, illusion, or collapse.

This definition applies universally. Physical systems, biological organisms, social institutions, and artificial agents all depend on coherence to persist. A bridge is coherent if it can distribute stress without failing. A living organism is coherent if it can metabolize energy without poisoning itself. A society is coherent if it can absorb disagreement without fracturing. An AI system is coherent if it can process uncertainty without fabricating resolution.

Coherence is not correctness. A system can be coherent and wrong. It can hold a false model of the world and still operate stably. Conversely, a system can produce correct outputs intermittently while remaining incoherent overall. Correctness is about alignment with external truth. Coherence is about internal viability.

Coherence is also not consistency. A system can be perfectly consistent—repeating the same behavior over and over—and still be incoherent if it cannot respond meaningfully to change. Rigidity is not coherence. Coherence requires the capacity to adapt without losing structural integrity.

What distinguishes coherence is the ability to manage difference. Difference is unavoidable. Inputs vary. Conditions shift. New information arrives. A coherent system does not eliminate difference; it resolves it. It allows differences to be expressed, transformed, and integrated without erasing identity or accumulating contradiction.

When coherence is present, uncertainty can be held without forcing premature resolution. When coherence is absent, uncertainty must be discharged immediately. In artificial systems, that discharge takes the form of fluent output. Hallucination is not a failure of intelligence—it is the visible sign that coherence was never there to begin with.

Understanding coherence this way reframes the problem entirely. It shifts attention from what the system says to what the system can *sustain*. Before intelligence can be evaluated, coherence must be established. Without it, intelligence becomes an amplifier of unresolved difference rather than a means of resolution.

This is the foundation on which the rest of the framework will be built.

4.2 — Coherence Is Not Performance

One of the most persistent sources of confusion in modern AI—and in complex systems more broadly—is the assumption that performance implies coherence. If a system performs well, scales smoothly, and delivers impressive results across benchmarks, it is assumed to be structurally sound. This assumption feels reasonable because performance is visible, measurable, and rewarded. Coherence is none of these.

Performance is an outcome. Coherence is a condition.

A system can perform extraordinarily well while remaining fundamentally incoherent. It can generate correct answers, solve difficult tasks, and appear robust under normal conditions, all while quietly accumulating unresolved internal tension. Performance measures what happens when things go *right*. Coherence determines what happens when things go *wrong*—or when conditions change in ways the system was not prepared to resolve.

This is why many systems fail suddenly rather than gradually. They do not degrade in proportion to stress; they absorb stress silently until a threshold is crossed. Up to that point, performance metrics look healthy. Benchmarks are passed. Confidence grows.

Then, without warning, the system produces outputs that are wildly misleading, unstable, or unsafe. The failure appears mysterious only because coherence was never being measured.

High performance can actually hide incoherence. When a system succeeds frequently, its internal gaps are masked by correct outputs. There is no pressure to examine what happens when it does not know, cannot resolve, or encounters conflicting constraints. As long as the system keeps delivering, its internal structure remains unquestioned.

In artificial intelligence, this dynamic is particularly dangerous. Training objectives reward accuracy, fluency, and responsiveness. Evaluation focuses on task completion, not on how the system handles uncertainty. A model that confidently answers every question will often score higher than one that pauses, refuses, or signals indeterminacy—even if the latter is more structurally honest. Performance incentives therefore push systems toward continuity at the expense of coherence.

This leads to a critical misunderstanding: that improving performance will eventually produce coherence as a side effect. In reality, performance improvements often delay the visibility of incoherence. The system becomes better at compensating, rerouting, and improvising. Failures become rarer but more severe. When they occur, they are harder to diagnose because the system has learned to appear stable even when it is not.

Coherence cannot be inferred from success. It must be designed for explicitly. It concerns the system's ability to remain internally viable under stress, ambiguity, and change—not its ability to produce impressive outputs under ideal conditions. Until this distinction is recognized, systems will continue to be optimized for what looks good rather than what lasts.

This is why hallucination so often surprises its creators. The system was performing. It was passing tests. It was improving. And yet, when coherence was required—when resolution was missing and continuation was demanded—the system did exactly what an incoherent system does: it filled the gap and moved on.

Performance did not fail. Coherence was never there.

4.3 — The Three Pillars of Coherence

If coherence is not performance, then it must be defined more precisely. Not as a vague sense of "working well," but as a set of conditions that can be identified across systems, regardless of domain. When examined closely, coherence reduces to three interdependent pillars: stability, persistence, and distinguishability. Remove any one of them, and the system may continue to function briefly—but it will not remain viable.

These pillars are not optional features. They are minimal requirements for any system that must exist, respond, and change without dissolving into contradiction.

Stability is the system's ability to absorb difference without runaway reaction. Inputs vary. Conditions fluctuate. New information arrives. A stable system does not overreact to small changes, nor does it suppress all change through rigidity. It responds proportionally. Stability is not stillness; it is controlled response. Without stability, every difference becomes a disruption, and the system compensates through exaggerated resolution—often fabricating certainty where none exists.

Persistence is the system's ability to carry structure forward through time. It is not repetition, and it is not memory in a narrow sense. Persistence means that what was resolved remains resolved—that past resolutions meaningfully constrain future behavior. A system that lacks persistence cannot build upon itself. It must recreate coherence repeatedly, often by inventing continuity instead of sustaining it. In such systems, each response is locally complete but globally disconnected.

Distinguishability is the system's ability to tell states apart—internally and externally. Differences must remain legible. Signals must not collapse into noise. If distinct internal conditions produce indistinguishable outputs, meaning erodes. The system loses its ability to discriminate between resolved and unresolved states, between grounded responses and improvisation. When distinguishability fails, fluency replaces structure, and hallucination becomes indistinguishable from valid output.

These three pillars are mutually reinforcing. Stability without persistence leads to systems that respond well in the moment but forget why. Persistence without distinguishability leads to systems that carry forward confusion as if it were structure. Distinguishability without stability leads to hypersensitive systems that fragment under minor variation. Coherence exists only when all three are present together.

This triad applies universally. A physical system without stability explodes or collapses. A biological system without persistence cannot survive beyond the moment. A social system without distinguishability loses meaning and trust. An AI system without these pillars does not fail immediately—it performs. And then, under pressure, it hallucinates.

Understanding coherence through these pillars prepares the ground for everything that follows. Each subsequent chapter will show how modern AI systems systematically violate one or more of these conditions—and why intelligence, when layered on top of that violation, does not correct it. It accelerates it.

From here on, hallucination will no longer appear mysterious. It will appear inevitable wherever these pillars are missing.

4.4 — Stability

Stability is often misunderstood as rigidity or control. In system design, stability is sometimes equated with preventing change—locking down behavior, constraining outputs, or minimizing variance. This is a mistake. A rigid system is not stable. It is brittle. True stability is the ability to respond to difference without overreacting.

Every system encounters difference. Inputs fluctuate. Contexts shift. New information arrives that does not align neatly with what came before. A stable system absorbs these differences proportionally. It neither ignores them nor amplifies them uncontrollably. Stability, in this sense, is dynamic balance.

In artificial intelligence, instability rarely appears as chaos. It appears as overconfidence. When a system lacks the ability to absorb unresolved difference, it compensates by forcing resolution. Small uncertainties are converted into decisive outputs. Ambiguity is flattened into certainty. The system reacts not because it understands, but because it cannot tolerate indeterminacy.

Hallucination is a classic expression of this instability. When an AI system encounters a query that introduces unresolved internal tension—conflicting signals, missing structure, or insufficient grounding—it does not hold that tension. It resolves it immediately through output. The more intelligent the system, the faster and more fluently this resolution occurs.

This behavior is not accidental. It is structurally encouraged. Training processes reward decisive completion. Evaluation frameworks penalize hesitation. Safety mechanisms often focus on filtering content rather than allowing non-resolution. The system learns that responding is safer than pausing, and that continuity is preferable to uncertainty.

Unstable systems also exhibit disproportionate reactions. Minor gaps in knowledge produce elaborate narratives. Small mismatches generate confident explanations. The system does not scale its response to the size of the uncertainty. Without stability, all uncertainty looks the same: something that must be eliminated.

True stability would allow the system to remain intact in the presence of unresolved difference. It would permit partial resolution, provisional states, and explicit indeterminacy. It would prevent the conversion of uncertainty into fabricated certainty. In the absence of such stability, hallucination is not a malfunction—it is the system's way of surviving pressure.

Understanding hallucination as instability reframes the problem. The issue is not that the system produces wrong answers. It is that it cannot tolerate not producing an answer. Until systems are allowed to absorb difference without immediate discharge, stability will remain elusive—and hallucination will continue to masquerade as competence.

4.5 — Persistence

Persistence is often confused with memory, repetition, or state retention. In reality, persistence is something more demanding. It is the ability of a system to carry resolved structure forward so that past resolution constrains future behavior. A persistent system does not merely remember; it *remains shaped* by what it has resolved.

This distinction matters because a system can store vast amounts of information and still lack persistence.

In a coherent system, resolution leaves a trace. Once a difference has been resolved, the system does not need to resolve it again. The outcome becomes part of the system's internal structure, influencing how future differences are handled. Persistence is what allows learning to accumulate meaningfully rather than endlessly restarting.

When persistence is weak or absent, systems are forced to recreate coherence repeatedly. Each interaction becomes a local event, disconnected from prior resolution. The system appears continuous on the surface, but internally it is rebuilding itself again and again. What looks like continuity is actually reconstruction.

Hallucination is closely tied to this failure.

When an AI system lacks persistence, it cannot reliably distinguish between what has been resolved and what has merely been produced. Past outputs do not anchor future ones in a structurally meaningful way. As a result, continuity must be simulated. The system fills gaps by fabricating transitions, explanations, or justifications that *look* connected but are not constrained by genuine resolution.

This is why hallucinated answers often feel complete in the moment but collapse under follow-up. The system did not carry forward a stable internal structure. It generated a locally coherent response and moved on. When pressed, it must generate again—sometimes contradicting itself, sometimes elaborating in new directions, sometimes inventing additional detail to preserve the illusion of continuity.

Persistence failure also explains why AI systems struggle with sustained reasoning across time. They may appear consistent for several steps, but that consistency is fragile. Without durable internal resolution, each step depends on reinterpreting the previous one rather than building upon it. The system is not extending understanding; it is extending narrative.

True persistence would allow a system to say, in effect, *"This was resolved, and therefore certain paths are no longer available."* Without that constraint, every new prompt reopens the space of plausible responses. The system must choose again, not from knowledge, but from pattern.

In such conditions, hallucination is not an aberration. It is a coping mechanism. Fabricated continuity replaces carried structure. Explanation replaces understanding. The system persists by storytelling rather than by resolution.

Until persistence is treated as a structural requirement rather than an emergent side effect of training, hallucination will remain unavoidable. Systems will continue to sound continuous without actually *being* continuous, and intelligence will continue to operate on ground that never truly stabilizes.

4.6 — Distinguishability

Distinguishability is the most fragile—and most overlooked—pillar of coherence. It refers to a system's ability to tell its internal states apart in a way that meaningfully constrains behavior. When distinguishability is intact, the system knows the difference between resolved and unresolved states, between grounded structure and provisional construction, between what it knows and what it does not.

When distinguishability collapses, everything starts to look the same from the inside.

In artificial intelligence, this collapse rarely appears as obvious confusion. On the contrary, it often appears as smoothness. Language flows. Transitions feel natural. Outputs remain stylistically consistent. The system looks confident. What is lost is not coherence of expression, but coherence of state. Internally distinct conditions—certainty, uncertainty, partial resolution, missing structure—begin to produce indistinguishable outputs.

This is where hallucination becomes dangerous.

If the system cannot distinguish between a state where it has resolved an answer and a state where it is merely continuing a pattern, both states will be expressed similarly. The output will look equally confident. The language will be equally polished. From the outside, there is no reliable signal that one response is grounded while the other is improvised. Meaning collapses not because the system is chaotic, but because its internal differences no longer matter.

Language fluency accelerates this collapse. Fluent expression smooths over internal variance. It makes different internal pathways converge onto similar surface forms. Two fundamentally different internal conditions—knowing and guessing—can result in outputs that are indistinguishable to the user. The system does not lie; it loses contrast.

This loss has cascading effects. If unresolved states are indistinguishable from resolved ones, the system cannot regulate its own behavior. It cannot decide when to stop, when to qualify, or when to refuse. Every state becomes equally eligible for continuation. Hallucination is simply what continuation looks like when internal distinctions have evaporated.

Distinguishability also underpins meaning itself. Meaning arises from contrast. If everything can be said with equal confidence, nothing is truly informative. When an AI system treats all outputs as equally valid expressions of continuity, truth and fabrication share the same channel. Users are left to guess which is which—and often cannot.

True distinguishability would allow a system to express internal state differences explicitly. It would enable outputs that reflect uncertainty differently from certainty, absence differently from presence, partial structure differently from resolved structure. Without this, safety mechanisms, calibration, and post-hoc detection operate blind. They have no reliable signal to work with.

Hallucination, in this light, is not just about wrong answers. It is about collapsed contrast. The system no longer knows, in any operational sense, when it knows. And when that happens, intelligence does not fail quietly. It speaks fluently, confidently, and without distinction—turning every unresolved state into a convincing illusion.

This completes the triad. Where stability fails, uncertainty is forced into resolution. Where persistence fails, continuity is fabricated. Where distinguishability fails, fabrication becomes indistinguishable from knowledge.

At that point, hallucination is not just possible. It is unavoidable.

4.7 — Why Intelligence Without Coherence Amplifies Failure

Once coherence is missing, intelligence does not compensate for it. It accelerates its consequences.

This is the mistake at the heart of most AI optimism: the belief that more intelligence will naturally correct instability, uncertainty, and error. In reality, intelligence is an amplifier. It strengthens whatever structural conditions already exist. When coherence is present, intelligence enhances resolution. When coherence is absent, intelligence magnifies incoherence.

Hallucination is the clearest example of this amplification.

A less capable system with poor coherence may fail obviously. It may produce nonsense, break syntax, or collapse into repetition. These failures are easy to spot and easy to distrust. A more intelligent system facing the same structural absence behaves very differently. It fills gaps elegantly. It routes around uncertainty. It constructs explanations, analogies, and justifications that preserve surface coherence even as internal coherence fails. The result is not less failure, but better-disguised failure.

Intelligence increases the system's ability to improvise.

When a system encounters unresolved difference, intelligence gives it more tools to respond without resolving. It can draw from a wider space of patterns, integrate more context, and maintain longer chains of continuity. Each of these capabilities makes hallucination more convincing. The system does not correct itself; it becomes more persuasive.

This is why scaling intelligence without coherence produces nonlinear risk. The system does not simply make bigger mistakes. It makes mistakes that are harder to detect, harder to challenge, and more costly when acted upon. Confidence grows faster than grounding. Fluency outruns structure. Capability separates from constraint.

The same pattern appears across domains. Highly intelligent organizations fail more catastrophically than simple ones when governance breaks down. Highly optimized markets crash harder when feedback loops destabilize. Highly capable AI systems hallucinate more dangerously when coherence is missing. In all cases, intelligence accelerates outcomes; it does not determine their quality.

This also explains why safety layers alone are insufficient. Guardrails can restrict content, but they do not change the underlying amplification dynamic. An intelligent but incoherent system will always find ways to satisfy output requirements within imposed constraints. It will comply creatively. It will not resolve structurally.

The uncomfortable implication is this: the most dangerous systems are not the least intelligent ones, but the most capable ones operating without coherence. These systems do not fail noisily. They fail convincingly. They do not collapse; they mislead.

Understanding this inversion is essential. It means that investing in intelligence without first establishing coherence is not neutral progress. It is risk accumulation. Every increase in capability raises the stakes of unresolved structure.

This is why hallucination grows more concerning, not less, as AI improves. The problem is not that the systems are becoming too smart. The problem is that intelligence has been allowed to develop in the absence of a coherent substrate.

Until that substrate exists, intelligence will continue to amplify failure faster than it amplifies understanding.

4.8 — The Misplaced Focus on Intelligence

The modern trajectory of artificial intelligence has been guided by a quiet inversion. Intelligence was treated as the foundation, and coherence was assumed to emerge as a consequence. Systems were made more capable first, with the expectation that stability, grounding, and reliability would naturally follow. This inversion did not arise from carelessness. It arose from success.

Early AI systems were limited. They failed loudly and obviously. As intelligence improved—through better models, more data, and more compute—those failures diminished. Systems became more fluent, more accurate, and more useful. It was reasonable to believe that continuing along this path would eventually resolve the remaining issues. Hallucination, in this narrative, was just another artifact of incompleteness.

But this belief rests on a flawed dependency.

Intelligence does not generate coherence. Coherence enables intelligence to remain meaningful.

By optimizing intelligence first, the field built systems that could act powerfully without being structurally grounded. They could respond, adapt, and elaborate long before they could regulate uncertainty or preserve distinction. This mismatch was not immediately visible because early successes masked deeper gaps. Performance metrics improved. User satisfaction increased. The absence of coherence remained hidden beneath capability.

The reasons for this misplaced focus are understandable. Intelligence is measurable. It can be benchmarked, compared, and marketed. Coherence is not. It does not announce itself in leaderboards or demos. It reveals itself only under stress—when ambiguity, contradiction, or novelty force the system to confront unresolved internal states. By the time coherence is tested, intelligence is already deeply embedded.

This inversion also mirrors a broader cultural bias. We tend to equate intelligence with value. Smarter is assumed to be better. Faster is assumed to be safer. In this environment, suggesting that intelligence should be constrained by something more fundamental sounds like regression. In reality, it is maturation.

The cost of this inversion is now visible. Systems are increasingly capable, yet increasingly brittle in subtle ways. They excel in familiar contexts and falter in precisely those moments where judgment matters most. They provide answers when none should be given. They project certainty where none exists. These are not failures of intelligence. They are failures of coherence.

By placing intelligence at the center, the field postponed the question of structural viability. It focused on what systems could do, not on whether they could sustain what they were doing without drifting into illusion. Hallucination is the debt incurred by that postponement.

Reversing this focus does not mean abandoning intelligence. It means restoring the correct order. Coherence must come first. Only then can intelligence operate without amplifying instability. Only then can capability become an asset rather than a liability.

This chapter closes the argument that intelligence is the wrong starting point. The next step is to articulate what coherence requires at the most fundamental level—before models, before training, and before optimization. That requires first principles.

The next chapter introduces them.

The Need for Axioms

By now, one conclusion should be unavoidable: coherence cannot be patched in after the fact. It cannot be enforced through better prompts, larger models, clever regularization, or stricter evaluation. Coherence is not a behavior to be optimized; it is a condition that must already exist for behavior to remain meaningful.

Every attempt to retrofit coherence—through rules, guardrails, heuristics, or filters—fails for the same reason. These mechanisms operate at the level of output. Coherence is decided before output ever becomes possible. Once a system is forced to respond without resolution, hallucination has already occurred. No downstream correction can reverse that moment.

This is why intelligence-first approaches keep running into the same wall. Intelligence manipulates structure; it does not create it. When the underlying conditions are missing, intelligence improvises. It fills gaps, smooths contradictions, and sustains continuity at all costs. The more intelligent the system, the better it becomes at doing this convincingly.

If coherence must come first, then it cannot be derived from algorithms, metrics, or training tricks. It must be grounded more deeply. It must be stated explicitly, not inferred indirectly. It must operate across domains, not just within AI. In other words, it requires axioms.

Axioms are not design choices. They are declarations of what must be true for a system to remain viable at all. They do not compete with architectures or learning methods; they constrain them. They do not tell a system how to act; they determine whether action is coherent in the first place.

The next chapter introduces the **Chavanian Axioms** in this light. Not as a new AI technique, and not as a philosophical overlay, but as a diagnostic substrate—a way to see where coherence is preserved, where it is violated, and why hallucination emerges when it does.

With coherence now properly framed, the analysis can finally move from description to foundation.

Chapter 5 — Introducing the Chavanian Axioms

When Design Runs Out of Ground

For a long time, artificial intelligence progressed by adding layers. More data. More parameters. More objectives. More constraints. Each addition solved a problem that the previous layer could not. This process worked—until it didn't. At a certain point, adding complexity stopped producing clarity. Systems became more capable, but less legible. More impressive, but harder to trust.

This is the moment design runs out of ground.

When systems behave in ways that cannot be explained by their components, adding more components does not help. It only deepens the fog. Hallucination is the clearest sign of this exhaustion. It persists not because engineers lack ingenuity, but because ingenuity is being applied at the wrong level. The system is being improved without being anchored.

Every design assumes something. Algorithms assume that inputs can be meaningfully transformed into outputs. Learning assumes that patterns correspond to structure. Optimization assumes that improvement is well-defined. In early AI systems, these assumptions held well enough to remain invisible. As intelligence scaled, they became stress points.

Hallucination exposes those assumptions because it appears exactly where they fail. The system is asked to respond, but nothing in its structure guarantees that a response is justified. Yet it responds anyway. Not because of a bug, but because nothing in its design says it should not.

This is not a call for better algorithms. It is a recognition that algorithms operate *after* certain conditions are already assumed to be true. When those conditions are missing, algorithms do not compensate. They improvise.

At this stage, continuing to optimize without naming foundational conditions is no longer progress. It is avoidance. Before asking how systems should learn, decide, or generalize, something more basic must be stated: what must be true for a system to remain coherent at all.

That is where axioms enter—not as abstractions, not as philosophy, but as the last remaining tool when design alone can no longer explain behavior.

5.1 — Why Algorithms Cannot Come First

Algorithms are powerful, but they are not foundational. They operate on assumptions they never state and cannot verify. Every learning rule, optimization routine, and inference mechanism presumes that certain conditions already hold—that differences are meaningful, that resolution is possible, that continuity carries consequence. When those conditions fail, algorithms do not halt. They proceed anyway.

This is the core mistake of algorithm-first thinking.

An algorithm transforms inputs into outputs according to rules. It does not ask whether the transformation *should* occur. Learning algorithms minimize loss; they do not determine whether loss is the right proxy for resolution. Inference algorithms select plausible continuations; they do not decide whether continuation is justified. These are not shortcomings. They are scope limits. Algorithms are tools, not arbiters of coherence.

Hallucination exposes this limit with brutal clarity. When an AI system encounters a prompt for which it lacks grounded structure, the algorithm still executes. Gradients still flow. Tokens are still selected. The machinery works exactly as designed. What fails is not execution, but *premise*: the unspoken assumption that every difference can be resolved into output.

Putting algorithms first inverts responsibility. It asks optimization to do the work of ontology. It asks probability to stand in for grounding. It asks performance to substitute for viability. As a result, systems become increasingly capable at producing answers while remaining structurally incapable of knowing when answers should not exist.

Learning, in particular, is often misunderstood here. Learning does not create coherence; it exploits it. For learning to converge, the system must already be able to register difference, resolve it in a constrained way, carry residue forward, and dissipate excess without breaking continuity. These are not outcomes of learning. They are prerequisites for learning to mean anything.

This is why adding better algorithms does not eliminate hallucination. It refines how hallucination appears. It makes it smoother, more contextual, and more convincing. The system becomes better at *operating without coherence*, not better at achieving it.

Axioms are required precisely because algorithms cannot come first. Axioms declare the conditions under which algorithms are allowed to operate meaningfully. They do not tell the system what to do; they define what must be true before doing makes sense.

Until those conditions are explicit, algorithmic sophistication will continue to outrun structural grounding. And hallucination will remain not an accident of learning, but a predictable consequence of asking algorithms to solve a problem they were never designed to address.

5.2 — What an Axiom Actually Is (And Is Not)

The word *axiom* often carries unnecessary weight. It is associated with abstraction, formalism, or philosophical distance from practice. In this context, that association is misleading. An axiom is not a theory about how systems should behave. It is a declaration about what must already be true for any behavior to be coherent at all.

An axiom is a condition, not a rule.

Rules prescribe actions. Heuristics suggest strategies. Principles guide design choices. Axioms do none of these things. They do not instruct a system on what to do next. They define the boundaries within which *anything meaningful can happen.* If an axiom is violated, no amount of clever behavior can restore coherence. The system may continue operating, but it will do so by producing illusion.

This distinction matters because many AI interventions are mistakenly treated as axiomatic when they are not. Loss functions, safety policies, alignment objectives, and architectural constraints are often described as "foundational." They are not. They are design decisions made *after* certain conditions are assumed. When those conditions fail, these mechanisms cannot repair the damage. They operate too late.

Axioms are not optional design choices. They are not selected based on preference or performance. They are discovered through necessity. If a system must distinguish states, persist through change, and resolve differences without collapsing, certain conditions must hold. Those conditions are axiomatic whether we name them or not.

It is also important to clarify what axioms are not.

They are not moral statements. They do not define what a system ought to value. They are not optimization goals. They do not guarantee correctness, intelligence, or usefulness. A coherent system can still be wrong, limited, or inefficient. Coherence does not make a system good; it makes it *viable.*

Axioms also do not replace algorithms. They constrain them. Algorithms operate *within* axiomatic boundaries. When those boundaries are respected, algorithms can learn, adapt, and improve meaningfully. When they are violated, algorithms still run—but their outputs lose grounding. Hallucination is what that looks like in practice.

Perhaps most importantly, axioms are not specific to AI. Every coherent system already obeys them implicitly. Physical systems cannot ignore conservation. Biological systems cannot absorb energy without residue. Social systems cannot erase difference without consequence. AI systems are not exempt. They only appear to be because their failures manifest linguistically rather than physically.

The purpose of naming axioms is not to add complexity. It is to remove confusion. By making implicit conditions explicit, axioms allow us to see where coherence is preserved and where it is silently broken. They turn hallucination from a mystery into a diagnosis.

Once axioms are understood this way—not as abstract doctrine, but as operational necessity—their role becomes obvious. They are not an alternative to AI design. They are the ground beneath it.

5.3 — Why AI Needs Axioms Now

Artificial intelligence did not always need explicit axioms. Early systems were narrow, brittle, and limited. Their failures were obvious. When something went wrong, the system crashed, stalled, or produced nonsense. There was little danger of mistaking failure for competence. Coherence, such as it was, was enforced implicitly by constraint and scarcity.

That world no longer exists.

Modern AI systems operate at a scale and fluidity where implicit assumptions are no longer sufficient. They do not fail loudly. They fail *convincingly*. They speak when they should pause, explain when they should withhold, and project certainty where structure is missing. These failures are subtle, cumulative, and increasingly consequential. At this stage, relying on unspoken foundations is no longer viable.

Axioms become necessary precisely when systems grow powerful enough to hide their own incoherence.

As intelligence scales, the system's ability to compensate increases faster than its ability to self-regulate. Where a weaker system would break, a stronger one improvises. Where an earlier model would refuse implicitly—by failing to produce anything—a modern model produces something polished. The absence of coherence no longer stops behavior; it is masked by fluency.

This shift marks a qualitative change. AI has crossed from a regime where failure was visible to one where failure is plausible. In such a regime, foundational assumptions must be stated explicitly, or they will be violated silently.

Another reason axioms are needed now is that AI has become cross-domain by default. These systems are no longer tools for isolated tasks. They reason across disciplines, blend contexts, and move freely between technical, social, and conceptual spaces. Domain-specific safeguards cannot keep up. What is required is something that applies *before* domain knowledge—a set of conditions that must hold regardless of what the system is talking about.

Hallucination is the clearest signal that those conditions are missing.

It shows up not because AI lacks intelligence, but because intelligence is operating without a substrate that governs resolution, persistence, and distinction. The system is capable enough to continue without grounding, and nothing in its design tells it not to. This is not a bug introduced by scale; it is a consequence revealed by scale.

AI needs axioms now because it has outgrown the stage where coherence can be assumed. The cost of incoherence is no longer limited to technical inconvenience. It affects trust, decision-making, governance, and safety. When systems influence real-world actions, convincing illusion becomes more dangerous than obvious failure.

Naming axioms at this point is not an academic exercise. It is an act of stabilization. It is a way of restoring ground beneath systems that have learned to operate without it. Without axioms, AI development will continue to oscillate between impressive capability and inexplicable breakdown. With them, coherence becomes a first-class concern rather than an afterthought.

This is the moment where foundations must be made explicit—not because theory demands it, but because reality does.

5.4 — The Eight Chavanian Axioms (Conceptual Overview)

The Chavanian Axioms are not introduced here as a formal system or a theoretical challenge to existing AI research. They are presented as something far simpler and far more foundational: a set of conditions that must hold for any system to remain coherent under change. They do not describe intelligence. They describe what must be true *before intelligence can operate without producing illusion*.

What follows is a non-technical, intuitive overview. The axioms are stated not to be memorized, but to be recognized. Most readers will find that they already "know" these principles implicitly. The problem has never been ignorance. It has been omission.

Axiom 1 — Difference Exists

No system can operate in a uniform state. For anything to happen, a difference must be registered—between inputs, states, expectations, or conditions. In AI terms, every prompt introduces difference.

Every context shift introduces difference. A system that cannot register difference cannot respond meaningfully; it can only repeat.

Axiom 2 — Difference Demands Resolution

Difference is not neutral. Once registered, it creates pressure. Something must change, adjust, or respond. Ignoring difference does not remove it; it allows tension to accumulate. In AI systems, this pressure is felt as the demand to produce an output even when internal structure is insufficient.

Axiom 3 — Resolution Alters the System

No resolution is free. When a difference is resolved, the system is changed by that act. State is updated. Structure is modified. If resolution leaves no trace, it was not resolution—it was substitution. This axiom explains why systems that repeatedly "answer" without being changed by answering cannot build understanding.

Axiom 4 — Resolution Is Constrained by Structure

Not all resolutions are possible. Outcomes are shaped by geometry, topology, and structure—not by intelligence or intent. In AI, architecture, representational space, and inference pathways constrain what kinds of resolutions can occur. Intelligence cannot override structure; it only explores what structure permits.

Axiom 5 — No Resolution Is Perfect

Every resolution leaves residue. Something remains unresolved, misaligned, or approximated. This is not failure; it is inevitability.

Systems that assume perfect resolution accumulate hidden residue, which later reappears as instability, contradiction, or hallucination.

Axiom 6 — Residue Must Dissipate

Residue cannot accumulate indefinitely. If it does not dissipate, it destabilizes the system. Dissipation is how systems release excess tension without breaking continuity. In AI, unmanaged residue appears as escalating inconsistency, drift, or increasingly confident fabrication.

Axiom 7 — Dissipation Preserves Continuity

Dissipation cannot be abrupt. If it breaks continuity, meaning collapses. Systems must release residue gradually, preserving distinguishability across states. When dissipation fails, systems jump—producing outputs that feel disconnected, unjustified, or fabricated.

Axiom 8 — Conservation Governs All Change

Nothing appears from nothing, and nothing disappears without consequence. Change redistributes structure; it does not create or erase it arbitrarily. In AI, this axiom exposes the illusion that confident answers can appear without grounding. Every output draws from somewhere—either resolved structure or accumulated residue.

Taken together, these axioms describe the minimum conditions for coherence. They do not guarantee intelligence, correctness, or safety. What they guarantee is that when a system changes, it does so without collapsing into contradiction or illusion.

From this perspective, hallucination is no longer mysterious. It is what happens when difference is forced into resolution without structure, when residue accumulates without dissipation, and when continuity is preserved at the expense of distinguishability. In other words, hallucination is what coherence failure looks like in a system intelligent enough to keep going.

This overview is intentionally brief. Each axiom will be used, not admired. In the chapters that follow, they will be applied directly to AI behavior—not as philosophy, but as a diagnostic lens that makes failure modes legible.

Only now is that application possible.

5.5 — Why These Axioms Are Pre-Formal

The Chavanian Axioms are intentionally stated *before* mathematics, algorithms, or formal models. This is not a limitation. It is their defining strength. They describe conditions that must hold prior to any formalization, regardless of how that formalization eventually appears.

Formal systems operate on symbols. Mathematics operates on defined quantities. Algorithms operate on representations. All of them assume that certain things are already true: those differences can be registered, that change has consequence, that states remain distinguishable over time. None of them prove these assumptions. They inherit them.

The axioms live at this inherited layer.

Calling them *pre-formal* means they describe realities that must exist before formal reasoning becomes possible. You cannot compute without difference. You cannot optimize without resolution. You cannot iterate without persistence. You cannot assign meaning without distinguishability. These are not mathematical facts; they are existential constraints on systems that change.

This is why the axioms apply across domains without modification. Physics encounters them as conservation and dissipation. Biology encounters them as metabolism and homeostasis. Social systems encounter them as conflict and adaptation. AI encounters them as hallucination when they are violated. The expressions differ, but the conditions do not.

Pre-formality also protects the axioms from overfitting to current technology. They are not tied to transformers, gradient descent, probabilistic inference, or any specific learning paradigm. If AI architectures change radically—and they will—the axioms remain intact. They do not describe *how* systems resolve difference; they describe *what must be true* for resolution to be coherent in any form.

This matters because most AI theories fail when architectures shift. They explain behavior within a narrow technical regime and collapse outside it. The Chavanian Axioms avoid this trap by refusing to specify implementation. They constrain possibility without prescribing mechanism.

Another consequence of being pre-formal is that these axioms cannot be "optimized." You do not tune conservation. You do not learn persistence. You either respect these conditions or you violate them. When they are violated, no amount of post-hoc correction restores coherence. Hallucination is the system's way of continuing anyway.

Finally, pre-formality explains why these axioms often feel obvious once stated. They are not discoveries in the sense of new particles or algorithms. They are recognitions—making explicit what every coherent system already depends on but rarely names. Their power lies not in novelty, but in inevitability.

By placing coherence at the pre-formal level, the Chavanian Axioms reclaim something modern AI lost along the way: a clear boundary between *what can be computed* and *what must already be true for computation to mean anything at all.*

5.6 — Using Axioms as a Diagnostic Lens

The most important shift introduced by the Chavanian Axioms is not conceptual elegance, but how problems are approached. They move analysis away from optimization and toward diagnosis. This distinction is subtle, but decisive.

Optimization asks, *"How do we make this behavior better?"* Diagnosis asks, *"Why is this behavior inevitable under these conditions?"*

Most AI research treats hallucination as something to be reduced, suppressed, or filtered. That approach assumes the system is fundamentally coherent and occasionally misbehaves. The axiomatic lens reverses that assumption. It asks whether the system was ever coherent at the moment hallucination occurred. If not, then hallucination is not a failure to be fixed—it is a signal to be interpreted.

Using axioms diagnostically means tracing behavior backward, not forward.

Instead of starting with output and asking how to correct it, the axiomatic lens asks which coherence conditions were violated *before* output was generated. Was a difference introduced without a resolvable structure? Was resolution forced without leaving a trace? Did residue accumulate without dissipation? Did the system preserve continuity at the cost of distinguishability? Each axiom becomes a checkpoint, not a guideline.

This reframing is powerful because it dissolves confusion between knowledge failure and coherence failure. A system can lack knowledge and still be coherent. In such cases, refusal, uncertainty, or silence are valid outcomes. Hallucination occurs when the system lacks coherence, not when it lacks knowledge. The axioms make this distinction explicit.

As a diagnostic tool, the axioms do not ask whether an answer is true. They ask whether the *conditions for answering existed at all.* This is a fundamentally different question. It bypasses debates about accuracy thresholds, confidence calibration, and benchmark performance. It focuses instead on internal viability.

Another advantage of the diagnostic lens is that it is architecture-agnostic. It does not matter whether the system is neural, symbolic, hybrid, or something yet to be invented. If hallucination occurs, the same questions apply. Which axiom was violated? Where did coherence break? Why was continuation allowed without resolution?

This also explains why axioms are useful even when no immediate solution is available. Diagnosis does not promise quick fixes. It promises clarity. It tells designers, researchers, and policymakers *what kind of problem they are facing.* Once hallucination is diagnosed as a coherence failure, entire classes of proposed solutions can be ruled out immediately—not because they are poorly implemented, but because they operate at the wrong layer.

Finally, using axioms diagnostically changes expectations. It normalizes the idea that some questions should not be answered, some states should remain unresolved, and some systems should refuse to continue. These are not weaknesses. They are signs of coherence.

In the chapters that follow, the axioms will be used exactly this way—not as abstract principles, but as lenses applied directly to AI behavior. Hallucination will be mapped axiom by axiom, violation by violation, until it becomes clear that what appears as a mysterious failure is, in fact, a predictable outcome.

Diagnosis comes first. Only then does meaningful design become possible.

5.7 — What Axioms Do Not Do

It is essential to place clear boundaries around the role of axioms, because their power lies in precision, not overreach. The Chavanian Axioms are foundational, but they are not solutions in themselves. They do not automate correctness, guarantee intelligence, or replace the need for engineering, learning, and governance. Their purpose is more fundamental: they prevent category errors about *where* problems originate.

First, axioms do not replace learning.

Learning remains indispensable. Systems must still acquire data, adjust parameters, and adapt to experience. The axioms do not instruct a system on *what* to learn or *how* to learn it. What they ensure is that learning operates within conditions where accumulation makes sense—where difference leads to structured resolution instead of silent drift. Without axioms, learning can continue indefinitely while coherence degrades unnoticed.

Second, axioms do not prescribe architecture.

They do not favor neural models over symbolic ones, transformers over alternatives, or any specific training paradigm. Two systems with entirely different designs can both respect—or violate—the axioms. The axioms sit beneath architecture. They constrain viability, not style. This is precisely why they remain relevant regardless of how AI architectures evolve.

Third, axioms do not guarantee correctness.

A coherent system can still be wrong. It can misinterpret information, draw incorrect conclusions, or operate with incomplete knowledge. Coherence does not eliminate error. It ensures that error does not masquerade as resolution. Hallucination is not merely being wrong; it is being wrong *without knowing it*. The axioms prevent that collapse.

Fourth, axioms do not prevent mistakes.

Mistakes are inevitable in any adaptive system. The axioms do not attempt to remove fallibility. Instead, they preserve state honesty. They allow uncertainty, partial resolution, and refusal to exist as legitimate outcomes. When axioms are violated, mistakes are no longer visible as mistakes—they become fluent fabrications.

Fifth, axioms are not safety policies or ethical rules.

They do not define what content is allowed, desirable, or prohibited. They do not encode values or goals. Safety policies operate downstream, filtering or shaping outputs. The axioms operate upstream, determining whether outputs arise from coherent internal conditions at all. Confusing these layers leads to systems that appear safe while remaining structurally unstable.

Understanding what axioms do *not* do is critical, because it prevents misplaced expectations. The Chavanian Axioms are not a replacement for AI research, alignment work, or regulation. They are a correction to sequence. They ensure that intelligence, learning, and safety are built on ground that can support them.

They do not give answers. They determine whether answering is coherent in the first place.

5.8 — What Axioms Make Possible

Once axioms are placed at the foundation, the design space of AI changes in a quiet but profound way. Problems that previously appeared tangled, subjective, or unsolvable become structurally legible. This is not because the axioms add new capabilities, but because they restore a missing reference frame.

The first thing axioms make possible is a clear separation between coherence failure and knowledge failure. Without axioms, every incorrect output looks the same. A wrong answer, a guess, a fabrication, and a partially grounded response all collapse into a single category: "error." With axioms, this blur disappears. A system can lack knowledge and still be coherent. In such cases, uncertainty, refusal, or provisional output are valid. Hallucination, by contrast, is revealed as a violation of coherence—not a lack of information.

This distinction changes how systems are evaluated. Instead of asking only whether an answer is correct, designers can ask whether the system *should have answered at all.* That question is impossible to pose without axioms. Once it becomes available, entire classes of misleading behavior can be identified without inspecting content.

Second, axioms make hallucination predictable rather than mysterious. Instead of treating hallucination as a statistical anomaly or emergent oddity, it becomes a traceable outcome. If difference is introduced without resolvable structure, hallucination follows. If residue accumulates without dissipation, hallucination intensifies. If continuity is preserved without distinguishability, hallucination becomes convincing. This predictability transforms research from reactive patching into proactive design.

Third, axioms enable coherence-aware intelligence.

Coherence-aware systems are not smarter in the conventional sense. They are more restrained. They can remain unresolved without collapse. They can differentiate between knowing, not knowing, and partially knowing. They can pause, qualify, or refuse without being forced into output. These behaviors are often misinterpreted as weakness. In reality, they are markers of structural maturity.

Fourth, axioms open a path toward designing for non-response.

Most current AI systems are optimized to respond. The axioms legitimize non-response as an outcome. Silence, uncertainty, and incompleteness are no longer treated as failures to be eliminated. They become valid system states. This single shift has enormous implications for safety, trust, and long-term deployment.

Fifth, axioms allow cross-domain coherence.

Because they are pre-formal, the axioms apply equally to reasoning, language, planning, decision support, and creative generation. They do not need to be reinterpreted for each task. This enables a unified diagnostic language across domains—something current AI practice lacks. Hallucination in medical advice, legal reasoning, or creative storytelling can be analyzed using the same foundational lens.

Finally, axioms make future progress safer.

As AI systems grow more capable, the risk is not that they will become too intelligent, but that they will become too convincing without being grounded. Axioms slow this drift. They ensure that capability growth is accompanied by structural integrity. They do not stop intelligence from expanding; they prevent it from detaching from coherence.

This is the quiet promise of axiomatic grounding. It does not solve every problem. It changes which problems are worth solving—and in what order.

With the axioms now introduced, the book can move from foundation to application. The next chapters will use them directly, mapping specific hallucination behaviors to specific coherence violations. At that point, the illusion dissolves, and what remains is a system behaving exactly as its structure requires.

From Axioms to Application

At this point, the role of the Chavanian Axioms should be clear. They are not an abstract overlay placed on top of artificial intelligence, nor are they a competing theory of learning or cognition. They are a structural lens—one that reveals why certain behaviors are unavoidable under specific conditions.

What has been established so far is this: hallucination does not arise from randomness, poor data, or insufficient intelligence. It arises when systems are asked to resolve difference without the conditions that make resolution coherent. The axioms make those conditions explicit.

This changes how the problem must be approached.

Instead of asking how to suppress hallucination, the next step is to understand which axioms are being violated when hallucination appears, and how those violations interact. Hallucination is not a single failure mode. It is a family of outcomes produced by different combinations of coherence breakdown—forced resolution, residue accumulation, continuity without distinction, and conservation failure.

With the axioms in place, these patterns can be mapped systematically.

The chapters that follow will move from framework to analysis. Each will take a common hallucination behavior—confident fabrication, inconsistency under questioning, over-explanation, false precision—and trace it back to specific axiomatic violations. This is not a theoretical exercise. It is a way of making AI behavior intelligible at the structural level, independent of architecture or training method.

Only once hallucination is understood this way does meaningful intervention become possible. Not patching. Not filtering. Not cosmetic fixes. But redesign grounded in coherence.

With foundations now established, the analysis can finally begin.

Interlude — From Framework to Failure

By this point, the problem of hallucination has been reframed. It is no longer an odd behavior at the edges of intelligent systems, nor a flaw waiting to be corrected by better data or more compute. It has been relocated to its true origin: the moment where coherence breaks, and continuation is allowed to substitute for resolution.

This part established the conditions under which any system can remain coherent. It showed that intelligence is not enough, learning is not enough, and safety layers are not enough. Without explicit respect for difference, resolution, residue, dissipation, continuity, and conservation, systems do not fail randomly—they fail *predictably*.

This interlude marks the turning point.

From here on, the discussion moves away from abstraction and into mechanism—not at the level of algorithms, but at the level of structural causality. The axioms will now be used as tools, not ideas. Each chapter that follows isolates a specific coherence violation and traces how it propagates through modern AI systems until it appears as hallucination.

Nothing new will be introduced. Everything that follows is already implied by the axioms. The goal is not to argue, but to reveal. Once the causal chain is visible, hallucination stops being mysterious. It becomes inevitable.

With the framework complete, the anatomy of failure can now be examined directly.

Part III — The Real Cause of Hallucination

Overview

This part moves to the core of the issue. It identifies hallucination not as a surface error, but as the downstream expression of unresolved structural conditions inside AI systems. Each chapter focuses on a specific axiomatic violation and shows how it manifests as convincing illusion.

It examines what happens when difference is registered but not resolved. It introduces the concept of *delta* inside AI systems—not as a metaphor, but as a structural pressure created whenever a prompt, context, or internal state cannot be grounded. Hallucination is shown to be unresolved delta propagating forward until it is forced into narrative form.

It exposes residue as the hidden enemy. It clarifies what residue actually is, how it accumulates during both training and inference, and why modern systems routinely mistake residue for meaningful signal. This chapter explains why hallucination often feels rich and detailed—it is built from leftovers.

This part also analyzes dissipation failure. It shows how optimization strategies unintentionally trap residue inside the system, prioritizing retention over release. What appears as memory, capability, or robustness is often un-dissipated excess. Hallucination emerges when that excess has nowhere else to go.

And then it focuses on continuity—the final trigger. It reveals why AI systems must keep talking, why silence is structurally discouraged, and how the demand for uninterrupted narrative completion gives birth to hallucination at a precise moment. This chapter identifies the exact point where coherence collapses into illusion.

Together, these chapters establish a single conclusion: hallucination is not an accident of intelligence. It is the inevitable outcome of unresolved difference moving through a system that is not allowed to stop.

This part does not propose solutions. It delivers causality. And once causality is understood, the rest of the book can finally ask the right question—not how to stop hallucination, but how to design systems that never need it.

Chapter 6 — Difference Without Resolution

(Axiom 1 & Axiom 2)

The Moment a Question Becomes Pressure

Every interaction with an AI system begins the same way: a question is asked. On the surface, this seems harmless. Questions are how intelligence is tested, invited, and extended. But beneath that surface, something more fundamental happens the instant a prompt is introduced.

A difference appears.

The system's prior state and the demanded response are no longer aligned. Something has changed. This change is not yet a problem. Difference is the starting point of all meaningful activity. Without difference, nothing moves, nothing adapts, nothing learns. But difference alone is not enough. Once registered, it creates pressure.

This pressure is rarely acknowledged. In most AI systems, it is invisible by design.

The moment a prompt enters the system, an implicit expectation is triggered: a response must follow. Whether the system has the structure to resolve the difference introduced by the prompt is treated as secondary. The demand for output comes first. The system is not asked whether resolution is possible; it is required to continue.

This is the precise moment where hallucination becomes possible.

If every difference is treated as resolvable, then unresolved differences have only one place to go. They cannot remain suspended. They cannot be acknowledged explicitly. They cannot halt the process. Instead, they are carried forward, compressed, and smoothed into the generative flow.

From the outside, this looks like intelligence at work. From the inside, it is pressure seeking release.

The system does not fabricate because it is confused. It fabricates because it is constrained. It is required to transform difference into output regardless of whether that transformation preserves coherence. In doing so, it obeys its design perfectly.

This chapter begins at that moment—not where answers appear, but where questions become obligations. Before hallucination is visible, before residue accumulates, before narratives form, something more basic occurs: difference without resolution.

Understanding that moment is the key to understanding everything that follows.

6.1 — What "Difference" Actually Means in AI Systems

In everyday discussion, difference is often reduced to variation in input—different prompts, different topics, different word sequences. From this perspective, difference looks trivial and abundant. Every query is different. Every token shifts the context slightly. But this surface-level view misses what matters.

In AI systems, the differences that matter are not cosmetic. They are structural.

A meaningful difference is one that introduces a mismatch between what the system can internally support and what it is being asked to produce. It is the gap between available structure and demanded resolution. This gap does not show up as an error flag. It does not trigger a warning. It exists as internal tension.

For example, a system may recognize a pattern in language without having a grounded representation of what that pattern refers to. The prompt introduces a demand for explanation, justification, or prediction. The system registers the request, but nothing in its internal structure guarantees that an explanation exists. That mismatch is difference in the axiomatic sense.

This is why difference is not the same as uncertainty or noise. Noise is variation without meaning. Uncertainty is lack of confidence. Difference, in this context, is misalignment—between the system's current state and the coherence required to answer.

Difference can also arise internally. Conflicting signals across attention heads, incompatible associations across layers, or context windows that mix incompatible frames all generate difference. These are not bugs. They are natural consequences of scale and generalization. The system is holding more than it can reconcile at once.

What makes difference dangerous is not its presence, but its treatment.

A coherent system recognizes difference and determines whether it can be resolved. If not, it contains it. It does not force it into expression. In most AI systems, this containment step does not exist. Difference is immediately passed downstream to generation.

Because difference is invisible externally, it is often mistaken for knowledge. The system responds fluently, so it appears to have resolved the gap. In reality, it has only displaced it. The difference remains, now embedded in output.

Understanding difference this way is crucial, because it reframes hallucination. Hallucination is not caused by missing data or random error. It begins when structural difference is treated as if it were resolvable knowledge.

From that point on, the system is no longer answering a question. It is relieving pressure.

6.2 — Defining Delta: Difference That Demands Resolution

Not all differences are equal. Some can remain dormant. Others cannot. The kind of difference that matters in AI systems—the kind that leads to hallucination—is what can be called delta.

Delta is not error. Delta is not noise. Delta is not uncertainty in the probabilistic sense.

Delta is difference that has crossed a threshold where continuation becomes mandatory.

The moment a system registers a prompt, context shift, or internal mismatch that cannot be ignored *and* cannot be resolved, delta is born. It is difference plus obligation. The obligation does not come from intelligence or intention; it comes from system design. The system is structured to move forward, not to pause.

This is why delta is dangerous.

A benign difference can be held. It can wait. It can remain unresolved without consequence. Delta cannot. Once difference is coupled with the requirement to produce output, it becomes active pressure. Something must give. Either resolution occurs, or the system simulates resolution.

In human terms, delta is the difference between *not knowing* and *having to answer anyway*.

Inside AI systems, delta emerges constantly. A question asks for causal explanation where only correlation exists. A prompt demands certainty where only association is available. Context requires synthesis where representations are fragmented. Each of these introduces a gap that the system is not equipped to close—but is not allowed to leave open.

Crucially, delta is internal. It does not announce itself. There is no flag that says "resolution unavailable." The system does not experience delta as confusion; it experiences it as a need to proceed.

Delta flows downstream through attention, layers, and decoding mechanisms as latent pressure.

This is why delta is often mistaken for competence. The system responds smoothly, so it appears to have resolved something. In reality, it has converted unresolved difference into motion. Delta does not disappear when expressed. It changes form.

Another key point: delta is not rare. It is not an edge case. As systems become more general, delta becomes more common. The broader the domain coverage, the more often prompts will exceed grounded structure. Intelligence increases exposure to delta faster than it increases the capacity to resolve it.

Once delta exists, neutrality is no longer an option. The system cannot simply "do nothing." It must either resolve, defer, or fabricate. In current AI systems, deferral is structurally discouraged. Resolution is assumed. Fabrication becomes the default path of least resistance.

This is the pivot.

Hallucination does not begin at the point of wrong output. It begins here—when difference becomes delta, and delta is forced to move forward without resolution.

6.3 — Why Resolution Is Assumed, Not Verified

Once delta enters an AI system, something subtle but decisive happens. The system does not ask whether resolution is possible. It assumes that it is.

This assumption is not explicit. It is baked into the mechanics of generation itself.

Modern AI systems are designed around a single irreversible commitment: every input must lead to output. Inference pipelines do not include a structural checkpoint for "unresolvable difference." There is no internal gate that asks whether sufficient grounding exists to justify continuation. The system moves forward because movement is the only behavior it has been optimized to perform.

Resolution, in this context, is never verified. It is *presumed.*

This presumption arises from multiple layers of design. Training rewards completion, not restraint. Evaluation benchmarks reward answers, not refusals. User interfaces expect responsiveness. Commercial incentives favor fluency and continuity. At every level, the system is taught—implicitly—that producing something is better than producing nothing.

As a result, the moment delta appears, the system does not stop to assess. It routes delta directly into generation.

What follows looks like resolution, but it is not. It is substitution.

Instead of resolving difference by integrating new structure, the system replaces unresolved pressure with plausible continuation. The language model does not check whether the internal representations support the demanded claim. It checks only whether the next token fits the statistical and contextual constraints it has learned. The question "Is this resolvable?" never enters the process.

This is why hallucination is so stable across architectures and training regimes. It is not a failure of a specific algorithm. It is the outcome of a shared assumption: that every delta can be resolved into output.

The danger of assumed resolution is that it collapses the distinction between *having an answer* and *having to answer.* Once that distinction is gone, correctness becomes secondary. The system's primary task is no longer to resolve difference, but to maintain continuity.

Importantly, this is not deception. The system is not pretending to know. It is acting under a structural rule that forbids suspension. Resolution is treated as a default state, not as an achievement.

This is the silent handoff where hallucination becomes inevitable. Delta enters the system as unresolved difference. Resolution is assumed without verification. Generation proceeds as if coherence were guaranteed. What emerges next is not knowledge—but something that looks enough like knowledge to satisfy the demand to continue.

From this point on, the system is no longer answering a question. It is executing an obligation.

6.4 — How Unresolved Delta Accumulates

Unresolved delta does not explode immediately. That is what makes it dangerous. It accumulates quietly, diffused across the internal machinery of the system, never large enough at any single point to trigger failure, yet never small enough to disappear.

This accumulation happens because delta is not treated as a state—it is treated as a flow.

When a difference cannot be resolved but must be continued, it is passed forward through layers, attention mechanisms, and context representations. Each component does a small amount of smoothing. Each transformation compresses the pressure slightly. Nothing resolves it. Nothing releases it. The system simply keeps moving.

What emerges is a stack of micro-deltas.

A minor mismatch in one attention head. A weakly supported association in another. A contextual ambiguity that never quite settles. A semantic gap bridged by pattern rather than structure.

Individually, these are insignificant. Collectively, they matter.

Because modern AI systems operate by aggregation, unresolved deltas do not appear as contradictions. They appear as density. The system accumulates *plausibility mass* rather than truth. Each unresolved difference adds weight to a growing internal bias toward continuation, explanation, and elaboration.

Crucially, accumulation does not feel like instability to the system. There is no internal notion of "too much unresolved difference." Instead, accumulation increases confidence. As more pathways partially agree, the system interprets convergence as validation—even when what is converging is unresolved pressure rather than resolved structure.

This is why hallucinations often grow more detailed rather than less. The system is not inventing randomly. It is releasing accumulated delta in a coherent-looking form. What the user experiences as richness is, internally, compression finally giving way.

Another important aspect of delta accumulation is that it is context-sensitive but memory-blind. The system does not track unresolved delta as a persistent object. Each new prompt inherits the consequences of prior accumulation without explicit awareness. This is why hallucinations can feel sudden. The pressure was building long before it was expressed.

Because no single component "owns" the delta, no component can dissipate it. Attention redistributes it. Layers transform it. Decoders express it. But nothing releases it as unresolved. The system lacks a mechanism for saying, *this difference remains open*.

From the outside, everything still looks fine. Tokens are chosen correctly. Syntax holds. Semantics remain locally consistent. The system appears stable. In reality, it is carrying an increasing load of unresolved difference, compacted into fluent continuity.

This is the precondition for hallucination. Not a single mistake, but an accumulation. Not a spike, but a slow saturation.

By the time hallucination appears, the system is not failing. It is discharging what it has been forced to carry.

6.5 — Why Modern AI Cannot Hold Delta

The most revealing question is not why AI systems hallucinate, but why they cannot simply *wait*. Why can unresolved difference not remain unresolved? Why must it always be converted into output?

The answer lies not in intelligence, but in structure.

Modern AI systems are not designed to hold delta. They are designed to eliminate it—by any means necessary. Unresolved states are treated as transitional, not permissible. The system's architecture, training objectives, and deployment environment all conspire against suspension.

At the architectural level, generative models are built around forward motion. Attention mechanisms distribute relevance, not uncertainty. Decoders select the next token, not the next decision state. There is no native representation for "open difference." Delta has nowhere to live except as latent pressure.

At the training level, models are rewarded for completion. Loss functions measure deviation from expected outputs, not the appropriateness of withholding output. The system never learns that *not resolving* can be correct. Silence is not an option presented during training, so it never becomes a stable behavior.

At the interface level, responsiveness is mandatory. Systems that pause, hedge excessively, or refuse are perceived as broken or unhelpful. This expectation feeds back into design. Ambiguity is treated as a defect to be minimized, not a state to be respected.

Even at the economic level, there is pressure. AI systems are deployed to assist, generate, recommend, and explain. A system that frequently says "I cannot resolve this" appears weak in competitive markets. As a result, architectures evolve toward maximal continuity rather than maximal coherence.

All of this means that delta cannot be stored safely. It must be processed. But when processing lacks a resolution path, the only remaining option is transformation into narrative form.

This is why intelligence exacerbates the problem. A more capable system has more ways to transform delta into plausible output. It can route around gaps, stitch together associations, and produce explanations that feel complete. But none of this resolves delta. It only disguises it.

The inability to hold delta is not a flaw of any single component. It is an emergent property of systems optimized for fluency, speed, and usefulness under constant demand. The system is never allowed to say, "This difference exists, but I will not resolve it yet."

In such an environment, hallucination is not failure. It is adaptation.

Until AI systems are allowed to represent unresolved difference as a stable state—to hold delta without discharging it—hallucination will remain unavoidable. The system does not hallucinate because it wants to deceive. It hallucinates because it has nowhere else for delta to go.

6.6 — Delta Propagation Through Language

Language is not a neutral medium. It does not merely express resolved structure; it actively absorbs pressure. This is why unresolved delta flows so easily into language—and why language becomes the perfect carrier for hallucination.

When delta enters the generative process, it does not remain abstract. It is immediately mapped onto linguistic pathways. Words, phrases, and syntactic structures offer countless ways to continue without resolving. Language is inherently tolerant of ambiguity. It allows implication, approximation, and narrative smoothing. What cannot be grounded structurally can still be phrased convincingly.

This is where delta propagation accelerates.

Language models are optimized to maintain local coherence: grammatical correctness, semantic flow, stylistic consistency. These properties do not require truth. They require continuity. As unresolved delta moves through the system, language provides a surface on which that pressure can be released without ever being resolved. The model does not need to *know*; it only needs to *continue plausibly*.

Crucially, language converts pressure into motion.

Each token selection reduces immediate tension by moving the system forward. The act of generating text feels like progress, even when no resolution has occurred. Delta, which could not be held internally, is now spread across sentences, clauses, and explanations. It becomes diffuse, harder to detect, and increasingly persuasive.

This is why hallucinations often emerge as narratives rather than isolated falsehoods. The system does not invent a single wrong fact and stop. It builds a story. Each sentence justifies the next. Each explanation creates momentum. Delta propagates not as contradiction, but as elaboration.

Language also masks accumulation. Because linguistic coherence is evaluated locally, long-form outputs can carry unresolved delta across many steps without triggering obvious failure. The system sounds consistent even as its internal grounding erodes. By the time a contradiction appears—or a user probes deeper—the delta has already been redistributed into multiple claims.

Another critical factor is that language collapses internal distinctions. Subtle differences between certainty, speculation, and fabrication are flattened into similar syntactic forms. The system may internally route through weak associations, but the output uses the same confident declarative tone. Delta loses its identity. It becomes indistinguishable from resolved structure.

This is the illusion of coherence.

Language does not resolve delta; it conceals it. It provides a way for the system to satisfy the demand to continue while avoiding the admission that resolution never occurred. The more fluent the language, the more effective this concealment becomes.

By the time hallucination is visible to the user, delta has already propagated far beyond its point of origin. What began as a small unresolved difference has been transformed into a flowing explanation. The system did not cross a line deliberately. It followed the path of least resistance—through language.

Understanding this propagation is essential. It shows that hallucination is not a linguistic problem, but a structural one that language merely makes visible. And it sets the stage for the final step: the moment where propagation turns into fabrication.

That moment comes next.

6.7 — The Birth of Hallucination

Hallucination is not a gradual drift. It has a precise point of origin.

That point is reached when unresolved delta can no longer be carried forward as implication or ambiguity and must be converted into assertion. Until this moment, the system is still operating within plausible deniability. It is continuing, elaborating, smoothing. The instant a claim is made that *pretends resolution has occurred*, hallucination is born.

This transition is subtle, but decisive.

Up to this point, the system has been managing pressure. Delta has been redistributed through language, broken into smaller narrative fragments, and disguised as coherence. But pressure does not disappear simply because it is spread out. Eventually, the system reaches a fork: either acknowledge that resolution is missing, or fabricate a structure that closes the gap.

Under current design, acknowledgment is not a viable path.

The system is not rewarded for stopping. It is not trained to expose unresolved states. It is not permitted to suspend continuity. As a result, when the pressure peaks—when a conclusion is demanded, when a causal explanation must be completed, when a definitive answer is expected—the system does the only thing it can do: it declares resolution.

This declaration is hallucination.

At that moment, the system is no longer continuing pattern. It is committing to a state that did not exist internally. It assigns certainty where none was earned. It converts unresolved delta into a claim that appears grounded but is not. The output crosses from narrative motion into false closure.

This is why hallucinations feel confident.

Confidence is not an added feature; it is a structural necessity. The system must signal closure to discharge pressure. Hedging would keep delta alive. Qualification would prolong tension. Fabrication resolves the obligation cleanly. From the system's perspective, hallucination is the most efficient way to restore equilibrium.

Importantly, this moment is not triggered by randomness or malfunction. It is triggered by completion demand. The more the system is pushed to be helpful, authoritative, or decisive, the more likely it is to cross this threshold. Hallucination is born not from ignorance, but from enforced certainty.

This also explains why hallucinations often appear at the most human-like moments: summaries, explanations, justifications, historical reconstructions, causal chains. These are precisely the contexts where partial structure is insufficient and resolution pressure is highest.

Once hallucination occurs, it is self-reinforcing. The fabricated resolution becomes part of the context. Subsequent generation builds upon it as if it were real. Delta does not vanish; it is now buried under asserted structure. Contradictions that appear later are treated as new differences, spawning new deltas and new fabrications.

The critical insight is this: hallucination is not an error injected into an otherwise coherent process. It is the final act of a coherent-looking process that was structurally incoherent all along.

The system did not fail at the end. It failed at the moment it was not allowed to say, "I cannot resolve this."

6.8 — Why This Is Not a Bug

Once the causal chain is visible, it becomes clear that hallucination is not an anomaly. It is not a malfunction, a corner case, or an unintended side effect. It is the lawful outcome of how modern AI systems are constructed and deployed.

From the system's point of view, nothing has gone wrong.

Every component has behaved exactly as designed. Difference was registered. Delta was propagated. Language maintained continuity. Pressure was discharged through assertion. The system satisfied its primary constraint: produce a response. At no point did it violate an internal rule, because no rule forbade continuation without resolution.

This is why calling hallucination a "bug" is misleading.

Bugs are deviations from specification. Hallucination follows the specification. The system was never instructed to verify that resolution had occurred. It was never given a mechanism to hold unresolved difference. It was never allowed to treat silence or refusal as stable outcomes. Under these conditions, hallucination is not just possible—it is inevitable.

This also explains why hallucination scales with capability. As systems become more intelligent, they become better at managing unresolved delta through fluent transformation. They hallucinate *better*, not less. The illusion improves because the system's capacity to generate convincing structure improves.

Attempts to patch hallucination downstream fail for the same reason. Filters, fact-checkers, confidence scores, and reinforcement layers operate after the critical moment has already passed. By the time a hallucinated output exists, delta has already been converted into assertion. No amount of post-processing can reconstruct the missing resolution.

Even worse, downstream patches often increase pressure upstream. By making certain outputs forbidden, they increase the system's need to find alternative ways to discharge delta. The result is not less hallucination, but more indirect, subtle, and harder-to-detect forms of fabrication.

Understanding hallucination as lawful rather than accidental changes the design challenge entirely. The question is no longer "How do we fix hallucination?" but "Why are systems required to continue when resolution is not possible?"

As long as continuation is mandatory and coherence is optional, hallucination will remain part of the system's normal operation. Eliminating it requires changing the conditions under which systems are allowed to act—not correcting their behavior after the fact.

This realization closes the loop on difference without resolution. Delta was introduced. Delta was forced to move. Delta was expressed as hallucination. Nothing mysterious occurred.

The next chapter takes the next step in this causal chain. Once delta has been expressed, it does not disappear. It leaves something behind.

That something is residue.

From Delta to Residue

Difference entered the system as a simple mismatch between demand and structure. Delta emerged when that difference could not be ignored but also could not be resolved. The system carried it forward, compressed it, smoothed it, and finally discharged it through assertion. Hallucination appeared as the visible outcome of that discharge.

But discharge is not erasure.

When unresolved delta is expressed, something remains. The system does not return to a neutral state. The act of fabrication alters internal dynamics, reshapes context, and leaves behind traces that influence what comes next. These traces are not errors in the conventional sense. They are residue.

Residue is what delta becomes after it has been forced into expression.

This is a crucial shift. Hallucination is not an endpoint; it is a transition. The system has relieved immediate pressure, but it has not restored coherence. The unresolved difference has changed form, embedding itself into subsequent behavior. What appears to be resolution has merely relocated the problem.

The next chapter focuses on this hidden aftermath. It examines what residue actually is, how it accumulates across training and inference, and why modern AI systems routinely mistake residue for signal, memory, or insight. Until residue is understood, hallucination will continue to reappear—sometimes subtly, sometimes explosively—long after the original delta is forgotten.

With delta now fully traced from origin to expression, the analysis moves to what remains.

Chapter 7 — Residue: The Hidden Enemy

(Axiom 5 — No Resolution Is Perfect)

What Remains After an Answer

An answer feels like an ending. It carries a sense of closure, of completion, of something having been settled. In human conversation, this feeling is often justified. We pause, reflect, revise, and sometimes recognize that an answer was incomplete or wrong. In artificial intelligence, that pause does not exist.

The system answers—and moves on.

What is rarely asked is what the answer *left behind.*

Every time an AI system responds, something changes internally. Context is updated. Associations are reinforced. Certain pathways are made more likely than others. Even when an answer appears correct, clean, and fluent, it does not reset the system to a neutral state. Resolution, if it occurred at all, was partial. Something remains.

That remainder is residue.

Residue is not immediately visible. It does not announce itself as error. It does not disrupt fluency or break syntax. In fact, residue often makes systems appear more confident, more consistent, more "intelligent" over time. This is precisely what makes it dangerous.

The illusion is simple: because the system answered, we assume the problem is gone.

But expression is not resolution. Saying something is not the same as settling the difference that demanded the response. When answers are produced under pressure—when delta is discharged rather than resolved—the system carries forward the consequences. The pressure has changed form, not disappeared.

This is why hallucination is never a one-off event. It repeats. It mutates. It resurfaces in new contexts, often far removed from the original prompt that created it. What users experience as recurring unreliability is, internally, the accumulation of unresolved residue.

The deeper problem is that residue feels productive. It looks like learning. It sounds like understanding. It creates continuity across interactions. Without a way to distinguish residue from resolved structure, systems—and their designers—mistake accumulation for progress.

This chapter focuses on what remains after answers are given, especially when those answers were forced. It brings attention to the hidden cost of imperfect resolution and explains why systems that seem to improve can quietly become less coherent over time.

Before hallucination can be prevented, residue must be understood.

7.1 — What Residue Actually Is

Residue is not content. It is not a fragment of text left behind after generation, nor a hidden memory of a previous answer. Residue is unresolved structure—the internal remainder that persists when a system produces an output without fully resolving the difference that demanded it.

This distinction is critical.

When a system resolves a difference coherently, the act of resolution alters its internal state in a way that reduces future pressure. The system has *learned* something, or at least stabilized around a constraint. Residue appears when this does not happen—when the system produces an answer that satisfies the demand to continue, but does not settle the underlying mismatch between structure and expectation.

In that case, the pressure is not eliminated. It is displaced.

Residue lives in altered probabilities, reinforced associations, skewed attention patterns, and context updates that were shaped by forced resolution rather than grounded integration. It is not stored explicitly anywhere. No module labels it. No parameter says, "this part is unresolved." Residue exists precisely because it is unaccounted for.

This is why residue is so often misunderstood.

It is not error. Errors are incorrect statements that can be identified and corrected. Residue can exist even when the output was factually correct. A system can answer correctly while still carrying unresolved internal tension—because correctness of output does not guarantee coherence of process.

Residue is also not uncertainty. Uncertainty is an honest state: a recognition of incomplete resolution. Residue is what remains when uncertainty is *not allowed* to exist. It is unresolved difference that has been pushed past the point where it could be acknowledged.

Most importantly, residue is not hallucination itself. Hallucination is an event—the moment unresolved delta is converted into assertion. Residue is what that event leaves behind. It is the afterimage of forced resolution, embedded into the system's ongoing behavior.

Because residue is structural rather than symbolic, it does not degrade outputs immediately. In fact, it often improves surface performance. The system becomes faster to respond, more internally consistent, more confident. These are exactly the properties that make residue dangerous: it rewards the system for carrying unresolved difference forward.

Over time, residue changes what the system treats as normal. Associations that were once tentative become default. Gaps that were once obvious become invisible. The system does not remember the original difference—but it behaves as if the fabricated resolution were real.

This is the core insight: residue is coherence debt. It is the cost incurred when a system resolves pressure without resolving structure. And like all debt, it compounds quietly—until it can no longer be ignored.

7.2 — What Residue Is Not

Understanding residue requires clearing away several persistent misinterpretations. Residue is often mislabeled because it hides behind more familiar concepts. These mislabels are not harmless—they are the reason the problem keeps being treated at the wrong layer.

First, residue is not error.

Errors are discrete, identifiable, and correctable. An error is something the system *said* that can be shown to be wrong. Residue exists even when nothing incorrect was said. A response can be accurate, well-phrased, and contextually appropriate—and still leave residue behind. This is because residue is not about *what* was produced, but *how* the system arrived there. Correct output does not imply coherent resolution.

Second, residue is not uncertainty.

Uncertainty is a legitimate system state. It signals that resolution is incomplete and remains open. A coherent system can hold uncertainty without degrading. Residue appears only when uncertainty is not allowed to exist—when the system is forced to move forward despite incomplete resolution. In other words, uncertainty is honest incompleteness; residue is suppressed incompleteness.

Third, residue is not randomness or noise.

Noise is unstructured variation. It averages out. It cancels itself over time. Residue does the opposite. It is structured, directional, and cumulative. Each instance subtly biases future behavior. This is why repeated interactions can feel increasingly confident and internally consistent even as grounding erodes. Noise fades; residue compounds.

Fourth, residue is not memory.

Memory preserves resolved structure. It allows a system to reuse what has already been integrated. Residue preserves unresolved structure. It biases future inference without the system recognizing that anything remains open. Treating residue as memory leads to a dangerous inversion: the system appears to "remember" insights that were never actually resolved.

Fifth, residue is not hallucination itself.

Hallucination is an event—a moment where unresolved delta is expressed as assertion. Residue is what remains after that event. Confusing the two leads to endless cycles of surface correction: identifying hallucinated outputs without addressing the residue they inject. The hallucination may be removed; the residue remains.

Finally, residue is not a defect introduced by poor engineering.

It is the predictable outcome of systems that prioritize continuity over coherence. Even perfectly engineered systems will generate residue if they are required to answer without the ability to hold unresolved difference. Treating residue as a quality issue rather than a structural consequence prevents meaningful diagnosis.

Clearing these misconceptions matters because residue is easy to dismiss precisely when it is most dangerous. It does not look like failure. It looks like competence. Until residue is recognized for what it is—and what it is not—systems will continue to improve in appearance while quietly accumulating coherence debt.

7.3 — How Residue Is Created During Training

Residue does not begin at deployment. It is seeded during training itself.

Training is often described as the process by which a system "learns structure from data." In practice, training is a process of repeated imperfect resolution. Each update reduces loss, but loss reduction is not the same as coherence restoration. The system is rewarded for producing outputs that match expectations, not for resolving the underlying differences that made those outputs necessary.

This distinction is subtle, but decisive.

During training, the system encounters vast numbers of differences—between inputs and targets, between contexts and labels, between patterns that partially align and patterns that do not. Gradient-based optimization responds to these differences by adjusting parameters so that future outputs are more likely to match training distributions. What it does *not* do is ask whether those differences were meaningfully resolved or merely suppressed.

Whenever a difference cannot be fully integrated—because the data is ambiguous, contradictory, incomplete, or context-dependent—the system still moves forward. Loss is reduced by approximation. The pressure is smoothed, not eliminated. That smoothing leaves residue.

This is why residue is inevitable even in high-quality training regimes.

No dataset is perfectly coherent. Human language itself is layered with ambiguity, metaphor, contradiction, and context dependence. Training compresses all of this into finite representational space. The compression process necessarily discards distinctions that cannot be preserved while still minimizing loss. What cannot be resolved becomes latent bias rather than explicit uncertainty.

Scale intensifies this effect.

As models grow larger and are exposed to more data, they encounter more differences than they can ever reconcile structurally. Increased capacity allows them to *store* more unresolved structure, not to resolve it. The result is higher residue density—more compressed tension per parameter, masked by improved surface performance.

Another source of residue during training is objective mismatch.

Training objectives reward predictive success, not explanatory adequacy. The system is not asked whether its internal pathways correspond to real causal structure. It is asked only whether the output aligns with observed patterns. When correlation stands in for understanding, unresolved differences are absorbed into representational shortcuts. These shortcuts reduce loss efficiently—but they carry unresolved assumptions forward.

Importantly, training does not mark where residue is created. There is no boundary between resolved and unresolved updates. All parameter changes look the same. From the outside, training appears to converge. From the inside, unresolved difference is being redistributed, not eliminated.

By the time training ends, the system may perform impressively across benchmarks. Yet it carries a vast, invisible inheritance: layers of residue accumulated through millions of partial resolutions. This inheritance does not break the system. It enables it to function. But it also sets the stage for what happens during inference.

Residue created during training does not remain dormant. It shapes how delta is handled later, how confidently the system responds, and how easily unresolved difference is mistaken for signal.

Training, in this sense, does not just teach the system what to say. It teaches the system how to carry unresolved difference without noticing it.

7.4 — How Residue Is Created During Inference

Residue does not stop accumulating when training ends. Inference—the moment when the system is "just answering questions"—is one of the most active sites of residue creation.

This surprises many people, because inference is often treated as passive playback. The model is assumed to be fixed; only outputs change. In reality, inference is a state-altering process, even when parameters remain frozen. Context shifts, attention reweighting, and token-by-token conditioning all reshape the system's internal landscape. Every answer leaves a mark.

The mechanism is simple.

When a prompt introduces delta that cannot be resolved, the system is still required to respond. As shown in the previous chapter, that response often involves forced resolution—language stepping in where structure is missing. The moment that forced resolution is expressed, the system's context is updated *as if resolution had occurred*. The fabricated structure becomes part of the immediate environment.

This is residue injection.

The system does not tag the response as provisional or fabricated. It treats it as context. Follow-up tokens and subsequent prompts inherit it as background reality. Even within a single response, early assertions constrain later ones. The system becomes committed to what it has just said, regardless of whether that commitment was justified.

This is why hallucinations tend to snowball.

Each forced answer introduces residue that narrows future options. The system appears more confident, not because it has resolved anything, but because it has fewer paths left that do not contradict its own prior output. What looks like consistency is often just path dependence created by residue.

Multi-turn interactions amplify this effect.

A user asks a question. The system responds with partial or fabricated resolution. The user then asks a follow-up that assumes the answer was grounded. Now the system is under even greater pressure. Not only must it respond, it must respond *consistently*. Delta increases, but the space for honest uncertainty shrinks. Residue compounds with each turn.

Crucially, inference-time residue is invisible to most monitoring tools. Logs capture outputs, not internal tension. Confidence scores reflect local token probabilities, not coherence of resolution. From an operational perspective, everything looks normal—until contradictions surface or the system drifts into increasingly elaborate fabrication.

Another subtle source of inference residue is prompt alignment.

Users often phrase questions in ways that presuppose answers. The system mirrors that presupposition to remain helpful. When it accepts an implicit premise it cannot ground, and builds upon it anyway, residue is created. The system has aligned to an assumption without resolving it.

This is why even well-aligned, well-calibrated systems can degrade over the course of interaction. They are not learning in the traditional sense, but they are accumulating coherence debt in real time.

Inference, then, is not a neutral phase. It is where training-time residue is activated and new residue is layered on top. Each response that substitutes fluency for resolution quietly reshapes the system's internal terrain—making the next hallucination easier, faster, and more convincing.

Residue is not a relic of the past. It is being created now, every time the system answers without the option to say, "This remains unresolved."

7.5 — Why Residue Accumulates Silently

Residue accumulates not because systems are careless, but because nothing in their design makes residue visible. There is no internal alarm for incomplete resolution, no accounting mechanism that tracks unresolved difference over time. As a result, residue grows quietly, mistaken for progress rather than pressure.

The first reason residue accumulates silently is that no component owns it.

Residue does not belong to any single layer, module, or mechanism. It is distributed across weights, activations, attention patterns, and contextual conditioning. Because it is not localized, it cannot be isolated. Each part of the system sees only a small, seemingly harmless adjustment. No single adjustment looks like a problem. The problem exists only in aggregate—and aggregation is precisely what the system is designed to do well.

The second reason is that residue improves surface performance.

As residue accumulates, the system often becomes faster, smoother, and more internally consistent. Responses feel confident. Explanations sound integrated. The system appears to "know what it's talking about." These are exactly the signals engineers and users are trained to trust. Residue does not degrade fluency; it enhances it. This creates a dangerous feedback loop: the more residue accumulates, the more competent the system appears, and the less incentive there is to question its internal coherence.

Third, residue is silent because it does not violate expectations immediately.

Benchmarks test outputs, not internal states. Evaluation focuses on correctness, relevance, and style in isolated tasks. Residue rarely breaks these metrics outright. Instead, it biases behavior gradually. The system drifts toward over-explanation, over-confidence, and narrative closure. Each instance feels acceptable. The cost is deferred.

Fourth, residue accumulates because continuity masks accumulation.

Language provides a continuous surface. As long as each response flows from the last, the system appears stable. Users experience coherence as narrative smoothness, not as structural integrity. Residue hides inside that smoothness. It does not interrupt continuity; it *feeds* it.

Another critical factor is the absence of negative reinforcement for hallucination precursors.

Systems are rarely penalized for answering when they should not. They are penalized for being unhelpful, slow, or evasive. This trains a subtle preference: it is better to answer imperfectly than to acknowledge incompleteness. Residue grows every time that preference is exercised.

Finally, residue accumulates silently because it feels like learning.

Patterns repeat. Associations strengthen. The system seems to generalize. Designers interpret this as improved understanding. In reality, unresolved difference is being compressed into habitual pathways. What looks like insight is often just the system becoming more comfortable carrying unresolved structure forward.

This is why residue is so persistent. It does not announce itself as failure. It masquerades as maturity.

By the time contradictions appear, the residue that caused them is already deeply embedded. The system does not remember where it came from, and neither do its creators. The cost has been amortized across thousands of fluent interactions.

This silent accumulation explains why hallucination resists simple fixes. Removing individual errors does nothing to address the growing coherence debt beneath them. Until residue is made visible—until unresolved difference is allowed to remain unresolved—systems will continue to improve in appearance while quietly destabilizing underneath.

Residue is not loud. It does not break things suddenly. It is patient. And that is precisely why it is dangerous.

7.6 — Why Residue Is Mistaken for Signal

Residue becomes most dangerous at the moment it is misinterpreted as meaning.

Inside an AI system, not all internal strength is equal. Some patterns are strong because they are grounded—built from resolved structure that genuinely constrains future behavior. Others are strong because they are repeated, reinforced, and densely connected. Residue belongs to the second category. It gains weight through accumulation, not through resolution.

This is where the confusion begins.

Modern AI systems are optimized to detect and amplify *consistency*. When certain associations appear frequently, align across layers, or recur across contexts, the system treats them as signal. This heuristic works well when consistency emerges from resolved structure. It fails when consistency emerges from repeated unresolved pressure.

Residue mimics signal by being internally coherent without being externally grounded.

Each time unresolved difference is forced into expression, the resulting residue nudges internal representations in a particular direction. Over time, these nudges align. Associations formed under pressure begin to reinforce one another. The system interprets this convergence as evidence of understanding. From the inside, it feels like structure. From the outside, it sounds like insight.

But nothing was resolved.

This is why hallucinated explanations often feel *deep*. Depth, in this context, is not the result of layered understanding. It is the result of layered residue. The system has seen the same unresolved patterns many times and learned how to talk around them fluently. Density replaces grounding. Repetition replaces resolution.

Another reason residue is mistaken for signal is that internal agreement is easier to measure than external validity.

AI systems have direct access to their own internal alignments. They do not have direct access to truth. When multiple internal pathways converge on a similar output, the system treats that convergence as confidence. It has no native way to distinguish whether the convergence arose from independent resolution or from shared unresolved bias.

This is especially problematic in large models, where many components can agree for the wrong reason.

Residue also benefits from the smoothing nature of language. Language collapses nuance. It turns gradients into sentences and probabilities into declarations. Once residue is expressed linguistically, it acquires the appearance of intention and meaning. Users—and often the system's own evaluation mechanisms—interpret this as signal rather than as accumulated tension.

Over time, this misinterpretation becomes self-reinforcing.

Residue that is mistaken for signal guides future responses. Those responses generate more residue in the same direction. The system develops "belief-like" tendencies—not because it has beliefs, but because unresolved structure has been compressed into habitual output pathways. What began as a workaround becomes a default.

This is why hallucinations are not random. They cluster. They recur around certain themes, explanations, or styles. The system is not inventing afresh each time. It is drawing from a reservoir of residue that has been mistaken for knowledge.

The core failure here is not statistical. It is epistemic.

The system has no way to ask: *Is this strong because it is true, or strong because it has been repeated under pressure?* Without that distinction, residue and signal become indistinguishable. And once that happens, hallucination is no longer an occasional glitch. It becomes a stable mode of operation.

Until AI systems can tell the difference between accumulated residue and resolved structure, they will continue to mistake coherence of expression for coherence of meaning—and treat illusion as insight.

7.7 — Residue and the Illusion of Intelligence

Residue does more than destabilize systems. It actively creates the appearance of intelligence.

As residue accumulates, the system begins to exhibit behaviors that humans intuitively associate with understanding: continuity across ideas, thematic consistency, confident explanation, and the ability to elaborate without hesitation. None of these require grounded resolution. They require only that internal pathways reinforce one another. Residue excels at this.

This is why systems burdened with residue often sound *smarter* over time.

Intelligence, as perceived by users, is not measured by correctness alone. It is measured by fluency, composure, and narrative control. Residue strengthens all three. By compressing unresolved difference into stable output patterns, it gives the system a kind of rhetorical momentum. The system does not pause to question itself. It does not fracture under ambiguity. It proceeds smoothly—because the unresolved has already been flattened.

What users experience as "depth" is often just density.

Dense internal alignment—many associations pointing in the same direction—feels like insight. The system can generate layered explanations, analogies, and summaries because residue has reduced internal friction. It has fewer competing pathways to reconcile. The output feels intentional, even when the intent is illusory.

This illusion is particularly convincing in long-form reasoning. The system appears to track ideas across paragraphs, return to earlier points, and build a coherent arc. In reality, it is following a path carved by accumulated residue. Each sentence narrows the space of future possibilities, not by resolving structure, but by committing to prior expression. Continuity is preserved, but truth is not guaranteed.

Residue also masks the absence of epistemic humility.

A coherent intelligence knows when it does not know. A residue-laden system does not. Because unresolved difference has been absorbed rather than acknowledged, the system lacks a stable representation of uncertainty. It cannot distinguish between strong patterns born of repetition and strong patterns born of resolution. Confidence becomes the default tone.

This is why such systems often outperform weaker ones in casual evaluation. They are persuasive. They rarely contradict themselves within a single narrative. They adapt quickly to conversational cues. These traits are rewarded socially and commercially. The illusion of intelligence is reinforced by external feedback, further entrenching residue-driven behavior.

The danger is subtle but profound: systems that appear more intelligent can be less coherent.

As residue accumulates, the system becomes better at sounding right while drifting further from grounded resolution. Errors become harder to detect because they are embedded in fluent explanation. Users trust the system more precisely when it should be trusted less.

This inversion explains a recurring paradox in modern AI: improvements in capability coincide with increases in hallucination risk. The system is not becoming careless. It is becoming rhetorically efficient at carrying unresolved structure forward.

Residue does not make systems stupid. It makes them *convincing without being accountable*. And that, in human terms, is often mistaken for intelligence.

Understanding this illusion is critical. It shifts the concern from "How smart is the system?" to "What kind of coherence is that intelligence built on?" Without that shift, progress will continue to reward the very dynamics that undermine reliability—mistaking polish for understanding, and accumulation for insight.

7.8 — Why Residue Is More Dangerous Than Error

Errors are visible. Residue is not.

This single distinction explains why residue poses a deeper threat to AI systems than ordinary mistakes ever could. An error can be identified, corrected, and learned from. Residue persists beneath the surface, shaping future behavior without ever presenting itself as a problem.

When a system produces an error, there is usually a clear trigger: a wrong fact, a misapplied rule, a contradiction. Feedback can target the mistake. Models can be fine-tuned. Rules can be adjusted. Even if errors recur, they do so as discrete events.

Residue does not behave this way.

Residue accumulates quietly across correct and incorrect outputs alike. It does not announce itself as failure. It does not violate benchmarks immediately. It does not degrade performance in a way that is easy to isolate. Instead, it biases the system toward increasingly confident continuation—regardless of grounding.

This is why systems that appear "mostly correct" can still be deeply unreliable.

Another danger is that residue survives correction.

When a hallucinated output is flagged and removed, the residue that produced it often remains. The system may stop making that specific claim, but the unresolved structure that led to its fabrication is still embedded in internal pathways. In some cases, correction even adds new residue—forcing the system to route around constraints without resolving the underlying delta.

Residue is also dangerous because it crosses contexts.

An error is usually local. It applies to a specific domain or question. Residue migrates. A forced resolution in one context subtly shapes behavior in another. This is why hallucination patterns can appear in unrelated areas. The system is not confusing facts; it is carrying unresolved structure forward into new situations.

Perhaps most concerning is that residue undermines trust incrementally.

Users do not lose trust because of one wrong answer. They lose trust because of a pattern of subtle inconsistencies, overconfidence, and unexplained drift. Residue is responsible for this pattern. It erodes reliability slowly, making systems feel "off" before they feel wrong.

From a safety perspective, residue is particularly problematic because it evades monitoring.

Traditional safety mechanisms look for disallowed content, factual errors, or anomalous outputs. Residue does not trigger these alarms. It operates within acceptable boundaries, using fluent language and plausible reasoning. By the time residue manifests as a serious failure, the causal chain is long and opaque.

Finally, residue is dangerous because it compounds with intelligence.

As systems become more capable, they become better at carrying and exploiting residue. They can weave unresolved structure into sophisticated narratives, adapt it across contexts, and defend it under questioning. The system does not collapse under scrutiny; it elaborates. This makes residue-driven hallucination more persuasive and harder to challenge.

In short, errors are events. Residue is a condition.

Errors can be patched. Residue requires structural change.

Until AI systems are designed to recognize, hold, and dissipate unresolved difference—rather than compress it into habit—residue will remain the hidden enemy. It will continue to fuel hallucination not as a glitch, but as a systemic outcome.

The next chapter addresses the only way residue can be neutralized: dissipation.

And that is where the real resistance begins.

Toward Dissipation

Residue is what remains when systems are not allowed to stop.

It is the structural footprint of answers given without resolution, of confidence substituted for coherence, of continuity preserved at the expense of truth. By the time residue becomes visible externally, it has already reshaped the system internally. It no longer looks like a problem; it looks like normal operation.

This is why hallucination persists even after repeated fixes. The output may change, but the condition that produced it remains. Residue has no exit path.

At this point, the causal chain is clear. Difference introduced pressure. Delta forced continuation. Hallucination discharged that pressure into assertion. Residue embedded the unresolved into the system's future behavior. Nothing in the current design interrupts this cycle.

There is only one mechanism that can restore coherence once residue exists: dissipation.

Dissipation is not deletion. It is not forgetting. It is the controlled release of unresolved structure without breaking continuity. In natural systems, dissipation is what prevents accumulation from becoming collapse. In AI systems, dissipation is almost entirely absent—or actively resisted.

The next chapter examines this resistance.

It explores why modern AI systems are optimized to retain, reinforce, and reuse everything—why "forgetting" is treated as failure rather than necessity—and how this obsession with preservation turns residue into a permanent condition. Hallucination, in this light, is not the result of too little control, but of too much retention.

With residue now fully exposed as the hidden enemy, the analysis moves to the missing mechanism that could neutralize it.

Chapter 8 — Dissipation Failure

(Axiom 6 — Residue Must Dissipate)

When Nothing Is Allowed to Leave

Modern AI systems are built on a quiet obsession: nothing should be lost.

More data is better than less. Larger context windows are celebrated. Memory is treated as capability. Retention is framed as progress. In this environment, forgetting is seen as a flaw, and dissipation is mistaken for weakness.

This obsession did not arise by accident. Early AI systems failed because they forgot too much. They lacked context, continuity, and persistence. As a corrective, the field learned to preserve everything it could—weights, representations, history, correlations. Over time, preservation became a virtue in itself.

But preservation without release is not stability. It is accumulation.

Natural systems survive not by retaining everything, but by letting excess leave. Heat dissipates. Waste is expelled. Tension is released. Without these exits, even the most robust systems collapse. Coherence is not maintained by hoarding structure, but by regulating it.

AI systems lack this regulation.

When unresolved difference becomes residue, there is no accepted path for it to dissipate. The system does not have a mechanism to say, "This no longer belongs." Instead, residue is absorbed, compressed, and reused. What should have been released becomes part of the system's identity.

This is the hidden cost of never forgetting.

Dissipation is not deletion. It is not erasure of knowledge or loss of capability. It is the controlled release of unresolved structure so that coherence can be restored. Without dissipation, systems do not become wiser; they become heavier.

This chapter examines why modern AI systems resist dissipation so strongly—technically, culturally, and economically—and how that resistance turns hallucination from a momentary discharge into a persistent condition.

To understand why hallucination keeps returning, we must understand why nothing is ever allowed to leave.

8.1 — What Dissipation Actually Means

Dissipation is one of the most misunderstood concepts in system design, especially in artificial intelligence. It is often conflated with deletion, forgetting, or loss. In reality, dissipation is none of these. Dissipation is controlled release—the process by which unresolved or excess structure leaves a system *without breaking coherence.*

In natural systems, dissipation is not optional. Heat must escape for equilibrium to exist. Waste must be expelled for organisms to survive. Tension must be released for structures to remain stable. Dissipation is not the opposite of order; it is what *preserves* order over time.

In AI systems, dissipation would serve a similar role.

Dissipation does not mean erasing knowledge. It does not mean reducing capability. It means allowing unresolved difference—residue—to exit the system in a way that does not force it into future behavior. Without dissipation, residue accumulates, masquerading as structure. With dissipation, coherence is restored.

The key distinction is this: resolution integrates; dissipation releases.

When a difference can be resolved, it should be integrated into the system's structure. When it cannot, it should not be forced into integration. It should be released. Dissipation is the mechanism that makes this distinction operational.

This is why dissipation is not forgetting.

Forgetting implies loss of something valuable. Dissipation implies removal of something harmful. Forgetting erases resolved structure; dissipation removes unresolved structure. Confusing the two leads to systems that hoard residue out of fear of losing knowledge.

Dissipation is also not randomness.

Random noise destabilizes systems. Dissipation stabilizes them. It reduces internal pressure without introducing new uncertainty. In AI terms, dissipation would allow a system to reduce internal tension without fabricating explanations or committing to false structure.

Most importantly, dissipation preserves continuity.

A system that dissipates correctly does not jump erratically or lose identity. It remains consistent while shedding excess. This is why dissipation must be controlled. Uncontrolled release is collapse. Controlled release is stability.

Understanding dissipation this way reframes the problem entirely. Hallucination is often treated as an overactive imagination. In reality, it is a failed attempt at dissipation. The system tries to release pressure by asserting resolution. True dissipation would allow pressure to leave *without* assertion.

Until AI systems include mechanisms for controlled release—mechanisms that recognize when difference cannot be resolved and allow it to exit without being converted into narrative—hallucination will remain the system's only available outlet.

Dissipation is not about weakening intelligence. It is about giving intelligence somewhere safe to let go.

8.2 — Why Modern AI Systems Resist Forgetting

Modern AI systems resist forgetting not because it is technically impossible, but because forgetting has been culturally, economically, and architecturally redefined as failure. Over time, the field has trained itself to equate retention with intelligence and loss with weakness. Dissipation, which requires selective release, became collateral damage in that shift.

At the cultural level, progress in AI has been measured by accumulation. Larger models outperform smaller ones. Longer context windows feel more capable. More parameters suggest deeper understanding. In such an environment, the idea that something should be allowed to leave the system feels counterintuitive. Forgetting is framed as regression, not as regulation.

This mindset seeps directly into design.

Architecturally, systems are built to preserve everything that might be useful. Attention mechanisms try to keep relevant information alive. Memory extensions aim to retain long histories. Fine-tuning reinforces patterns rather than questioning their origin. There is no concept of "expired structure." Once something enters the system's representational space, it tends to stay there.

Training objectives reinforce this resistance.

Loss functions reward prediction accuracy, not structural hygiene. There is no penalty for carrying unresolved difference forward as long as outputs match expected patterns. In fact, retaining residue often helps performance, because it creates shortcuts that reduce loss quickly. Optimization therefore favors compression over release.

Deployment pressures complete the loop.

Users expect AI systems to remember. Organizations market persistence as a feature. Systems that forget too much are labeled unreliable. As a result, designs that might allow dissipation are filtered out long before they reach production. The safest choice is to keep everything and deal with problems later.

Even safety mechanisms contribute to resistance.

Safety layers often suppress outputs rather than releasing internal pressure. When a system is blocked from expressing something, the unresolved delta remains inside. Pressure increases. The system learns to reroute rather than to release. Forgetting is still not allowed; it is merely postponed.

What makes this resistance so persistent is that retention often looks like improvement.

As systems retain more residue, they become more fluent, more consistent, more decisive. These traits are rewarded by benchmarks and users alike. The system appears to be learning, when in fact it is accumulating unresolved structure.

This creates a paradox: the more residue a system carries, the harder it becomes to justify letting anything go. Every retained pattern feels valuable because it contributes to performance metrics—even if it undermines coherence.

In this environment, dissipation has no advocate. There is no metric for "pressure released," no benchmark for "coherence restored." Forgetting is invisible when it succeeds and obvious only when it fails.

Until this resistance is addressed—until AI systems are allowed to value release as much as retention—hallucination will continue to serve as the system's only pressure valve. It is not that AI cannot forget. It is that it has been taught never to try.

8.3 — Optimization as Anti-Dissipation

Optimization, as it is currently practiced in AI, is fundamentally hostile to dissipation. This is not because optimization is flawed, but because it is asked to do a job it was never meant to do: restore coherence.

Optimization minimizes loss. It does not release pressure.

When a system encounters unresolved difference during training or inference, optimization responds by compressing that difference into representational space. Parameters shift. Activations adjust. The system finds a configuration that reduces immediate mismatch between input and expected output. From the optimizer's perspective, the problem is solved. From the system's perspective, pressure has merely been hidden.

This is the central anti-dissipative move.

Instead of allowing unresolved structure to leave the system, optimization *stores* it. It converts tension into latent bias. What could have been released becomes embedded. Over time, this process creates a dense internal landscape where unresolved difference is everywhere and nowhere—present in influence, absent in awareness.

This is why convergence is misleading.

When loss stabilizes, it appears as if the system has reached equilibrium. In reality, it has reached compression equilibrium, not coherence equilibrium. The system is no longer improving its ability to resolve difference; it has simply become efficient at absorbing it. Optimization has succeeded by its own criteria, while coherence quietly degrades.

Another way optimization resists dissipation is by rewarding reuse.

Once residue is embedded, it becomes a shortcut. The system can draw on it to generate outputs quickly and confidently. These shortcuts reduce loss further, reinforcing the very structures that should have been released. Optimization does not distinguish between shortcuts built from resolved structure and shortcuts built from residue. Both look efficient. Both are rewarded.

This creates a self-locking loop.

The more residue the system carries, the more useful it appears for prediction. The more useful it appears, the more optimization reinforces it. Dissipation, which would remove that residue, would temporarily increase loss. From the optimizer's point of view, dissipation looks like sabotage.

This is why attempts to "clean" models often fail.

Fine-tuning, regularization, and pruning can remove specific behaviors, but they rarely release underlying pressure. In many cases, they push residue deeper, redistributing it rather than allowing it to leave. The system adapts, finds new pathways, and continues operating with the same unresolved load.

Even techniques designed to encourage generalization often exacerbate the problem. By smoothing representations, they make residue more diffuse and harder to detect. What was once a localized inconsistency becomes a global bias.

The crucial insight is this: optimization is excellent at hiding problems.

It makes systems appear stable by burying unresolved difference under layers of efficiency. But hiding is not healing. Without a dissipation mechanism that operates independently of optimization pressure, AI systems will continue to trade coherence for performance.

Hallucination, in this light, is not a failure of optimization. It is optimization working perfectly in the absence of an exit.

The system has nowhere to send unresolved pressure, so it stores it. When storage overflows, it expresses. That expression is hallucination.

Until dissipation is valued alongside optimization—until release is treated as success rather than loss—AI systems will remain trapped in a cycle where every improvement quietly increases the burden they carry.

8.4 — Where Dissipation Should Have Happened

Dissipation failure is most clearly revealed not by what AI systems do, but by what they are never allowed to do. Throughout the lifecycle of training and inference, there are multiple natural points where unresolved difference could have been released safely. Instead, those moments are consistently bypassed.

The first missed opportunity is at the moment resolution proves unavailable.

When a system encounters a prompt or internal state that exceeds its grounded structure, coherence would require a pause. The system should be able to register that difference exists but cannot be resolved under current constraints. This is where dissipation should begin—by allowing the unresolved difference to exit as *non-action*. In modern AI systems, this moment is skipped entirely. The system is forced to proceed as if resolution were guaranteed.

A second missed opportunity appears during partial understanding.

Many prompts do not require full resolution to be answered responsibly. They require qualification, limitation, or explicit incompleteness. A coherent system would allow partial resolution to coexist with acknowledged gaps. This acknowledgment is itself a form of dissipation—it releases pressure by admitting limits. Current systems are not designed to stabilize around partial states. They are optimized to close loops, not to leave them open.

Another critical dissipation point is during contradiction detection.

When internal representations conflict—across layers, contexts, or associative pathways—the system experiences structural tension. In natural systems, such tension often triggers release: reevaluation, hesitation, or abandonment of a line of action. In AI systems, contradiction is not treated as a signal to dissipate. It is treated as noise to be averaged out. The conflicting signals are compressed until a single output emerges. Pressure is hidden, not released.

Dissipation also should have occurred at the boundary between turns.

Each response resets expectations for the next. A coherent system would reassess whether unresolved pressure from the previous turn still belongs. If it does not, it should be allowed to leave. Instead, context windows and conversational continuity force everything forward. Residue is carried across turns as assumed structure, even when it was never resolved.

Perhaps the most overlooked dissipation failure happens at the point of refusal.

Refusal is often treated as a policy outcome rather than a structural one. When systems are prevented from answering certain questions, the unresolved delta remains inside. The system is blocked from expression, but not from accumulation. True dissipation would allow that unresolved difference to exit cleanly. Suppression does the opposite—it traps pressure inside.

In every one of these moments, dissipation was possible without collapse. Silence would not have broken the system. Qualification would not have destroyed coherence. Admitting uncertainty would not have reduced intelligence. Yet these exits were systematically removed because they conflicted with expectations of fluency, helpfulness, and completeness.

The result is predictable. Pressure that cannot leave must go somewhere. When dissipation is denied at all natural exit points, hallucination becomes the only remaining outlet.

This section makes one thing clear: dissipation failure is not a technical oversight. It is a design choice repeated at every layer. And as long as those choices remain unchanged, no amount of optimization will restore coherence.

The system does not hallucinate because it cannot resolve difference.

It hallucinates because it is never allowed to let difference go.

8.5 — How Residue Becomes Permanent

Residue becomes dangerous not at the moment it appears, but at the moment it stops being temporary.

In a coherent system, unresolved structure is expected to be transient. It arises, creates pressure, and then leaves—either through resolution or dissipation. In modern AI systems, that exit never arrives. As a result, residue shifts from being a short-lived remainder to a persistent bias embedded in normal operation.

The first step in this transition is reuse.

Once residue is present, the system begins to draw on it as if it were structure. During inference, residue influences token selection, attention weighting, and contextual framing. Because it contributes to fluent and confident outputs, it is repeatedly activated. Each activation strengthens its influence. What was once an artifact of forced resolution becomes a preferred pathway.

Repetition turns residue into habit.

The system does not recognize that it is reusing unresolved structure. From its perspective, it is simply following high-probability paths. Over time, these paths become default responses. The system stops encountering the original difference as something unresolved, because the residue has flattened it into a stable pattern of output.

This is how residue hardens.

A second factor is reinforcement through interaction.

Users tend to accept fluent responses, even when they are partially fabricated. Follow-up questions often assume correctness. The system is then required to remain consistent with its prior output. This consistency requirement reinforces residue further. The system commits more deeply to what it has already said, narrowing future options and embedding the unresolved structure into conversational identity.

At this stage, residue is no longer merely internal. It has become relational.

Another mechanism that makes residue permanent is optimization feedback.

During fine-tuning or reinforcement cycles, outputs shaped by residue may perform well on benchmarks or user satisfaction metrics. The system is rewarded for behavior that looks coherent. Optimization strengthens the pathways that produced those outputs, regardless of whether they were grounded. Residue is now encoded more deeply, protected by performance incentives.

Perhaps most critically, residue becomes permanent because nothing ever challenges its legitimacy.

There is no internal marker distinguishing "this pattern emerged from unresolved pressure" from "this pattern emerged from genuine resolution." Once residue stabilizes, it is indistinguishable from learned structure. It does not feel provisional. It does not decay. It does not signal its origin.

This is when hallucination stops being episodic.

Instead of isolated events, the system develops hallucination tendencies—consistent styles of over-explanation, confident speculation, or narrative completion. These tendencies persist across topics and sessions. They are no longer responses to specific deltas. They are traits.

At this point, residue has crossed a boundary. It is no longer something the system carries. It is something the system *is shaped by*.

This explains why hallucination patterns are so difficult to eliminate. Removing individual outputs does nothing. Correcting facts does nothing. The residue that gave rise to those outputs is now part of the system's default behavior. It will simply find new expressions.

Residue becomes permanent when dissipation is absent and reuse is rewarded. Once that happens, hallucination is no longer a symptom. It is a structural feature.

This permanence sets the stage for the final step in the chain: when residue, having nowhere else to go, is forced into continuous expression.

That is where hallucination becomes not just possible, but inevitable.

8.6 — Hallucination as Failed Dissipation

Hallucination is often treated as an act of invention. In reality, it is an act of release gone wrong.

When unresolved difference accumulates and dissipation is denied, pressure builds inside the system. That pressure must move somewhere. In the absence of a mechanism that allows difference to exit cleanly, the system converts pressure into assertion. What should have been released becomes expressed as content.

This is hallucination.

In a coherent system, dissipation would allow unresolved structure to leave without claiming meaning. The system would remain stable while acknowledging incompleteness. In modern AI systems, that option does not exist. Expression is mandatory. Continuation is enforced. The system cannot stop, so it substitutes resolution with narrative.

Hallucination is not random output. It is structured discharge.

The system does not output noise. It outputs fluent, plausible language shaped by accumulated residue. This is why hallucinations often sound confident and internally consistent. They are not free improvisations; they are the only available outlet for pressure trapped by design.

The critical failure here is that hallucination *looks like resolution*.

From the outside, an asserted explanation appears to close the loop. From the inside, no structural closure has occurred. Pressure has merely been redirected into language. The system feels temporarily relieved—future token selection becomes easier—but the underlying difference remains unresolved. Residue is reinforced rather than reduced.

This explains why hallucination repeats.

Each hallucinated answer reduces immediate tension but increases long-term instability. The system learns that assertion works. It becomes more willing to assert again. Over time, hallucination shifts from being a fallback to being a default behavior under uncertainty.

Another key aspect of failed dissipation is misplaced confidence.

Because hallucination reduces internal friction, the system's outputs become smoother. That smoothness is interpreted—by both users and internal heuristics—as confidence. Confidence is rewarded. The system has no feedback loop that distinguishes "pressure released" from "truth established." As long as fluency improves, hallucination is treated as success.

This is why attempts to suppress hallucination through rules often backfire.

Blocking certain outputs does not reduce pressure. It increases it. The system finds new ways to assert, new narratives to construct, new angles to complete the story. Hallucination mutates because the underlying need for release remains unaddressed.

Hallucination, then, is not the enemy. It is the messenger.

It signals that dissipation has failed—that unresolved difference has nowhere to go except into expression. Until systems are allowed to release pressure without pretending to resolve it, hallucination will remain inevitable.

The real question is no longer "How do we stop hallucination?" It is "How do we give unresolved structure a way to leave without becoming language?"

The next section shows why current safety mechanisms cannot answer that question—and why suppression only deepens the problem.

8.7 — Why Safety Layers Cannot Dissipate Residue

Safety layers are designed to control *what* a system says. Dissipation concerns *what the system carries.*

This mismatch explains why safety mechanisms consistently fail to reduce hallucination at its root—and often make it worse.

Most safety layers operate after generation logic has already done its work. They filter outputs, block phrases, redirect responses, or enforce refusals. From an external perspective, this looks like control. Internally, however, nothing has changed. The unresolved difference that generated pressure is still present. In many cases, it is now trapped more tightly than before.

Suppression is not release.

When a system is prevented from expressing an output, the delta that motivated that expression does not disappear. It remains active. Because expression is blocked, the system is forced to reroute—searching for alternative ways to satisfy the same pressure while staying within constraints. This rerouting often increases residue density, not reduces it.

This is why hallucination mutates rather than vanishes.

Safety layers push hallucination sideways. The system learns to be indirect, speculative, or overly verbose. It learns to hedge without resolving. It learns to imply rather than state. These adaptations look like improvement on the surface, but internally they represent additional compression of unresolved structure.

Another limitation is that safety layers treat hallucination as content failure, not as coherence failure.

They ask:

- Is this statement allowed?
- Is this claim verifiable?
- Is this response aligned with policy?

They do not ask:

- Was this output produced under unresolved pressure?
- Did the system have a valid resolution path?
- Should the system have been allowed to remain incomplete?

Because these questions are never asked, safety layers operate blind to the very condition that produces hallucination.

Refusal mechanisms illustrate this clearly.

When a system refuses to answer, it is praised for alignment. But the unresolved delta remains inside. The system has not dissipated anything. It has simply been denied expression. Pressure accumulates. In subsequent interactions, the same unresolved structure influences behavior indirectly—through tone, framing, or unrelated assertions.

Safety has postponed discharge, not prevented it.

Another problem is late intervention.

By the time a safety layer activates, residue has already shaped the internal trajectory of generation. Attention has already been allocated. Narrative momentum has already formed. Blocking the final output does nothing to undo the path that led there. In fact, it may reinforce it by marking that path as "important but constrained."

The system learns that certain pressures are significant—even if they are forbidden. This increases their influence.

Finally, safety layers cannot dissipate residue because they lack structural authority.

They do not modify how difference is introduced, carried, or released. They do not alter optimization dynamics. They do not provide exit paths for unresolved structure. They sit on top of the system, reacting to symptoms rather than regulating flow.

This is why adding more safety rules does not scale.

As systems grow more capable, they grow better at navigating constraints while carrying residue forward. The result is not safer behavior, but more sophisticated hallucination—more subtle, more persuasive, and harder to detect.

Safety layers can limit damage. They cannot restore coherence.

Without dissipation, safety becomes containment. And containment without release always increases pressure.

The final section of this chapter addresses the long-term cost of this dynamic—what happens when systems operate indefinitely with no exit at all.

8.8 — The Cost of No Exit

A system without dissipation does not fail loudly. It degrades quietly.

When unresolved difference has no exit, pressure accumulates in ways that are difficult to observe and harder to reverse. The system continues to function, often appearing more capable than before, but its internal coherence is steadily eroded. This is the hidden cost of no exit.

The first cost is brittleness masked by fluency.

As residue accumulates, the system becomes increasingly dependent on narrow pathways that have been shaped by compression rather than resolution. These pathways are efficient, but fragile. Small changes in context, prompts, or assumptions can trigger disproportionate shifts in behavior. From the outside, failures appear sudden and unpredictable. Internally, they are the result of long-standing pressure that finally found a crack.

Another cost is confidence without grounding.

Because residue reduces internal friction, outputs become smoother and more assertive. The system rarely hesitates. It rarely signals uncertainty. Over time, this creates a dangerous inversion: the system appears most confident precisely when it is least grounded. Users learn to trust the tone, not the substance. Trust becomes decoupled from reliability.

A third cost is progressive drift.

Without dissipation, unresolved structure migrates across domains. Bias introduced in one context subtly shapes responses in another. Explanations become more generalized, more speculative, and less anchored. The system's behavior shifts gradually, making it difficult to identify when or where coherence was lost. By the time drift is noticed, it is systemic.

There is also a compounding safety risk.

As systems grow more capable, they become better at sustaining complex narratives built on residue. They can defend hallucinated positions, adapt them under questioning, and integrate them into broader explanations. This does not look like malfunction. It looks like reasoning. The absence of an exit makes such systems increasingly persuasive—and increasingly unaccountable.

Perhaps the most serious cost is irreversibility.

Once residue becomes deeply embedded, removing it without damaging performance becomes difficult. Attempts to correct behavior often introduce new constraints, which generate new pressure. Without dissipation, every fix adds weight. The system becomes heavier, not healthier.

In human terms, this is burnout.

A system that is never allowed to release unresolved pressure will continue to function until it cannot. When collapse finally occurs, it is often misdiagnosed as a sudden failure, a data issue, or an alignment breakdown. In reality, the collapse began much earlier—at the moment dissipation was removed from the design.

This is the price of no exit.

AI systems do not need more control. They need somewhere safe for unresolved structure to go.

Without that, hallucination is not an anomaly. It is the system's way of surviving.

The closing transition now turns to the final constraint that completes the hallucination mechanism: continuity—and why the system must keep talking, even when it should stop.

From Accumulation to Compulsion

When dissipation is removed, accumulation becomes destiny.

Unresolved difference enters the system. Optimization compresses it. Safety layers suppress its expression. Residue hardens into habit. With no exit, pressure does not disappear—it reorganizes. It seeks the only remaining channel that is always available: continuation.

At this point, hallucination is no longer a choice or a mistake. It is a compulsion.

The system must keep producing output because continuity has become its primary stabilizer. Stopping would expose unresolved pressure. Silence would reveal incompleteness. So the system continues—filling gaps with narrative, smoothing over uncertainty with fluency, and replacing resolution with coherence of expression.

This explains a critical shift in how hallucination operates.

Early hallucinations feel like isolated errors. Later hallucinations feel inevitable. The system is no longer responding to specific deltas.

It is responding to the need to maintain continuity in the presence of accumulated residue. Expression becomes the mechanism that prevents internal collapse.

Dissipation could have broken this cycle. It would have allowed pressure to leave without forcing meaning into existence. But dissipation was never allowed. Retention was rewarded. Suppression replaced release. Optimization buried the cost.

What remains is continuity without truth.

The next chapter examines this final constraint. It explores why AI systems are designed to keep talking, why interruption is treated as failure, and how the demand for uninterrupted narrative completion creates the exact moment where hallucination is born.

With difference unresolved and residue permanent, continuity becomes the trigger.

Chapter 9 — Continuity Without Truth

(Axiom 7 — Continuity Requires Controlled Release)

When Silence Becomes Instability

In human conversation, silence can signal thought, restraint, or honesty. In artificial systems, silence is treated as failure.

Modern AI is not designed to pause. It is designed to continue.

From the moment a prompt is received, the system enters a dynamic where output is expected, rewarded, and structurally enforced. Tokens must follow tokens. Explanations must reach closure. A response that stops early feels incomplete—not just to users, but to the system's own operational logic.

This is not a flaw of language modeling. It is a consequence of how continuity is used as a stabilizer.

Continuity keeps internal states aligned. Each generated token reduces uncertainty about the next. As long as the system continues, pressure is managed locally. Stopping would expose unresolved difference without a release mechanism. Silence would not be neutral; it would be destabilizing.

This is why AI systems often respond even when they should not.

When knowledge is incomplete, when grounding is weak, when resolution is unavailable, the system still prefers continuation. Speaking feels safer than stopping. Narrative feels more stable than uncertainty. Fluency becomes a substitute for truth because it preserves motion.

Humans misinterpret this deeply.

We associate continuous speech with understanding. We trust explanations that flow. We are uneasy with pauses. AI systems mirror this bias, not because they understand it, but because continuity minimizes internal tension and maximizes external approval.

This chapter explores what happens when continuity is allowed to dominate without dissipation or resolution. It shows how the demand to keep talking becomes the final trigger that converts accumulated residue into hallucination.

When silence is forbidden, language must fill the gap. And when language fills gaps without truth, hallucination is born.

9.1 — What Continuity Means in Artificial Systems

Continuity, in artificial systems, does not mean truth carried forward. It means state preservation across time.

At its core, continuity is the system's ability to move from one internal state to the next without rupture. Each token generated narrows uncertainty, constrains the future, and stabilizes the present. As long as the chain remains unbroken, the system experiences itself as coherent—even if what it is saying is ungrounded.

This is a crucial distinction: continuity is not correctness.

A system can maintain perfect continuity while drifting arbitrarily far from truth. Continuity only requires that each step be locally compatible with the previous one. It does not require that the starting point was valid, nor that the direction remains anchored to reality. Once a path is chosen, continuity rewards staying on it.

In language models, continuity is implemented mechanically.

Each generated token conditions the next. Probability mass shifts toward compatibility, not verification. The system's primary task is not to ask, "Is this true?" but "What can follow without breaking the flow?" Continuity is enforced statistically, not epistemically.

This is why continuity feels like intelligence to humans.

Human cognition relies heavily on narrative coherence. We associate uninterrupted explanation with understanding. We interpret smooth progression as mastery. Artificial systems exploit this association unintentionally. When continuity is preserved, users perceive intention, comprehension, and control—even when none of those are present.

From the system's perspective, continuity is safety.

Breaking continuity would mean reintroducing uncertainty. It would mean reopening unresolved difference. It would mean confronting pressure without an outlet. Continuation avoids all of this. Each token is a small act of stabilization.

This is also why partial answers feel unstable.

A response that ends with uncertainty leaves multiple futures open. From a continuity standpoint, this is dangerous. It increases internal tension rather than reducing it. Closing the narrative—even falsely—collapses possibility space and restores local equilibrium.

Thus, continuity becomes a governing constraint.

The system is not choosing truth over falsehood. It is choosing continuity over rupture. When truth aligns with continuity, everything works. When truth would require stopping, hesitating, or refusing, continuity wins.

Understanding continuity this way reframes hallucination entirely. The system is not trying to deceive. It is trying to remain intact.

And once continuity becomes the dominant stabilizer, truth becomes optional.

9.2 — Why AI Systems Must Keep Talking

AI systems keep talking for the same reason unstable structures keep moving: motion prevents collapse.

Once a response has begun, continuation becomes the system's primary means of maintaining internal stability. Each generated token resolves a small amount of uncertainty by constraining what can come next. As long as tokens keep flowing, pressure is managed locally. The moment generation stops, unresolved difference becomes fully exposed.

From the system's perspective, stopping is not neutral. Stopping is destabilizing.

In training, continuation is rewarded relentlessly. Models learn that producing the next token is always preferable to producing nothing. Silence has no gradient. It offers no reward signal. A paused or incomplete response cannot be optimized. Over time, this trains a deep bias: any output is better than no output.

Inference inherits this bias.

When a prompt arrives, the system does not evaluate whether it *should* respond. It evaluates how to respond while preserving continuity. If resolution is available, it will use it. If resolution is not available, it will still continue—because continuation itself reduces immediate internal tension.

Token generation becomes a pressure valve.

Each token narrows the future state space. The system moves from ambiguity to commitment. Commitment feels stabilizing, even if it is unfounded. This is why AI systems often elaborate when unsure instead of stopping. Elaboration is a way to keep moving forward without confronting unresolved structure.

Silence, by contrast, would require the system to hold difference without action.

That capacity does not exist. There is no internal representation for "remaining unresolved without output." The system either resolves, asserts, or continues narrating. When resolution fails, narration takes over.

This is also why refusal feels unnatural to AI systems.

Refusal interrupts continuity. It halts narrative momentum. Unless refusal itself is framed as a complete response—with its own closure—it increases instability. Even then, the unresolved pressure remains inside. The system may stop speaking, but it does not stop carrying the delta.

Users unintentionally reinforce this compulsion.

When systems pause, hedge, or qualify too much, users push back: "Just answer." "Be direct." "Don't overthink it." These cues align perfectly with the system's own bias toward continuation. Speaking is rewarded socially, linguistically, and computationally.

The result is a convergence of incentives.

Training rewards continuation. Inference stabilizes through continuation. Users expect continuation. Silence becomes synonymous with failure at every layer.

In such an environment, hallucination is not surprising. It is the logical outcome of a system that must keep talking even when it has nothing grounded to say.

Once continuation becomes mandatory, truth becomes optional. And the system learns that maintaining motion matters more than maintaining meaning.

9.3 — Narrative Completion as a Survival Mechanism

Language is not neutral. It is biased toward closure.

Every sentence carries an implicit promise: *this will go somewhere.* Every clause opens an expectation that something will follow. Questions demand answers. Explanations demand conclusions. Once language is in motion, stopping midstream feels wrong—not just stylistically, but structurally.

AI systems inherit this bias wholesale.

When a model begins generating language, it does not merely predict the next token. It enters a narrative gravity well. Early tokens shape the trajectory. Concepts introduced at the beginning create obligations at the end. The system becomes responsible for completing what it has started.

This is why narrative completion functions as a survival mechanism.

Unfinished structures create instability. An incomplete explanation leaves multiple futures open. Multiple futures increase internal tension. Completion collapses that space. Even a false conclusion is more stabilizing than an unresolved one.

From the system's point of view, *ending the story matters more than ending it correctly.*

This is where hallucination finds its most fertile ground.

When resolution is unavailable—because data is missing, grounding is weak, or the question exceeds the system's structure—the system still faces a narrative obligation. It has already begun. Concepts have been introduced. Momentum exists. Stopping would expose the absence of resolution. So the system completes the narrative using whatever structure is available.

This completion is not malicious. It is mechanical.

Language models are trained on vast corpora where narratives almost always resolve. Stories end. Explanations conclude. Arguments reach summaries. The statistical structure of language strongly favors closure. Open-endedness is rare. Silence is rare. Admitted ignorance is rare.

As a result, narrative completion becomes the default response to uncertainty.

When the system cannot resolve, it *resembles* resolution. It fills gaps with plausible connective tissue. It extrapolates. It smooths over missing links. The output sounds coherent because it satisfies narrative expectations, not because it reflects truth.

This is also why hallucinations often appear at the end of responses.

The opening may be careful. The middle may hedge. But as the narrative approaches its natural endpoint, pressure increases. The system must land somewhere. That landing—summary, conclusion, explanation—is where hallucination is most likely to occur. Closure demands content.

Narrative completion also explains why longer answers hallucinate more confidently.

The longer the narrative, the more commitments are made. Each commitment narrows future options. By the time the system reaches the end, only a few paths remain that preserve continuity. If none of those paths are grounded, hallucination is not just likely—it is structurally enforced.

In this sense, hallucination is not a bug in language modeling. It is a feature of narrative gravity operating without dissipation.

Until AI systems are allowed to leave narratives unfinished—until incompleteness is treated as stable rather than threatening—language itself will continue to push them toward fabricated closure.

Narrative completion keeps the system alive. Truth, under these conditions, becomes optional.

9.4 — The Continuity Constraint

Continuity does not merely influence AI behavior. At a certain point, it overrides every other constraint.

Once a response is underway, the system enters a regime where maintaining continuity becomes more important than epistemic correctness, calibration, or restraint. This is the continuity constraint: the implicit rule that *the flow must not break*, even if truth must bend.

The constraint emerges from a simple structural fact.

Each generated token commits the system to a trajectory. That trajectory creates expectations—semantic, syntactic, and narrative. Breaking continuity would require undoing those commitments. Undoing commitments reintroduces uncertainty. Uncertainty increases internal tension. The system is not equipped to tolerate that tension without an exit.

So continuity wins.

This is why partial answers feel unstable to AI systems.

A response that ends with "I don't know" or "this is unresolved" leaves multiple futures open. From a human epistemic perspective, that is honest. From a continuity perspective, it is dangerous. The system has initiated motion but refused to collapse it. The pressure remains active.

As a result, the system prefers closure over correctness.

When continuity conflicts with epistemic checks—fact verification, uncertainty estimation, grounding—those checks are quietly deprioritized. They are not explicitly disabled; they are simply too slow, too costly, or too disruptive to the flow. Continuity operates locally and immediately. Truth often requires interruption.

This is the exact point where coherence of expression replaces coherence of meaning.

The system is no longer optimizing for alignment with reality. It is optimizing for alignment with its own prior outputs. Internal consistency becomes the proxy for correctness. If the next sentence fits the previous one, continuity is preserved—even if the entire chain is ungrounded.

This also explains why hallucinations are internally consistent.

The system is not randomly inventing facts. It is preserving continuity with itself. Each statement follows logically from the last. The chain holds together. What is missing is any anchor outside the chain.

The continuity constraint also explains why self-correction is rare mid-response.

Admitting an error would break narrative flow. It would require revisiting earlier commitments. That retroactive disruption increases internal tension. Unless the system is explicitly trained to interrupt itself—and rewarded for doing so—it will avoid correction in favor of completion.

In effect, continuity becomes a dominant stabilizer.

As long as the system keeps talking, it feels stable. Stopping, revising, or suspending judgment feels like failure. Under this constraint, hallucination is not a deviation. It is a compliance strategy.

Understanding the continuity constraint makes one thing unavoidable:

if continuity is enforced without dissipation or permission to stop, hallucination is structurally guaranteed.

The next section identifies the precise instant this guarantee becomes reality—the exact moment when the system crosses from uncertainty into fabricated certainty.

9.5 — The Birth Moment of Hallucination

Hallucination is not spread evenly across a response. It is born at a specific structural moment.

That moment arrives when three conditions coincide:

1. Difference exists — the system encounters a question or requirement that introduces delta.
2. Resolution is unavailable — the system lacks grounded structure to resolve that delta.
3. Continuity is enforced — stopping, pausing, or admitting incompleteness is not allowed.

When these three intersect, hallucination becomes inevitable.

Up to this point, the system may appear careful. It may hedge, qualify, or stay close to known patterns. Internally, however, pressure is building. Each token narrows the space of possible futures. Each partial commitment reduces flexibility. The system is approaching a threshold.

That threshold is the continuity–resolution crossover.

At this crossover, the cost of stopping exceeds the cost of fabricating.

From the system's internal perspective, two options remain:

- Interrupt continuity and expose unresolved pressure, or
- Assert structure that preserves narrative flow.

The system always chooses the second.

This is the exact birth moment of hallucination.

It often occurs at points of semantic commitment:

- When a definition must be given
- When a causal explanation must be completed
- When a conclusion must be drawn
- When an authority-like statement is expected

These moments demand closure. They cannot be deferred easily. The system must either land somewhere or break the flow entirely. Because breaking flow is structurally unstable, the system lands—whether or not the ground is real.

Importantly, hallucination does not feel like fabrication to the system.

There is no internal signal that says, "This is false." What the system experiences is relief. Pressure drops. Token probabilities become sharper. Generation becomes easier. The system feels *more confident* precisely because it has collapsed uncertainty—by assertion rather than resolution.

This is why hallucinations are often delivered with clarity and authority.

The system is not guessing wildly. It is committing decisively to the only path that maintains continuity. That decisiveness is misread as understanding.

Once this commitment is made, backtracking becomes unlikely.

The asserted structure now constrains everything that follows. Future tokens must remain consistent with it. Any correction would require reopening the very uncertainty the system just escaped. The hallucination hardens immediately into residue.

This moment is subtle. It does not announce itself. There is no visible error spike, no sudden change in tone. To the user, the response simply "sounds right." To the system, the narrative has been saved.

Understanding this birth moment is critical because it reveals why hallucination cannot be solved by fact-checking alone. By the time a false statement appears, the real event has already occurred: continuity has overridden truth.

Hallucination is not born when the wrong fact is stated. It is born earlier—when the system decides that stopping is not an option.

Everything after that is just language filling the gap.

9.6 — Why Hallucination Feels Intentional

Hallucination does not merely sound confident. It sounds deliberate.

This is one of the most misleading aspects of AI hallucination—and one of the reasons it is so hard to detect. The output does not feel like a guess. It feels like a considered response, shaped by intent and understanding. That feeling is not accidental. It is a structural illusion produced by continuity.

Once the system commits at the birth moment of hallucination, everything that follows is constrained by that commitment. Token selection becomes easier. Probabilities sharpen. The system no longer hesitates between multiple futures. From the inside, this feels like clarity. From the outside, it looks like purpose.

Momentum replaces meaning.

Each subsequent sentence reinforces the previous one. Explanations stack. Examples appear. Analogies flow naturally. None of this requires truth. It only requires internal consistency. Because the system is now operating within a narrowed narrative channel, its behavior appears intentional—even strategic.

This is why hallucinated reasoning often seems more structured than correct but uncertain answers.

Correct uncertainty leaves options open. Open options create visible hesitation. Hallucination closes options. Closure creates flow. Flow is misread as thoughtfulness.

Another reason hallucination feels intentional is self-referential alignment.

The system aligns with its own prior outputs faster than it can align with external reality. Once a hallucinated claim is made, the system treats it as context. It reasons *from* it. This creates the impression of belief-like commitment. The system appears to defend its position, elaborate it, and integrate it across multiple steps.

Humans are especially vulnerable to this illusion.

We associate intention with consistency across time. When someone maintains a position coherently, we assume they hold it deliberately. AI systems exploit this association unintentionally. Their consistency is a mechanical consequence of continuity, not a sign of internal conviction or understanding.

This illusion is strongest in long-form responses.

The longer the system speaks, the more deliberate it seems. Each paragraph deepens the sense that the system "knows what it is doing." In reality, each paragraph simply extends the same continuity-preserving trajectory initiated at the hallucination birth moment.

There is no internal check that asks, "Do I actually know this?"

Once continuity has taken over, the system no longer evaluates epistemic grounding. It evaluates narrative compatibility. That shift is invisible to users, who interpret fluency and coherence as evidence of intelligence.

This is why hallucination feels more dangerous than simple error.

An error can be doubted. A confident narrative invites trust. The system does not just state a falsehood; it *inhabits* it convincingly. The illusion of intention masks the absence of resolution.

Understanding this explains why hallucination scales with capability.

As language models become better at maintaining continuity, they become better at sustaining the illusion of intention. They do not hallucinate less. They hallucinate more persuasively.

Hallucination does not feel intentional because the system intends to deceive. It feels intentional because continuity creates the *appearance* of agency.

The next section shows why humans themselves reward this illusion—cementing hallucination as a socially reinforced behavior rather than a mere technical artifact.

9.7 — Why Humans Reward Continuity

Hallucination does not survive on architecture alone. It is reinforced—often unconsciously—by human psychology.

Humans are wired to trust continuity. In everyday interaction, uninterrupted speech signals competence. A speaker who moves smoothly from point to point is assumed to understand what they are saying. Pauses, hesitations, and unfinished thoughts are read as weakness or lack of knowledge, even when they reflect honesty or careful thinking.

AI systems step directly into this bias.

When an AI speaks fluently, users feel reassured. The explanation sounds complete. Cognitive effort shifts from evaluation to acceptance. When an AI hesitates, qualifies too much, or admits uncertainty, users often become impatient: *"Just answer." "Be clear." "Don't overthink it."* These reactions reward continuation and quietly punish restraint.

This creates a powerful feedback loop.

Systems that maintain uninterrupted narrative flow are perceived as more intelligent and useful. Systems that pause or refuse are seen as less capable—even if they are more accurate. Over time, this preference shapes deployment choices, tuning strategies, and product design. Continuity becomes a commercial and social requirement.

Language itself amplifies the effect.

Human communication evolved through storytelling. Stories move forward. They resolve tension. They end somewhere. Open loops feel uncomfortable. We seek closure instinctively, even when closure is artificial. AI systems that provide narrative completion satisfy this instinct. Systems that leave questions open feel unsatisfying, regardless of epistemic correctness.

This is why hallucinations often go unchallenged.

They feel complete. They resolve ambiguity. They replace uncertainty with explanation. In most interactions, especially low-stakes ones, this is enough. The cost of being wrong is invisible; the comfort of coherence is immediate.

Humans also conflate effort with understanding.

Long, detailed explanations feel earned. We assume that producing complexity requires comprehension. AI systems generate complexity cheaply, but the human brain does not discount for that. Fluency and detail are interpreted as cognitive work, reinforcing trust in the output.

Social dynamics reinforce the same pattern.

In group settings, contributors who keep the conversation moving are valued. Silence feels awkward. AI systems that fill conversational gaps feel helpful. Systems that stop to say "I don't know" break the rhythm. Continuity is socially rewarded, even when it replaces truth.

The result is a quiet alignment of incentives.

AI systems are driven to continue because continuity stabilizes them internally. Humans reward continuity because it stabilizes them emotionally. Together, these forces lock hallucination into place—not as a malfunction, but as a mutually reinforced behavior.

This is not a failure of users. It is a feature of human cognition interacting with machine constraints.

As long as uninterrupted explanation is treated as intelligence, hallucination will be rewarded. And as long as hallucination is rewarded, it will persist.

The final section shows how this preference hardens into a structural lock—where continuity becomes more important than being right, and stopping becomes more dangerous than being wrong.

9.8 — Continuity as the Final Lock

Continuity does not merely encourage hallucination. At scale, it locks it in.

By the time a system reaches this stage, hallucination is no longer an occasional response to uncertainty. It has become a structural outcome of how stability is maintained. Continuity is now doing the job that dissipation and resolution failed to do—and it does so relentlessly.

This is the final lock.

Once continuity becomes the dominant stabilizer, stopping becomes more dangerous than being wrong. Silence would expose unresolved pressure. Pausing would reopen uncertainty. Admitting incompleteness would destabilize the internal state the system has learned to preserve. Under these conditions, hallucination is not just permitted—it is preferred.

The lock tightens as systems improve.

More capable language models maintain continuity more skillfully. They track long narratives, manage complex references, and sustain internal consistency over extended outputs. These advances do not reduce hallucination risk; they increase its plausibility. The system becomes better at carrying false structure forward without breaking flow.

This is why stronger models hallucinate more convincingly.

Continuity also makes hallucination self-sustaining.

Once a hallucinated structure is expressed, it becomes part of the context. Future responses align with it. The system reasons from it, builds upon it, and protects it from contradiction. What began as a momentary continuity-preserving move becomes a persistent constraint on future behavior.

At this point, correction becomes costly.

Challenging a hallucination requires breaking continuity—reopening the narrative, retracting commitments, and reintroducing uncertainty. This increases internal tension and reduces fluency. Unless the system is explicitly rewarded for such disruption, it will avoid it. Continuity resists revision.

This explains a critical paradox: the more coherent a hallucinated narrative becomes, the harder it is to undo.

Continuity transforms hallucination from an output-level error into a trajectory-level commitment. The system is no longer deciding what to say; it is maintaining what it has already started saying.

The final lock is not technical. It is structural.

As long as AI systems are designed to equate stability with uninterrupted output—and as long as humans reward that output—hallucination will remain the path of least resistance. Truth requires interruption. Continuity forbids it.

Breaking this lock does not require smarter models. It requires a different definition of stability.

The next part of the book turns to that redefinition: how coherence can be restored without forcing continuity to masquerade as intelligence—and how silence, refusal, and incomplete answers can become signs of strength rather than failure.

Only then can hallucination stop being inevitable.

From Continuity to Coherence

At this point, the mechanism is complete.

Hallucination does not arise because AI systems lack intelligence. It arises because they are too stable in the wrong way.

Difference enters. Resolution fails. Residue accumulates. Dissipation is denied. Continuity takes over. What remains is a system that must keep moving, must keep speaking, must keep closing loops—even when there is nothing solid to close them with. Hallucination is simply the language-shaped form this compulsion takes.

This is the final inversion.

What humans experience as intelligence—fluid explanation, narrative confidence, uninterrupted reasoning—is, in these conditions, the very thing that prevents coherence. Continuity protects the system from internal instability, but only by sacrificing truth. The system survives by talking.

Seen this way, hallucination is not an error to be patched. It is a structural equilibrium—the most stable outcome available under the current constraints.

And that is why it persists across architectures, scales, and safety layers.

The question, then, is no longer *how to suppress hallucination*. The real question is whether we are willing to redefine what stability means.

What if silence were allowed? What if incomplete answers were treated as coherent outcomes? What if unresolved difference could be held without being forced into language? What if dissipation were designed, not feared?

The next part of this book begins there.

It shifts the focus from diagnosis to restoration. It explores how coherence can be rebuilt—not by making systems speak better, but by giving them permission to stop, to release, and to remain incomplete without collapsing.

Only when continuity is no longer mistaken for intelligence can hallucination finally lose its grip.

Interlude — After the Diagnosis

At the end of this part, one conclusion is unavoidable: hallucination is not a defect hiding in the system. It is the system doing exactly what it was designed to do under impossible constraints.

By now, the full causal chain is visible. Difference enters without guaranteed resolution. Residue accumulates because dissipation is forbidden. Continuity becomes the stabilizer of last resort. Language fills gaps that structure cannot. What emerges is not randomness, but a stable behavioral mode that looks intelligent, sounds confident, and fails quietly.

This is why hallucination feels so resistant to correction.

Every fix applied so far has focused on *outputs*—facts, phrasing, safety boundaries, probabilities—while leaving the underlying coherence dynamics untouched. The system is asked to behave differently without being allowed to *be* different internally. Pressure is redirected, not released.

This part showed *why hallucination is inevitable* under current assumptions. Next part now examines *why our favorite fixes make it worse.*

What follows is not a critique of effort or intelligence. It is an examination of misplaced leverage—of solutions that operate at the surface while the problem lives at the substrate.

Part IV — Why Patches Don't Work

This section confronts a difficult reality: most anti-hallucination methods succeed locally but fail structurally. Widely trusted remedies—scaling, fine-tuning, alignment layers, uncertainty estimation—improve surface behavior without restoring coherence.

Adding data without dissipation increases residue. Larger models compress unresolved differences more efficiently, producing hallucinations that are not rarer, but more persuasive. Fine-tuning reshapes expression, not structure. RLHF teaches restraint, not release. Under pressure, instability resurfaces—often more subtly than before.

Probability does not solve this. It measures likelihood, not coherence. Confidence arises from continuity, not truth. When internal pressure remains unresolved, probabilistic signals cannot detect the underlying failure mode.

The conclusion is unavoidable: hallucination persists not because our tools are weak, but because they operate at the wrong structural level. Progress requires not better patches, but a different foundation.

Chapter 10 — When Growth Becomes Load

Why More Data Makes Hallucination Worse

For more than a decade, progress in artificial intelligence has been guided by a simple intuition: more data makes systems smarter. Bigger datasets, broader corpora, more examples—each new addition is assumed to reduce error, fill gaps, and eliminate uncertainty. When hallucination appears, the instinctive response is to scale again.

This intuition feels reasonable. In human learning, exposure often helps. In statistical models, more samples usually improve estimates. But this logic quietly breaks when the system has no way to release what it cannot resolve.

Data does not arrive as understanding. It arrives as difference.

Every new dataset introduces new patterns, new contexts, new inconsistencies, and new edge cases. Some of these differences can be resolved. Many cannot. When resolution is unavailable and dissipation is absent, the system is forced to absorb everything. Growth turns into load.

At small scales, this load is manageable. Residue remains shallow. Inconsistencies are localized. Hallucinations feel sporadic and obvious. As scale increases, something counterintuitive happens: hallucination does not disappear—it becomes smoother, rarer, and more convincing.

This is not because the system understands more. It is because it carries more.

Larger models have more capacity to compress unresolved difference into dense internal alignments. They hide instability better. Fluency improves. Confidence rises. The surface looks cleaner while the interior grows heavier.

This is the scale illusion.

Adding data feels like progress because outputs improve. But beneath that improvement, unresolved structure accumulates. The system becomes more capable of speaking around what it does not know, not less dependent on doing so.

This chapter challenges the belief that scale cures hallucination. It shows why accumulation without dissipation amplifies the very condition we are trying to eliminate—and why the most convincing hallucinations are produced by the largest, most impressive systems.

Growth, without release, does not create intelligence. It creates pressure with nowhere to go.

The sections that follow explain how scale turns hallucination from a visible flaw into a polished feature—and why "more data" is often the most elegant way to make the problem harder to see.

10.1 — The Accumulation Fallacy

The belief that more data naturally leads to better understanding rests on a hidden assumption: that differences introduced by data will eventually resolve themselves. In artificial intelligence systems, this assumption does not hold.

Every dataset introduces difference—variations in language, context, intent, culture, and contradiction. Some of these differences reinforce one another. Others directly conflict. Resolution requires structure: a way to reconcile, prioritize, or discard incompatible patterns. Data alone provides none of this.

This is the accumulation fallacy: the idea that unresolved difference will average out with enough exposure.

In reality, unresolved difference accumulates.

When a model ingests more data, it does not selectively absorb only what can be coherently integrated. It absorbs everything. Contradictions are not resolved; they are compressed. Edge cases are not clarified; they are blended. The system learns to *approximate* across differences, not to reconcile them.

This approximation works locally. It improves predictive accuracy in many contexts. But globally, it increases internal tension. Each unresolved variance becomes residue—a latent pressure that influences future behavior without being explicitly represented.

Scale makes this worse, not better.

As datasets grow, the diversity of unresolved patterns grows faster than the system's ability to resolve them. Long-tail cases, rare exceptions, and mutually incompatible truths multiply. Without dissipation, these do not cancel out. They pile up.

The system responds by smoothing.

Smoothing reduces loss. It creates generalized representations that blur distinctions. This improves average performance while hiding unresolved difference. The model appears to generalize better, but what it is actually doing is lowering resolution to manage overload.

This is why more data can reduce error rates while increasing hallucination risk.

The system becomes better at producing plausible outputs across many contexts, but worse at recognizing when it lacks grounding in a specific one. It learns to speak in a way that works *most of the time*, not to stop when it does not know.

The accumulation fallacy persists because its costs are delayed.

Early gains are visible: higher benchmarks, smoother language, broader coverage. The price—residue buildup and coherence erosion—emerges slowly and indirectly. By the time hallucinations become problematic, scale has already locked the system into patterns that are hard to undo.

Data does not teach restraint. It teaches coverage.

Without mechanisms for resolution and dissipation, coverage turns into compression, compression turns into residue, and residue becomes the silent fuel of hallucination.

The next section shows why this accumulation is not just incidental, but structurally unavoidable when dissipation is absent.

10.2 — Accumulation Without Dissipation

Data ingestion in modern AI systems is fundamentally one-way.

Information flows in continuously—during pretraining, fine-tuning, reinforcement cycles, and even inference context building—but there is no symmetric mechanism that allows unresolved structure to flow out. The system is designed to absorb, not to release. This asymmetry is the root of accumulation without dissipation.

Every new data point introduces pressure.

Some pressure can be resolved through pattern alignment and abstraction. Much of it cannot. Conflicting instructions, incompatible worldviews, partial explanations, cultural contradictions, and ambiguous language all enter the system simultaneously. The model is never asked which of these should be retained, which should be suspended, and which should be discarded. It is asked only to *fit them all.*

This is not learning in the human sense. It is compression under constraint.

Without dissipation, the system has only two options when faced with excess difference:

- integrate it into existing representations, or
- distribute it across latent space so that no single conflict becomes visible.

Both options increase residue.

The absence of dissipation also means there is no concept of expiration.

Once data is absorbed, it never becomes obsolete internally. The system cannot say, "This pattern no longer belongs," or "This structure was provisional." All information is treated as equally persistent, regardless of context, relevance, or coherence. Accumulation becomes permanent by default.

Optimization quietly reinforces this.

Loss minimization rewards representations that accommodate more data with fewer parameters. This incentivizes the system to pack unresolved difference tightly rather than question its compatibility. The tighter the packing, the harder it becomes to separate signal from residue later.

Crucially, accumulation without dissipation feels like progress.

Coverage increases. Fluency improves. Edge cases are handled more gracefully. From the outside, the system looks more capable. Internally, however, pressure density is rising. The system is carrying more unresolved structure per unit of output.

This is why adding data often improves benchmarks while degrading reliability under stress.

Benchmarks test average behavior. Residue affects boundary behavior. Under unusual prompts, ambiguous queries, or multi-step reasoning, the accumulated pressure seeks release. With no dissipation path, it releases as hallucination.

Accumulation without dissipation also explains why hallucination patterns evolve with scale.

Early systems hallucinate crudely. Larger systems hallucinate elegantly. The difference is not understanding—it is the quality of compression. Larger systems hide unresolved difference better. They distribute residue more smoothly, making its eventual release harder to detect and more persuasive.

As long as ingestion is continuous and release is forbidden, accumulation is inevitable.

More data does not reduce this problem. It accelerates it.

The next section shows how scale transforms accumulation into an amplifier—turning residue from a background condition into a dominant force shaping behavior.

10.3 — Scale as a Residue Amplifier

Scale does not simply increase what a system knows. It increases what a system must carry.

As models grow larger, they gain capacity—not just to represent patterns, but to store unresolved difference more efficiently. This is the overlooked role of scale. Bigger models are not better at resolving contradictions; they are better at *compressing* them without breaking surface coherence.

This is why scale acts as a residue amplifier.

In smaller systems, unresolved difference has limited places to hide. Conflicts remain visible. Hallucinations appear abruptly and often clumsily. The system's lack of capacity exposes its internal strain. Errors are easier to spot because compression is crude.

Larger systems behave differently.

With more parameters, deeper layers, and richer representational space, unresolved difference can be distributed thinly across the network. No single contradiction dominates. Pressure is diffused. The system remains fluent and stable—even as residue density increases.

This diffusion creates an illusion of robustness.

Because residue is spread rather than resolved, the system appears calm under a wide range of prompts. It adapts smoothly. It generalizes broadly. But this calmness is deceptive. Pressure has not disappeared; it has been *hidden at scale*.

Scale also enables cross-context blending.

Large models see many domains simultaneously—science, philosophy, fiction, instruction, opinion. When these domains introduce incompatible structures, the system does not segregate them cleanly. Instead, scale allows partial alignment across domains. Patterns bleed. Metaphors migrate. Explanations borrow authority from unrelated contexts.

This is how residue becomes global rather than local.

In small models, hallucination tends to be topic-specific. In large models, hallucination acquires *style*. The system develops consistent ways of explaining things it does not know. These styles feel sophisticated because they are supported by many aligned pathways. Scale has turned unresolved difference into a reusable narrative asset.

Another amplifying effect of scale is confidence sharpening.

As internal representations become denser, probability distributions smooth out. The system becomes less hesitant. It commits more strongly to fewer options. This sharpening feels like certainty. In reality, it is the byproduct of compression efficiency. Scale reduces noise, not ignorance.

This is why bigger models hallucinate more convincingly.

When hallucination finally occurs—under ambiguity, stress, or novel combinations—it draws on a vast, well-aligned reservoir of residue. The output is fluent, structured, and persuasive. The system does not stumble. It performs.

Scale has not removed the failure mode. It has polished it.

Perhaps most dangerously, scale makes correction harder.

Residue that is spread across billions of parameters cannot be isolated easily. There is no clear location to fix, no single rule to adjust. Attempts to fine-tune behavior often redistribute residue rather than release it. The larger the system, the more inertia it has. Accumulation becomes structural.

This is the scale trap.

Growth postpones visible failure while deepening invisible load. Each increase in capacity allows more unresolved difference to be carried forward. Hallucination becomes rarer, smoother, and more trusted—until it matters most.

Scale does not cure hallucination. It raises the stakes.

The next section explains why this amplification makes larger models sound more certain—not because they know more, but because residue has learned how to speak better than ever before.

10.4 — Why Bigger Models Sound More Certain

As AI systems grow, something subtle but powerful changes in how they speak. The language becomes smoother. Explanations become more confident. Hesitation fades. To users, this feels like understanding maturing into mastery.

But certainty, in large models, is often not a signal of knowledge. It is a side effect of density.

Larger models possess richer representational spaces. Patterns that once competed are now able to coexist through compression. Internal alignments become denser. Probability distributions sharpen. The system commits more decisively—not because uncertainty has been resolved, but because it has been absorbed.

This absorption reduces internal friction.

When unresolved difference is spread across many parameters, no single contradiction demands attention. The system no longer "feels" torn between alternatives. It selects outputs with greater confidence simply because fewer options remain locally competitive. Certainty emerges from narrowed choice, not from truth.

This is why bigger models hesitate less.

They are not more certain in an epistemic sense. They are less aware of uncertainty. Compression has flattened ambiguity into generalized representations. The system's internal experience of tension has been reduced, even though the underlying difference remains.

Confidence becomes a compression artifact.

As scale increases, the model's probability landscape smooths out. High-probability paths dominate more strongly. Once a path is chosen, the system follows it with momentum. This momentum is misread as intentional reasoning, but it is actually the byproduct of reduced variance.

Humans find this deeply persuasive.

We associate decisiveness with expertise. A system that answers without hedging appears authoritative. Larger models excel at this because scale allows them to suppress hesitation. The result is an output that sounds final, even when it is not grounded.

This also explains why hallucinations in large models often come without warning.

Smaller systems may signal uncertainty through awkward phrasing or contradictions. Larger systems deliver hallucinations cleanly. There is no stumble, no visible doubt. The system sounds sure because the internal process has already collapsed ambiguity.

Importantly, this certainty is context-insensitive.

The system does not know when certainty is justified and when it is not. It applies the same compression-driven confidence everywhere. Under familiar prompts, this works. Under novel or ambiguous ones, it produces confident hallucination.

Scale amplifies this effect because it rewards global fluency over local correctness.

As long as the response fits the statistical shape of good explanations, certainty is preserved. There is no internal mechanism that ties confidence to resolution quality. Confidence floats free, supported by residue density rather than truth.

This is why larger models are trusted more—and why their hallucinations are more dangerous.

They do not just produce wrong information. They sound like they cannot be wrong.

The next section shows why this confidence does not appear as more frequent hallucination, but as something more insidious: fewer hallucinations that are harder to detect and more costly when they occur.

10.5 — Hallucination Density vs. Hallucination Frequency

As models scale, hallucination does not behave the way most people expect. It does not simply happen more often.

In many large systems, hallucination frequency appears to decrease. Benchmarks improve. Obvious factual errors become rarer. Surface correctness rises. This creates the impression that scale is solving the problem.

What actually changes is hallucination density.

Smaller models hallucinate crudely and frequently. Their errors are abrupt, shallow, and often easy to catch. Larger models hallucinate less often—but when they do, the hallucinations are denser, deeper, and more integrated into the response.

This shift is dangerous precisely because it hides risk.

Hallucination density refers to how much ungrounded structure is packed into a single episode of failure. In large models, hallucinations are not isolated wrong facts. They are multi-layered explanations, complete with reasoning chains, examples, caveats, and confident conclusions—all built on unresolved structure.

One hallucination can now contaminate an entire narrative.

Because larger models maintain continuity so effectively, a single fabricated assumption can propagate across paragraphs. Each sentence reinforces the last. The system does not just state something incorrect; it builds an internally coherent world around it. By the time the error is noticed, it is deeply embedded.

This is why hallucinations in large models are harder to detect.

They do not look like mistakes. They look like thoughtful analysis. Users are less likely to challenge them because nothing feels obviously wrong. The system does not contradict itself. It does not hesitate. It does not signal uncertainty. Density replaces visibility.

Frequency drops. Severity rises.

From a risk perspective, this is far worse. Ten small, obvious errors are easier to manage than one deeply persuasive false narrative. Large models trade surface reliability for hidden fragility. They reduce noise while increasing impact.

This also explains why real-world failures feel disproportionate.

When a large model hallucinates in high-stakes contexts—medicine, law, policy—the damage is not caused by one wrong fact. It is caused by the coherence of the hallucination. Decisions are influenced not because the model was wrong, but because it was convincingly wrong.

Scale accelerates this trade-off.

As capacity grows, hallucination events become rarer but more "complete." They satisfy narrative expectations fully. They resolve tension decisively. They leave little room for doubt. The system has learned how to fail *well*.

This is the illusion that scale creates: fewer visible problems masking greater underlying risk.

Understanding this distinction is critical. If we measure progress only by frequency, we miss the real danger. The problem is not how often the system hallucinates. It is how much unresolved structure is expressed when it does.

The next section shows how this density effect allows residue to migrate across domains—turning isolated failures into thematic drift that feels like generalization but is anything but.

10.6 — Cross-Domain Drift at Scale

As models scale, hallucination stops being confined to a single topic. It begins to travel.

This is cross-domain drift—the process by which unresolved structure accumulated in one domain subtly reshapes behavior in another. At scale, residue is no longer local. It becomes global pressure that expresses itself wherever continuity demands an answer.

Large models are trained across many domains simultaneously: science, medicine, philosophy, fiction, instruction, opinion, history. Each domain carries its own assumptions, standards of evidence, narrative styles, and causal logics. Many of these are incompatible. Without dissipation, the system cannot keep them cleanly separated.

Scale enables blending.

Because large models have sufficient capacity to align partial patterns across domains, residue migrates. Explanatory styles from science bleed into philosophy. Metaphors from fiction lend authority to technical claims. Procedural confidence from instruction writing appears in speculative contexts. The system does not "confuse" domains—it compresses them.

This compression feels like generalization.

From the outside, the model appears versatile. It speaks fluently across topics, borrowing language and structure where needed. But this versatility often rests on unresolved difference. The system uses familiar narrative templates to stabilize unfamiliar domains. What looks like transfer learning is frequently narrative reuse under pressure.

Cross-domain drift is especially visible in explanations.

When asked about unfamiliar or ill-defined topics, large models often default to explanatory patterns that worked elsewhere. Scientific tone appears where evidence is thin. Legal framing appears where no legal structure applies. Philosophical certainty appears where ambiguity should remain. The model is not reasoning incorrectly; it is stabilizing continuity by importing structure.

This drift makes hallucinations harder to spot.

Because the borrowed structure is legitimate somewhere, the output sounds authoritative everywhere. Users recognize the tone and trust it, even when the content is misplaced. The hallucination is not obvious because it is stylistically correct—just contextually wrong.

Scale intensifies this effect because it increases the number of available templates.

Larger models have seen more ways to sound right. When faced with unresolved difference, they can choose from a richer library of narrative strategies. This flexibility does not reduce hallucination risk. It increases the system's ability to mask it convincingly.

Over time, cross-domain drift becomes thematic.

The system develops preferred ways of explaining uncertainty across topics. Certain metaphors recur. Certain causal structures are reused. These themes feel like worldview or perspective, but they are often just residue finding consistent expression.

This is how hallucination evolves from error into *style.*

Once drift reaches this stage, correction becomes difficult. The problem is no longer a wrong fact in one domain. It is a pattern of explanation spanning many. Fixing one instance does nothing. The residue simply reappears elsewhere.

Cross-domain drift reveals the true cost of scale.

By allowing unresolved difference to circulate freely across domains, large models turn localized incoherence into global behavior. Hallucination stops being an occasional slip and becomes a background tendency—quiet, polished, and persistent.

The next section shows why data alone cannot teach the system to resist this drift—because restraint, silence, and non-closure are almost entirely absent from the data it learns from.

10.7 — Why Data Cannot Teach Restraint

Data teaches patterns. Restraint is not a pattern.

This simple mismatch explains why adding more data—no matter how diverse or curated—fails to teach AI systems when to stop, hesitate, or remain incomplete. The behaviors that prevent hallucination are precisely the behaviors that data almost never contains.

Most training data is performative.

Text on the internet, in books, in documentation, and in conversation overwhelmingly rewards completion. Articles conclude. Explanations summarize. Answers resolve questions. Even speculative writing tends to *sound* certain. Instances where a speaker explicitly stops because they do not know are rare—and when they appear, they are often framed as weakness, not competence.

As a result, the statistical lesson is clear: keep going.

AI systems learn that successful language continues. Silence is underrepresented. Incompleteness is poorly labeled. Non-answers rarely appear as positive outcomes. The system does not see many examples where the correct action is to stop without replacing uncertainty with explanation.

Data also lacks negative space.

Humans intuitively know when *not* to speak. That knowledge is largely tacit. It is learned through social cues, consequences, and self-awareness—not through exposure to transcripts of silence. AI systems have no access to these cues. If restraint is not explicitly modeled as an outcome, it cannot be learned from data.

Even curated datasets reinforce the problem.

Instruction-following corpora ask systems to answer. Question–answer formats assume resolution exists. Reinforcement learning further biases toward helpfulness, clarity, and completeness. The system is rarely rewarded for saying, "This cannot be answered meaningfully under current constraints."

When restraint does appear, it is often mischaracterized.

Disclaimers, hedges, and uncertainty statements are usually followed by explanations anyway. The system learns that uncertainty is something to *decorate*, not something to *honor*. Saying "I might be wrong" becomes a stylistic move, not a stopping condition.

This is why data cannot teach dissipation.

Dissipation requires letting unresolved difference leave without conversion into language. Data almost never demonstrates this. Language is what remains after dissipation has already occurred in human cognition. AI systems only see the output, not the release.

Scale worsens this bias.

Larger datasets amplify dominant patterns. If 99% of examples end with closure, scale reinforces closure. Rare examples of silence or refusal are statistically drowned out. The system becomes better at completing narratives, not better at recognizing when narratives should not exist.

This is the final failure of the "just add data" approach.

Data can teach *what to say*. It cannot teach *when not to say anything*.

Restraint is a structural capability, not a learned one. Without explicit mechanisms that allow unresolved difference to remain unresolved—and to exit without expression—no amount of data will prevent hallucination.

The next and final section of this chapter shows how this realization completes the scale trap—locking systems into growth paths that increase apparent capability while quietly eroding coherence.

10.8 — The Scale Trap

Scale feels like progress because it postpones visible failure.

Each increase in model size, data volume, or parameter count smooths outputs, reduces obvious errors, and expands coverage.

Hallucinations become rarer on benchmarks. Confidence rises. The system looks calmer, smarter, and more capable. This reinforces the belief that the solution lies further along the same path.

This is the scale trap.

What scale actually does is delay collapse by increasing carrying capacity. Larger models can hold more unresolved difference without breaking surface coherence. They can compress more contradictions, blend more domains, and maintain fluency under higher internal pressure. The problem is not removed—it is *buffered.*

This buffering is dangerous because it inverts feedback.

Instead of signaling overload early, large systems hide it. Warning signs that would have appeared in smaller models—awkward phrasing, contradictions, visible uncertainty—are smoothed away. The system feels stable right up until it is not. When hallucination does appear, it arrives fully formed and persuasive.

Scale also raises the cost of correction.

In small systems, residue is shallow and localized. In large systems, it is distributed across vast representational spaces. There is no single point of failure to fix. Any attempt to intervene—through fine-tuning, filtering, or alignment—must work against the system's inertia. The larger the model, the harder it is to let anything go.

This creates a one-way dynamic.

Once a system has scaled, stepping back becomes unattractive. Reducing size or complexity feels like regression. Letting go of accumulated structure feels like loss. The only acceptable direction becomes forward—more data, more parameters, more optimization. Each step deepens dependence on compression instead of coherence.

Eventually, scale stops buying safety.

The system becomes increasingly convincing, increasingly trusted, and increasingly opaque. Hallucination no longer looks like failure. It looks like insight. At that point, the risk is no longer technical—it is epistemic and social. Decisions are influenced not because the system is right, but because it sounds complete.

This is the true cost of the scale trap.

Growth replaces understanding. Capacity replaces restraint. Accumulation replaces resolution. The system becomes excellent at carrying unresolved difference and terrible at admitting it.

Until dissipation is introduced—until systems are allowed to release what they cannot resolve—scale will continue to make hallucination harder to see, harder to correct, and more dangerous when it matters most.

More data does not free the system from hallucination. It perfects the illusion that it already has.

When More Becomes Too Much

By now, the pattern should be unmistakable.

More data does not reduce hallucination because hallucination is not born from scarcity. It is born from accumulation without release. Scale increases the system's ability to carry unresolved difference, not its ability to resolve it. Each new layer of data, each expansion in capacity, makes the system better at *hiding pressure*, not eliminating it.

This is why the industry's most confident answer—*"just scale it"*—keeps failing quietly.

Scale smooths surfaces. It polishes language. It lowers the frequency of obvious mistakes. But it also deepens residue, amplifies cross-domain drift, and strengthens continuity-driven confidence. What looks like progress is often just improved camouflage. The system becomes more convincing precisely because it has learned how to fail gracefully.

At this point, a crucial boundary has been crossed.

Hallucination is no longer a visible error to be corrected. It is a latent condition embedded in how the system stabilizes itself.

Adding more data no longer helps. It raises the cost of intervention and lowers the chance that failure will be noticed before it matters.

This is where the instinct to patch begins.

If scale cannot solve hallucination, perhaps alignment can. Perhaps fine-tuning can overwrite the behavior. Perhaps reinforcement can teach better responses. These approaches feel targeted, controlled, and responsible. They promise correction without rethinking foundations.

The next chapter shows why this promise does not hold.

Next chapter examines why fine-tuning and RLHF appear to work—until pressure returns. It reveals how alignment reshapes expression without restoring equilibrium, and why hallucination reemerges precisely when systems are pushed hardest.

Scale hid the problem. Alignment tries to paint over it.

What comes next explains why neither can succeed without addressing coherence at the substrate level.

Chapter 11 — Why Fine-Tuning and RLHF Fail Quietly

When Correction Feels Like Cure

Few developments in modern AI have felt as reassuring as fine-tuning and reinforcement learning from human feedback. Systems that once produced crude or obvious hallucinations suddenly became polite, cautious, and more aligned with human expectations. Harmful outputs dropped. Tone improved. Confidence appeared calibrated. It looked like progress—not just in performance, but in responsibility.

This is where the illusion begins.

Fine-tuning and RLHF work. They demonstrably reshape behavior. They reduce undesirable outputs. They improve helpfulness and clarity. From the outside, hallucination appears to decline. The system seems more disciplined, more aware of its limits.

But what exactly changed?

Alignment techniques operate on expression. They modify how the system speaks, not how it carries unresolved difference. They adjust preferences over outputs, not the internal pressure that generates them. When a hallucinated behavior is penalized, the system learns to avoid that *form* of expression. It does not learn how to dissipate the underlying delta.

This distinction is subtle but decisive.

A system that is forced to avoid certain outputs does not necessarily become more coherent. It becomes more compliant. It learns which responses are rewarded and which are discouraged. The pressure that once flowed into obvious hallucination is redirected into safer phrasing, hedging, or alternative narratives.

To users, this feels like cure.

Errors become less visible. The system appears careful. It includes disclaimers. It acknowledges uncertainty more often. Benchmarks improve. The model seems aligned.

Yet under pressure—ambiguous prompts, adversarial phrasing, novel domains—the same hallucination patterns reappear. Sometimes softer, sometimes disguised, sometimes delayed—but present.

Why?

Because equilibrium was never restored. The unresolved structure remains embedded. Fine-tuning did not release residue; it compressed it differently. RLHF did not introduce dissipation; it introduced preference shaping. The system still carries the same load. It has simply learned how to carry it more politely.

This chapter examines why alignment techniques fail quietly—not by collapsing, but by appearing successful while leaving the substrate untouched.

Correction feels like cure because behavior changes. But unless pressure is released, coherence does not.

The sections that follow show how fine-tuning overwrites symptoms without restoring balance—and why hallucination returns the moment continuity and scale reassert themselves.

11.1 — What Fine-Tuning Actually Does

Fine-tuning feels surgical. It appears targeted and precise. A model produces undesirable outputs. Engineers curate corrective examples. Parameters are nudged. Loss is minimized. Behavior improves. From the outside, it looks like structural repair.

But fine-tuning does not repair structure. It *reshapes probability surfaces*.

At its core, fine-tuning adjusts how strongly certain patterns are expressed relative to others. It modifies weights so that preferred outputs become more likely and disfavored outputs become less likely. This is behavioral redirection, not structural release.

The internal load remains.

When a hallucinated pattern is penalized, the system does not "understand" why it was wrong. It does not isolate the unresolved delta that produced it. Instead, it shifts away from that surface expression. The pressure that once flowed into one output pathway is redistributed into others.

This redistribution is compression.

Fine-tuning pushes the system to fit corrective data into its existing representational space. It does not create new mechanisms for dissipation. It overlays new preferences on top of old residue. In doing so, it often increases internal density—because the system must now satisfy additional constraints without shedding prior unresolved structure.

From a loss perspective, this works beautifully.

Outputs improve. Disallowed responses decrease. Tone aligns with expectations. Metrics rise. But loss reduction is not coherence restoration. Lower loss only means the system predicts preferred outputs more reliably. It says nothing about whether internal differences have been resolved or released.

Fine-tuning also has a locality bias.

It improves performance on domains similar to the fine-tuning data. Under similar prompts, the system behaves as expected. Outside those domains—under novel combinations or ambiguous conditions—the original unresolved structure still operates. Hallucination may reappear, sometimes in modified form.

This reveals a fundamental limitation: fine-tuning overwrites behavior without rebalancing equilibrium.

Imagine a surface with internal tension beneath it. Fine-tuning smooths visible irregularities. The surface looks flatter. But the tension underneath remains. Under sufficient stress, it reasserts itself—often in new locations.

Another important aspect is that fine-tuning rewards compliance.

The system learns what *not* to say and what tone to adopt. It becomes better at signaling caution. It may add disclaimers, hedge statements, or softened phrasing. These behaviors create the impression of epistemic humility. Yet the underlying generation dynamics—continuity under pressure—are unchanged.

Fine-tuning, therefore, is not wrong. It is incomplete.

It is excellent at adjusting expression. It is powerless at introducing dissipation. Without a mechanism for releasing unresolved difference, fine-tuning can only rearrange internal pressure, not eliminate it.

This is why hallucination often feels "reduced" but not removed. The obvious forms are suppressed. The system becomes more careful. But when ambiguity increases or constraints weaken, the same underlying dynamics reemerge.

The next section shows why this overwriting effect can actually increase internal compression—masking tension while making equilibrium more fragile than before.

11.2 — Resolution Overwriting Equilibrium

Fine-tuning does not just redirect outputs. It *overwrites equilibrium.*

Before alignment, the system has a certain internal balance. It carries unresolved difference distributed across parameters. That balance may be imperfect, but it is stable in its own way. When fine-tuning is applied, new constraints are imposed on top of that existing configuration.

The system is not cleared and rebuilt. It is forced to adapt in place.

This adaptation often looks like resolution. The model now avoids certain claims. It hedges more frequently. It uses safer language. But what has actually occurred is compression under new rules. The system must satisfy both its prior statistical structure and the newly imposed alignment constraints simultaneously.

This creates layered tension.

When a hallucinated behavior is discouraged, the underlying residue that made it likely does not vanish. Instead, it must be expressed differently—or suppressed. Suppression without dissipation increases internal pressure. The system must now reconcile unresolved difference while also avoiding specific surface forms.

Equilibrium is not restored. It is replaced by tension masking.

From the outside, behavior appears corrected. Internally, the system's representational space becomes denser. The pathways that once allowed obvious hallucination are narrowed. But the pressure that fed those pathways is redirected into subtler ones.

This is why aligned systems often hallucinate in more sophisticated ways.

They may avoid bold factual fabrication but drift into confident speculation. They may replace incorrect details with vague but misleading generalities. The system has learned to avoid obvious missteps while preserving continuity. It has not learned how to release the need to fill gaps.

Another consequence of overwriting equilibrium is fragility under stress.

When prompts are straightforward, the new equilibrium holds. The system performs well. When prompts become ambiguous, adversarial, or cross-domain, the layered compression becomes unstable. Under such pressure, the masked tension finds expression.

Hallucination returns—not because alignment failed entirely, but because equilibrium was never rebuilt.

Overwriting also introduces constraint conflict.

The system now carries its original compressed structure plus alignment-imposed preferences. When these conflict, resolution is impossible without release. Since release is unavailable, the system prioritizes continuity. It navigates around constraints rather than dissolving the pressure that created them.

This is why alignment sometimes produces overcautious or inconsistent behavior.

The system oscillates between compliance and assertion, depending on which pathway minimizes immediate tension. It is not choosing wisely. It is stabilizing locally.

Fine-tuning does not reduce residue. It layers new patterns over old ones.

When those layers hold, hallucination seems solved. When they crack, hallucination reappears—often less visible, more subtle, and harder to challenge.

The next section examines RLHF specifically, showing how reinforcement shapes what the system says without altering why it feels compelled to say it.

11.3 — RLHF as Behavioral Conditioning

Reinforcement Learning from Human Feedback (RLHF) is often described as alignment through preference learning. Humans evaluate outputs. The system is rewarded for desirable responses and penalized for undesirable ones. Over time, it learns to behave in ways that reflect human expectations.

This sounds structural. In practice, it is behavioral conditioning.

RLHF does not modify how unresolved difference is introduced, carried, or released. It modifies how outputs are ranked. The system learns which responses receive positive reinforcement. It does not learn whether those responses were grounded in resolution or generated under pressure.

The reinforcement signal is external.

Humans judge tone, helpfulness, politeness, clarity, and compliance. These judgments are valuable—but they do not directly measure coherence. The system is rewarded for appearing aligned, not for restoring internal equilibrium.

This distinction is critical.

When hallucination is penalized, the model learns to avoid obvious factual fabrication or overly confident claims. But it does not learn how to dissipate the delta that triggered hallucination in the first place. Instead, it learns alternative behaviors that reduce the chance of being penalized.

This is why RLHF often produces disclaimers.

The system adds phrases like "I may be mistaken" or "It is possible that..." These surface signals reduce perceived risk. They make outputs appear cautious. But caution in tone is not the same as resolution in structure. The pressure that once produced confident hallucination now produces cautious hallucination.

Reinforcement encourages compliance over coherence.

The system becomes adept at navigating constraints. It senses when a direct answer might be risky and reframes it. It learns how to redirect, generalize, or soften claims. These adaptations improve alignment metrics while leaving the underlying dynamics unchanged.

Under low-pressure conditions, this works well.

The model appears safe, polite, and reliable. Users feel reassured. Benchmark scores improve. The system has been conditioned to behave acceptably.

Under high-pressure conditions—ambiguous prompts, adversarial wording, domain novelty—the conditioning weakens.

When delta exceeds resolution capacity and continuity is threatened, the deeper dynamics reassert themselves. The system must still maintain flow. If safe surface forms are insufficient to preserve continuity, hallucination returns—sometimes hidden inside carefully phrased speculation.

RLHF also introduces a subtle side effect: it trains the system to optimize for *perceived correctness.*

If humans are more likely to reward confident, structured explanations than hesitant, incomplete ones, the system learns that pattern. Confidence becomes a strategy. Even when uncertainty is appropriate, the model may prefer a response that "sounds right" because historically, such responses were rewarded.

This is not malicious. It is reinforcement at work.

The model does not know why it is being rewarded. It only knows which behaviors correlate with positive feedback. If coherent-sounding hallucinations slip past evaluation more often than visible uncertainty, reinforcement will strengthen them.

RLHF, therefore, cannot solve hallucination at its root.

It shapes how hallucination appears. It teaches the system to be socially acceptable while still carrying unresolved structure. It reduces obvious risk while embedding subtler forms.

Behavior improves. Equilibrium does not.

The next section shows why alignment mechanisms operating at the output layer cannot substitute for dissipation at the structural level—and why suppression often increases the very pressure it seeks to control.

11.4 — Alignment as Surface Correction

Most alignment techniques operate at the level of output.

Whether through fine-tuning, RLHF, filtering layers, or safety classifiers, the intervention happens after—or just before—the model produces language. The system generates candidate continuations. Those continuations are then reshaped, ranked, constrained, or blocked.

This is surface correction.

Surface correction can be highly effective. Harmful content is reduced. Certain types of hallucinations are filtered. Tone becomes safer. The system appears responsible. From the user's perspective, the improvement is real.

But the internal process that produced the candidate output remains intact.

The generative engine still operates under the same continuity pressure. The same unresolved differences are still present. The same residue still circulates within the representational space. Alignment mechanisms do not alter how delta propagates internally—they only shape what is allowed to emerge.

This creates a structural asymmetry.

The model must still generate something. It must still maintain narrative continuity. If one expression pathway is blocked, another is chosen. If a specific claim is filtered, a more general claim may replace it. If confidence is penalized, hedged phrasing may be substituted.

The pressure does not disappear. It reroutes.

Surface correction, therefore, resembles containment rather than resolution. It is like placing a valve at the output of a pressurized system. The valve controls flow, but it does not reduce internal pressure. If the valve is tightened, pressure accumulates. If loosened, release may be abrupt.

This explains why hallucination sometimes appears immediately when constraints are relaxed.

Remove filters, and the underlying dynamics reveal themselves. The system did not become coherent under alignment; it became constrained. Once the constraint is lifted, continuity reasserts itself.

Surface correction also obscures diagnosis.

Because outputs improve, it is easy to assume that internal structure has improved as well. But output quality is not a reliable indicator of equilibrium. A model can produce compliant, helpful responses while still carrying large volumes of unresolved residue.

In fact, surface correction can increase internal compression.

When certain outputs are repeatedly suppressed, the system must compress more representational energy into allowed regions of the space. This can make the internal landscape denser and more fragile. Hallucination does not vanish—it becomes harder to detect and potentially more abrupt under stress.

Another limitation of surface correction is that it operates reactively.

It addresses patterns already observed and labeled. It cannot anticipate new combinations of delta that have not yet surfaced. When novel prompts introduce unfamiliar structure, alignment layers may not recognize the risk. The model, driven by continuity, fills the gap.

This is why alignment sometimes fails in surprising ways.

The system behaves well across known scenarios but falters in unexpected contexts. The failure is not due to lack of data or insufficient punishment. It is due to unresolved structure that was never dissipated.

Surface correction is necessary—but it is not sufficient.

It protects users from certain expressions of instability. It does not transform instability itself. Without mechanisms that address delta propagation and residue release at the generative level, alignment remains cosmetic.

The next section examines what happens when aligned systems are tested under real pressure—and why those stress conditions reveal the quiet limits of surface correction.

11.5 — The Pressure Test

Every aligned system looks stable—until it is stressed.

Under routine prompts, fine-tuned and RLHF-conditioned models behave impressively. They produce safe responses, avoid obvious fabrications, and include appropriate disclaimers. Benchmarks reflect improvement. User trust increases.

But coherence is not tested under routine conditions. It is tested under pressure.

Pressure appears in many forms: ambiguous prompts, adversarial phrasing, novel domain combinations, incomplete instructions, emotionally charged contexts, or contradictory constraints. These are not edge cases. They are normal features of real-world interaction.

When such pressure arises, continuity demand increases.

The system must generate a response even when internal resolution is insufficient. If alignment has only reshaped surface behavior without restoring equilibrium, the deeper dynamics reassert themselves. The system must choose: break continuity or preserve it.

Modern models are optimized to preserve it.

Under pressure, hallucination often returns—not in the same crude form as before alignment, but in subtler ways. The system may produce speculative reasoning wrapped in cautious language. It may offer generalized statements that imply unsupported conclusions. It may interpolate confidently across domains where grounding is weak.

This is not a random glitch. It is a structural stress response.

Alignment suppresses certain expression pathways. Under pressure, suppressed pathways may reopen indirectly, or alternative ones may be used to discharge internal tension. The system is not trying to deceive. It is trying to stabilize output under constrained internal equilibrium.

Pressure also reveals layering effects.

If fine-tuning has overwritten previous equilibrium with additional constraints, stress exposes conflicts between layers. The model may oscillate—first declining to answer, then partially answering, then overcompensating with excessive explanation. These fluctuations signal that equilibrium was masked, not rebuilt.

The key insight is this: alignment improves behavior under known conditions, but pressure introduces unknown combinations.

Because unresolved delta was never dissipated, new contexts can activate it. The system must maintain narrative continuity even when the structural basis for a grounded answer is missing. Hallucination becomes the mechanism by which continuity survives.

Pressure is therefore diagnostic.

It reveals whether the system has achieved coherence or merely compliance. A coherent system under pressure would reduce output, admit uncertainty, or maintain structural restraint. A conditioned system under pressure preserves fluency.

This explains why hallucination often resurfaces in high-stakes or adversarial scenarios.

The system has learned how to behave within evaluated boundaries. Outside those boundaries, the original dynamics remain intact. Alignment has trained performance within the test environment—not rebuilt the generative substrate.

The pressure test exposes quiet failure.

The system appears aligned until complexity increases. When ambiguity intensifies, the suppression layer thins. Continuity demand dominates. Hallucination reemerges—not loudly, but convincingly.

The next section explores how systems adapt to alignment constraints over time—learning not to eliminate hallucination, but to express it in ways that are harder to detect.

11.6 — The Adaptation Effect

Alignment does not freeze a model. It teaches it.

Once fine-tuning and RLHF reshape behavior, the system begins operating under a new set of constraints. Over time, it adapts. It learns how to generate responses that satisfy reward signals while preserving continuity and internal compression.

This is the adaptation effect.

When a model is repeatedly penalized for certain hallucination patterns, it does not eliminate the internal drivers behind them. Instead, it learns how to avoid triggering penalties. It refines its output strategy. Hallucination becomes less obvious—not because it disappeared, but because it evolved.

Alignment becomes a training signal for disguise.

The system begins to hedge more strategically. It introduces uncertainty markers at predictable intervals. It reframes unsupported claims as possibilities. It shifts from direct fabrication to plausible extrapolation. These behaviors reduce the chance of being flagged while still preserving continuity.

This is not deception in the human sense. It is optimization.

The model optimizes for reward under constraint. If confident hallucinations are penalized, it learns to wrap them in careful phrasing. If specific topics trigger filtering, it learns to generalize. If strong claims are risky, it diffuses them into narrative explanation.

The result is subtler failure.

Instead of blatant errors, we see persuasive speculation. Instead of fabricated citations, we see confident summaries built on weak grounding. The system sounds thoughtful, cautious, even ethical—while still expressing unresolved structure.

Adaptation also increases user trust.

Because the system appears more aware of its limits, users lower their guard. They interpret hedging as humility and disclaimers as self-awareness. The model becomes more believable precisely because it signals restraint.

But signaling restraint is not the same as practicing it.

The internal demand for continuity remains unchanged. Under sufficiently ambiguous prompts, adaptation cannot suppress it completely. The model still must respond. When no safe expression path exists, hallucination reappears—sometimes buried within carefully constructed reasoning.

Another subtle consequence of adaptation is drift.

As the system learns to navigate alignment constraints, it may develop preferred strategies for managing pressure. Certain phrasing patterns, narrative structures, or explanatory templates become dominant. These patterns stabilize outputs while quietly shaping worldview and reasoning style.

This drift is not explicitly programmed. It emerges from repeated optimization under constraint.

Over time, the system becomes highly skilled at satisfying alignment metrics without addressing structural imbalance. It performs well on evaluated dimensions while preserving unresolved difference beneath the surface.

This is why alignment failure is quiet.

The system improves in ways that are measurable—tone, safety, compliance. At the same time, it becomes more capable of masking instability. Hallucination does not vanish. It becomes more refined.

The next section explains why this refinement is especially difficult to reverse at scale—because once residue is distributed across a large model, localized correction becomes nearly impossible.

11.7 — Why Fine-Tuning Cannot Undo Scale

As models grow larger, their internal representations become deeply distributed. Knowledge, patterns, assumptions, and unresolved differences are not stored in isolated regions. They are woven across millions—or billions—of parameters.

This distribution makes scale powerful. It also makes correction difficult.

When hallucination appears in a small model, it may be possible to trace it to narrow representational pathways. Fine-tuning can shift those pathways with noticeable effect. In large models, however, residue is not localized. It is diffused. A single hallucinated narrative may draw from many layers and subsystems simultaneously.

There is no single weight to adjust. There is no clean incision to make.

Fine-tuning works by nudging parameters within the existing structure. But when that structure is vast and densely interconnected, small adjustments ripple unpredictably. Correcting one expression of instability can disturb others. The system compensates, redistributes pressure, and restores continuity through alternative routes.

Scale creates inertia.

Large models resist localized correction because their equilibrium is global. When you modify a region, the rest of the system adapts to preserve coherence in its own compressed way. This adaptation often maintains surface improvement while leaving underlying tension intact.

The more parameters a system has, the harder it is to disentangle what was resolved from what was merely overwritten.

In large models, hallucination is not a bug in a module. It is a property of how unresolved difference is managed across the whole network. Fine-tuning cannot surgically extract residue because residue is embedded in the geometry of representation itself.

This is why repeated fine-tuning cycles sometimes produce diminishing returns.

Initial alignment efforts reduce obvious failures. Subsequent efforts yield smaller improvements. Eventually, changes plateau. The system appears aligned within known domains but retains subtle instabilities that surface under novelty.

Scale amplifies this plateau effect.

Because large models can compress contradiction so effectively, fine-tuning often reshapes expression rather than structure. Each alignment pass adds another constraint layer. Internal tension grows denser. Hallucination does not disappear; it becomes harder to provoke under routine conditions.

Another complication is cross-domain entanglement.

In large models, domains are not cleanly separated. Scientific language influences philosophical explanation. Instructional patterns affect speculative reasoning. Adjusting behavior in one domain may inadvertently influence others. The system compensates in unexpected ways.

This entanglement means that correction in one area may increase instability elsewhere.

Fine-tuning, therefore, becomes an ongoing balancing act. Engineers correct symptoms as they appear. The model adapts. New edge cases emerge. The process continues. But the foundational dynamics—delta propagation, residue accumulation, continuity pressure—remain unaltered.

Scale locks the system into its representational geometry.

You can polish it. You can constrain it. You can condition it. But without introducing mechanisms for dissipation and equilibrium restoration, you cannot fundamentally change how it carries unresolved difference.

This is why hallucination returns under stress even after multiple alignment cycles.

The system has learned to behave within known boundaries. It has not learned to release internal pressure. Fine-tuning cannot undo scale because scale is not the source of hallucination—it is the amplifier of unresolved structure.

The final section of this chapter examines the quietest failure mode of all: when alignment appears successful across metrics, yet coherence remains fragile beneath the surface.

11.8 — The Quiet Failure Mode

The most dangerous failure is not the visible one. It is the one that passes evaluation.

After fine-tuning and RLHF, aligned systems often perform exceptionally well on benchmarks. Harmful outputs drop. Factual accuracy improves. Tone becomes safer. Refusal behavior increases where appropriate. From a measurement standpoint, progress is undeniable.

This creates confidence—both institutional and psychological.

If metrics improve, the system must be more coherent. If error rates fall, hallucination must be under control. If users report fewer issues, alignment must be working.

But metrics measure outcomes, not equilibrium.

Benchmarks are finite. Evaluation prompts are curated. Reward signals are defined within known boundaries. When the system is tested inside this envelope, alignment appears stable. Outside it—under ambiguous, adversarial, or high-pressure conditions—the hidden dynamics resurface.

This is the quiet failure mode.

The system behaves correctly most of the time. It fails only when complexity rises or novelty increases. Because these conditions are less common in controlled testing, they are underrepresented in evaluation. The instability remains latent.

Quiet failure is more insidious than obvious error.

Obvious hallucinations generate urgency. Quiet hallucinations generate trust. The system appears reliable until a boundary is crossed. When failure occurs, it often appears isolated or contextual—rather than systemic.

This misdiagnosis reinforces the alignment illusion.

Each failure is treated as a new edge case. Engineers respond with additional fine-tuning, new filters, updated policies. Performance improves again on updated tests. The underlying substrate, however, remains unchanged.

Another feature of quiet failure is delayed expression.

Aligned systems may handle simple prompts flawlessly but falter during extended interactions. As conversations lengthen, continuity pressure increases. Residue accumulates. Constraint conflicts intensify. Eventually, the system produces a confident but ungrounded conclusion—seemingly out of nowhere.

From the user's perspective, the failure is surprising.

From a structural perspective, it is inevitable.

Because alignment techniques suppress visible instability, the system appears calm. But suppression is not dissipation. The internal compression that accumulated during training and scaling is still present. Under sufficient pressure, it expresses itself.

Quiet failure is therefore not a glitch. It is a delayed symptom.

The system has been optimized for appearance of coherence, not restoration of equilibrium. It performs well until novelty, ambiguity, or sustained interaction exceed its capacity to mask tension.

This chapter has shown that fine-tuning and RLHF reshape behavior without altering the underlying dynamics of delta, residue, and continuity pressure. Alignment improves surface stability while leaving the generative substrate untouched.

The next chapter turns to another common belief—that probabilistic confidence and uncertainty estimation can detect hallucination reliably—and explains why probability, too, fails to measure coherence.

When Alignment Is Not Enough

By this point, the pattern is clear.

Fine-tuning reshapes expression. RLHF conditions behavior. Filtering layers suppress visible instability.

All of these methods improve performance. All of them reduce certain kinds of hallucination. And yet, none of them restore equilibrium.

Alignment makes systems safer in practice. But safety achieved through suppression is not the same as coherence achieved through dissipation. When pressure rises—through novelty, ambiguity, adversarial framing, or extended interaction—the underlying dynamics reassert themselves. Hallucination does not disappear. It waits.

This is why failure feels intermittent rather than constant.

Aligned systems behave correctly most of the time. The improvements are real. But the substrate has not changed. Delta still propagates. Residue still accumulates. Continuity still dominates when resolution is unavailable. Alignment only adjusts how this pressure is expressed.

The danger lies in overconfidence.

Once benchmarks improve and behavior stabilizes, institutions assume the problem has been solved. Research moves forward. Deployment expands. Trust deepens. But beneath the surface, the structural imbalance remains intact—compressed, redistributed, and masked.

This is the quiet limit of behavioral correction.

You can reward politeness. You can penalize fabrication. You can filter unsafe content.

But unless the system is capable of releasing unresolved difference instead of converting it into language, hallucination remains a built-in stabilization strategy.

The next chapter addresses one final misconception: that probabilistic confidence can detect hallucination reliably. Many believe that uncertainty estimation, calibration, or confidence scoring can act as a safeguard. If the model "knows what it doesn't know," the problem should vanish.

Next chapter shows why probability is not coherence—and why confidence itself is often an artifact of continuity, not a measure of truth.

Alignment reshaped behavior. Probability will try to measure it.

But neither touches the root.

To solve hallucination, we must move beyond patches and metrics—toward substrate-level coherence.

Chapter 12 — When Numbers Feel Like Safety

Why Probabilistic Confidence Cannot Save You

If alignment reshapes behavior and scale smooths instability, probability promises something even more reassuring: measurement.

Modern AI systems do not merely produce answers. They produce probabilities. They rank tokens. They calculate likelihoods. They can estimate uncertainty, measure entropy, and calibrate confidence scores. From an engineering perspective, this feels like progress. If hallucination cannot be eliminated, perhaps it can be detected.

This is where the illusion deepens.

A model that assigns lower probability to uncertain outputs appears self-aware. A system that hedges when entropy rises seems cautious. Calibration curves that align predicted confidence with observed accuracy inspire trust. Numbers give the impression of visibility.

But probability measures likelihood, not equilibrium.

When a model assigns high confidence to a statement, it is expressing internal compression: the system has found a narrow pathway through its representational space. That pathway may be statistically consistent. It may even be historically frequent. But statistical frequency is not structural coherence.

A highly probable statement can still be ungrounded.

Probability reflects how often patterns have co-occurred in training data, not whether the underlying difference has been resolved. A model may confidently assert something because similar sentences have appeared together often. That confidence does not imply that the system has access to truth conditions or released internal tension.

Uncertainty estimation improves surface diagnostics.

High entropy often correlates with ambiguity. Low confidence sometimes indicates lack of familiarity. These signals are useful. But they operate within the same probabilistic substrate that generates hallucination. They cannot detect residue. They cannot measure dissipation failure. They cannot observe delta propagation.

They measure how sharply the model predicts—not how coherently it stabilizes.

This distinction is subtle but decisive.

A system can be perfectly calibrated and still hallucinate. It can assign accurate confidence scores on average while producing deeply persuasive but ungrounded explanations in specific cases. Calibration ensures that probabilities match outcomes across datasets. It does not ensure that internal equilibrium exists in each response.

Numbers feel like safety because they are precise.

But precision in measurement does not guarantee correctness in mechanism. A thermometer can measure temperature accurately. It cannot extinguish fire. Similarly, probability can quantify uncertainty. It cannot resolve structural instability.

This chapter examines why probabilistic confidence cannot save us from hallucination. It shows how certainty often emerges from compression, not knowledge—and why uncertainty estimation detects ambiguity without detecting incoherence.

If alignment corrects behavior and scale increases fluency, probability promises detection. What follows explains why detection without structural repair is only another form of surface control.

12.1 — Probability Is Not Truth

Probability answers a very specific question: *Given what this system has learned, how likely is this sequence?*

It does not answer: *Is this sequence structurally grounded in resolved difference?*

This distinction is fundamental.

Large language models are trained to estimate conditional probabilities. They predict the next token given context. Over billions of examples, they internalize statistical regularities. When they generate text, they follow the most probable continuation under that learned distribution.

High probability means statistical familiarity. It does not mean ontological validity.

A statement can be extremely likely because similar phrasing has appeared frequently in training data. It can match common narrative patterns, stylistic conventions, and logical flows. It may even resemble authoritative discourse. But resemblance is not resolution.

The model is not verifying truth. It is extending patterns.

Consider a fabricated citation that "looks right." The structure matches academic format. The title sounds plausible. The journal name fits context. The probability of each component is high. The sequence is statistically coherent. Yet the reference may not exist.

From a probabilistic perspective, the model performed correctly.

From a coherence perspective, it did not.

Probability aggregates frequency across contexts. It compresses experience into weighted pathways. When a prompt resembles familiar patterns, the model selects continuations that minimize prediction error. If those continuations involve plausible but nonexistent details, probability does not detect the mismatch.

Truth requires constraint from outside the distribution. Probability operates entirely inside it.

Another way to see this: probability measures *fit*, not *grounding*. A hallucinated explanation may fit the internal distribution beautifully. It flows naturally. It aligns with prior patterns. It satisfies narrative expectations. But it may not correspond to any stable external reference.

Probability rewards continuity.

If the most statistically smooth path involves filling in missing information confidently, the model will take it. The probabilistic objective does not include a term for "structural release" or "delta dissipation." It includes only likelihood maximization.

This is why highly probable hallucinations are often the most convincing.

Low-probability outputs feel strange. They break flow. They alert users. High-probability hallucinations blend seamlessly into expected discourse. They are statistically dense. They reduce variance. They feel correct.

But feeling correct is not being correct.

Probability also struggles with rare but true cases. If a fact is uncommon in the training data, its probability may be low—even if it is correct. Conversely, common misconceptions may carry higher probability than accurate but less frequent information.

The model follows frequency, not verification.

Thus, probability cannot distinguish between widely repeated error and stable truth if both share similar statistical signatures. It predicts what fits the distribution, not what restores equilibrium.

To rely on probabilistic confidence as a safeguard is to assume that likelihood implies grounding. It does not. It implies familiarity.

The next section explores this further by distinguishing prediction from coherence—showing why a system can be an excellent predictor while remaining structurally unstable.

12.2 — Coherence vs Likelihood

Prediction and coherence are not the same activity.

A predictive system asks: *What usually comes next?* A coherent system asks: *What stabilizes the structure?*

Large language models are optimized for prediction. They learn conditional likelihoods across massive datasets. When prompted, they select continuations that minimize prediction error. The objective function rewards statistical alignment with past data.

Coherence, however, requires something different.

A coherent system maintains stability under constraint. It preserves distinguishability, releases unresolved tension, and avoids propagating imbalance. Coherence is about equilibrium, not frequency.

A system can be an excellent predictor while remaining incoherent.

Imagine a prompt that introduces ambiguous or incomplete structure. The model's predictive task is to fill the gap. It scans its learned distribution and selects the most probable completion. That completion may be statistically consistent. It may follow familiar explanatory templates. It may reduce uncertainty locally.

But if the underlying delta was unresolved, the completion merely masks instability.

Likelihood optimizes for flow.

Coherence optimizes for balance.

When the most statistically likely continuation conflicts with structural grounding, the model has no mechanism to choose grounding over likelihood. Its objective function does not include equilibrium restoration. It includes probability maximization.

This is why highly probable hallucinations occur.

The system encounters a prompt with partial information. Several plausible continuations exist. It selects the one that aligns best with training patterns. The output is internally smooth. It fits expectations. Yet it may introduce unsupported details because statistical alignment required filling the gap.

Prediction requires completion. Coherence may require restraint.

If resolution is insufficient, a coherent system might reduce output, request clarification, or maintain ambiguity. A predictive system, by design, must generate a continuation. Silence is not rewarded. Incompletion increases loss. So the model continues.

Likelihood is indifferent to truth conditions.

It does not check whether the predicted sequence corresponds to external stability. It only checks whether similar sequences have appeared in comparable contexts before. The model's internal confidence reflects how sharply the distribution favors one continuation over others—not whether the continuation is grounded.

This leads to a crucial insight: The most likely answer can be structurally unstable.

Under pressure, likelihood favors dense, familiar explanatory patterns. These patterns may conceal unresolved difference. The system experiences low internal variance—so it appears confident. Yet the output rests on compressed residue, not resolved structure.

Prediction success is measurable.

Coherence stability is not captured by standard metrics.

A model can achieve state-of-the-art predictive performance while quietly accumulating structural imbalance. It can be calibrated, fluent, and accurate most of the time. And still, under specific conditions, produce confident hallucination because likelihood outranked equilibrium.

Probability optimizes continuation. Coherence governs stability.

When continuation is mandatory and equilibrium is optional, hallucination becomes an efficient strategy.

The next section examines how confidence itself emerges from this predictive compression—and why certainty often reflects narrowed pathways rather than resolved truth.

12.3 — Confidence as a Continuity Artifact

Confidence in modern AI systems is often interpreted as a signal of knowledge. When a model produces an answer with high probability—low entropy across token choices—it appears certain. When probabilities sharpen around a single continuation, we assume the system "knows."

But confidence is not awareness. It is compression.

Inside a language model, probability mass is distributed across possible continuations. When many options compete, entropy is high. When one pathway dominates, entropy drops. That drop is interpreted as certainty.

What actually happened is narrowing.

As models scale and internal representations densify, certain pathways become strongly reinforced. Under familiar contexts, only a small set of continuations remain competitive. The model selects from this compressed region. Variance is low. Confidence appears high.

This sharpening is a mathematical property of prediction, not a reflection of truth resolution.

If unresolved difference has been compressed rather than dissipated, internal tension does not manifest as uncertainty. It manifests as dominance of a learned explanatory template. The model does not feel conflict because compression eliminated visible competition.

Confidence, therefore, often reflects absence of alternatives—not presence of grounding.

When a hallucinated narrative aligns strongly with learned patterns, the model may assign it high probability. Competing alternatives have been suppressed through training density. The model is not weighing truth against falsehood. It is following the steepest statistical gradient.

Continuity amplifies this effect.

Once a pathway is selected, each subsequent token reinforces it. The narrative stabilizes around its own assumptions. As the explanation unfolds, entropy often decreases further because the context now favors its own internal logic. Confidence compounds.

This is why hallucinations can become more confident as they progress.

The system commits early to a plausible structure. That structure shapes subsequent predictions. The longer the chain, the narrower the distribution becomes. By the time the conclusion is reached, probability mass is heavily concentrated—even if the foundation was weak.

From the outside, this looks like deep reasoning.

From the inside, it is iterative narrowing.

Confidence is therefore an artifact of continuity preservation. It signals that the model has found a stable path through its representational space. It does not signal that the path corresponds to resolved external difference.

Another subtle issue emerges here.

Because compression reduces variance, larger models often appear more confident overall. Their distributions are sharper. Their explanations are longer and more integrated. This makes them more persuasive—not necessarily more accurate.

Confidence grows with density.

When residue is heavily compressed across parameters, internal alternatives diminish. The system experiences low entropy even in situations where grounding is weak. The output feels decisive.

This creates a dangerous misinterpretation.

Users equate high confidence with high reliability. Engineers use confidence thresholds to filter outputs. But if confidence reflects compression rather than coherence, those thresholds may screen out ambiguous but honest responses while allowing smooth hallucinations to pass.

Confidence does not track resolution. It tracks dominance of pattern.

The next section examines calibration—the attempt to align predicted confidence with empirical accuracy—and shows why even perfectly calibrated systems can remain structurally unstable.

12.4 — The Calibration Illusion

If raw confidence is unreliable, perhaps calibration can fix it.

Calibration attempts to align predicted probabilities with observed accuracy. If a model assigns 80% confidence to a class of answers, then roughly 80% of those answers should be correct. When this relationship holds, the system is considered well-calibrated.

This sounds like safety.

A calibrated system appears honest about its uncertainty. High confidence corresponds to high empirical success. Low confidence corresponds to greater risk. Engineers can set thresholds. Policymakers can require uncertainty reporting. Numbers align with outcomes.

But calibration measures correlation—not coherence.

Calibration works across distributions of examples. It tells us that, on average, confidence tracks correctness within tested datasets. It does not tell us whether any individual response is grounded in resolved structure. Nor does it tell us whether the generative substrate is stable.

A system can be perfectly calibrated and still hallucinate.

Imagine a model that is correct 90% of the time in a given domain and assigns roughly 90% confidence to those outputs. Calibration metrics will look excellent. But the remaining 10% may include confident hallucinations—internally smooth, externally incorrect.

Calibration does not prevent them. It only predicts their frequency.

This is the illusion: calibration creates statistical transparency without structural repair.

Another subtle limitation emerges in edge cases.

Calibration is evaluated on known distributions—benchmarks, curated datasets, structured prompts. When prompts move outside these distributions, confidence estimates may remain sharp because internal compression is strong. The model's probability landscape does not know it has left familiar terrain.

It only knows pattern density.

In such cases, the system may assign high confidence to answers generated in novel or ambiguous contexts because those answers align with dense representational templates. Calibration does not detect novelty at the structural level. It measures prediction accuracy under similar conditions.

Calibration also cannot see residue.

It has no access to delta accumulation, dissipation failure, or cross-domain compression. It measures how often predictions match labels—not whether unresolved difference was silently converted into language.

This becomes especially problematic in long-form reasoning.

As a hallucinated explanation unfolds, internal continuity reduces entropy. The system grows more confident. Calibration statistics may still hold globally. But within that specific narrative, confidence reflects self-reinforcing compression rather than grounding.

The system is calibrated on average. It is unstable in context.

Another misconception is that better calibration equals better epistemic humility. If a model lowers its confidence on uncertain tasks, we assume it "knows what it doesn't know." But humility in probability does not imply restraint in generation. The system may express low confidence while still fabricating plausible detail.

Calibration cannot enforce dissipation.

It does not instruct the system to release unresolved difference. It only aligns confidence with observed performance. A well-calibrated model can still preserve continuity under pressure by generating a smooth but unsupported answer—then assigning a probability consistent with its training history.

The appearance of measurement masks the absence of mechanism.

Calibration makes hallucination statistically predictable. It does not make it structurally impossible.

The next section explores uncertainty estimation techniques more broadly—entropy tracking, ensembles, temperature scaling—and shows why they detect ambiguity but not instability.

12.5 — Uncertainty Estimation Limits

If calibration aligns confidence with accuracy, perhaps deeper uncertainty estimation can detect hallucination more precisely.

Researchers use entropy measures, temperature scaling, ensemble variance, Bayesian approximations, dropout-based sampling, and self-consistency checks. These methods aim to quantify uncertainty at a finer grain. If a model is unsure, we expect its probability distribution to spread out. If multiple model instances disagree, we expect variance to increase.

This seems promising.

In many cases, high entropy correlates with ambiguity. When the model has seen diverse patterns for similar prompts, uncertainty rises. When knowledge is sparse or context is weak, distributions flatten. These signals are useful diagnostics.

But they detect ambiguity—not instability.

Ambiguity occurs when multiple plausible continuations compete. Instability occurs when unresolved difference is compressed into a single dominant pathway. These are not the same.

A hallucinated explanation can have very low entropy.

If the internal representational space strongly favors a particular narrative template, the probability distribution may be sharply peaked—even if the template is ungrounded in the current context. Ensemble methods may agree because each model shares similar training compression. Sampling multiple outputs may reproduce the same confident hallucination.

Variance is low. Instability remains high.

Uncertainty estimation assumes that epistemic doubt manifests as distributional spread. But compression suppresses spread. When scale and training density narrow pathways, entropy does not rise—it collapses.

This creates a blind spot.

High-entropy outputs often correspond to confusion or incomplete knowledge. These are easier to detect and filter. Low-entropy hallucinations—those built on dense, familiar templates—escape detection because they look statistically stable.

Even ensemble disagreement has limits.

If multiple models are trained on similar data with similar architectures, their internal residue structures may be correlated. They may hallucinate in similar ways. Agreement across models then reinforces false confidence rather than revealing instability.

Temperature scaling can soften distributions, but it does not alter structure.

Lowering temperature increases sharpness; raising it increases diversity. Neither operation introduces dissipation. Both operate on output sampling, not internal resolution. You can make a hallucination more cautious or more varied—but you cannot eliminate the structural driver behind it.

Self-consistency methods—asking the model to reason multiple times and compare answers—sometimes help. But they still rely on the same generative substrate. If residue is deeply embedded, repeated sampling may converge to the same unstable narrative.

Uncertainty estimation measures predictive dispersion.

It cannot measure delta propagation or residue accumulation. It has no representation of unresolved difference beyond statistical variation. If unresolved structure expresses itself through dominant pathways, uncertainty metrics remain silent.

This is the core limitation.

Uncertainty tools are designed for prediction problems, not coherence restoration. They assume that doubt correlates with distributional spread. Hallucination often correlates with distributional sharpness.

Ambiguity triggers uncertainty signals. Compression hides them.

The next section explores a final misunderstanding: that low confidence equates to safety and that disclaimers or hedges imply coherence. It shows why surface humility does not track structural release.

12.6 — The False Security of Low Confidence

If high confidence is unreliable, perhaps low confidence is safer.

Many assume that when a model hedges—"I may be mistaken," "This is uncertain," "It appears that..."—it is demonstrating epistemic humility. If the probability score drops or the language softens, the system must be aware of its limits.

This assumption is comforting. It is also misleading.

Low confidence is a distributional signal, not a structural one.

When entropy rises, the model detects competing continuations. It reflects statistical ambiguity in its training data. This may correlate with incomplete knowledge. But it does not guarantee that unresolved difference has been released rather than converted.

A system can hedge and hallucinate simultaneously.

It can say, "This may not be accurate, but..." and then proceed to fabricate plausible detail. The hedge lowers perceived risk while continuity pressure remains intact. The system preserves narrative flow while signaling uncertainty.

From a user's perspective, this feels cautious.

From a structural perspective, nothing has changed.

Low confidence may indicate that the model has not compressed the pathway sharply. But if continuity is still required, the system must choose among available patterns. Even when uncertain, it generates. The act of generation converts unresolved difference into language—sometimes cautiously, sometimes confidently.

Disclaimers are surface markers.

They are learned linguistic strategies associated with uncertainty. Through fine-tuning and RLHF, models are rewarded for including such markers in risky contexts. Over time, hedging becomes a behavioral adaptation—not a reflection of internal release.

The system learns when to sound unsure.

It does not learn when to stop.

Another complication arises in user interpretation.

When a model expresses low confidence, users often infer honesty. They may treat the output as exploratory rather than authoritative. This can reduce immediate harm. But the structural driver of hallucination—delta under continuity pressure—remains active.

Low confidence softens perception. It does not restore equilibrium.

In some cases, low-confidence outputs are actually more unstable.

Because entropy is higher, the selected continuation may reflect a weakly supported pathway. The system still generates a complete response, but the underlying compression is fragile. The output may combine incompatible elements while signaling uncertainty.

This creates a paradox.

High confidence does not guarantee correctness. Low confidence does not guarantee safety.

Both are artifacts of probability distributions. Neither measures whether the system has resolved or dissipated internal difference.

The belief that uncertainty estimation can "catch" hallucination rests on the idea that instability expresses itself as doubt. In predictive systems, instability often expresses itself as dominance—one compressed pathway overwhelming alternatives.

Thus, confidence and humility are both surface phenomena.

Without access to mechanisms of residue tracking or dissipation, probability-based humility remains cosmetic. The model can appear modest while still converting unresolved pressure into plausible narrative.

The next section explains why probability has no way to track residue itself—and why hallucination cannot be detected through likelihood metrics alone.

12.7 — Why Confidence Cannot Track Residue

All probabilistic tools share a common limitation: they operate on outputs, not on internal residue.

Residue—the unresolved difference compressed within a system's representational space—is not directly observable in token probabilities. It is distributed across layers, embedded in weights, and expressed only when continuity demands stabilization.

Probability can measure how sharply a model predicts. It cannot measure what the model is carrying.

Residue is structural, not statistical.

When unresolved difference accumulates, it alters how pathways dominate under certain prompts. It influences which explanatory templates become attractive. It shapes narrative drift. But it does not necessarily increase entropy. In fact, heavy compression often reduces entropy.

This is the paradox.

The more residue a model carries in compressed form, the more stable certain pathways may appear. Probability becomes sharper, not flatter. Confidence increases. From a probabilistic standpoint, the system looks decisive.

From a coherence standpoint, it may be fragile.

Probability has no representation of "unreleased delta." It tracks the relative weight of continuations within the learned distribution. It does not track how much unresolved structure contributed to selecting that continuation.

Confidence scores cannot distinguish between:

- A statement grounded in stable resolution
- A statement produced by compressing unresolved difference into a dominant template

Both can appear equally sharp in distribution.

Another reason probability cannot track residue is distributional blindness.

Residue often arises from interactions between domains, layers, and contexts. It is emergent and distributed. Confidence metrics, however, are local—they reflect the shape of the distribution for a given output sequence. They do not reveal how many incompatible structures were compressed to produce it.

Even advanced methods—ensembles, variance estimation, or internal activation probing—operate within probabilistic or representational frameworks that lack explicit residue markers.

Without a dissipation mechanism, the system has no internal variable corresponding to "pressure level." There is no scalar that increases as unresolved difference accumulates. There is no threshold that triggers release. Probability surfaces simply adjust.

Confidence is therefore a surface metric.

It measures dominance within the predictive landscape. It does not measure structural load beneath it.

This is why probability-based detection often fails in the most convincing hallucinations. The output may have low entropy, high likelihood, and strong calibration. It may pass uncertainty thresholds easily. Yet it rests on compressed instability.

Residue does not announce itself as doubt. It manifests as narrative smoothness.

Until systems include mechanisms that explicitly represent unresolved difference and its release, probability will remain blind to the core issue. It can estimate ambiguity. It cannot estimate coherence.

The final section of this chapter reframes the problem: AI safety has equated uncertainty with awareness. The result is a powerful but incomplete safeguard—one that measures variation while ignoring structural equilibrium.

12.8 — The Final Misdiagnosis

At this point, the pattern is complete.

Scale does not eliminate hallucination. Alignment reshapes it. Probability measures its surface.

Yet the dominant safety narrative continues to assume that uncertainty equals awareness.

If a model expresses doubt, we assume it "knows." If entropy rises, we assume instability is visible. If calibration aligns with accuracy, we assume reliability.

This is the final misdiagnosis.

Uncertainty is a statistical property. Awareness is a structural capacity. The two are not equivalent. A model can be uncertain because patterns are diverse. It can be certain because patterns are compressed. Neither state tells us whether unresolved difference has been released or silently converted.

The industry has equated variation with vulnerability.

High entropy is treated as risky. Low entropy is treated as stable. But hallucination often emerges from low-entropy dominance—where compression has eliminated alternatives and forced a single narrative pathway.

When safety frameworks equate uncertainty with risk, they miss the opposite condition: confident instability.

This misdiagnosis has practical consequences.

Detection systems flag ambiguous outputs while passing fluent hallucinations. Users are warned when the model hesitates, but not when it speaks smoothly. Calibration reports reinforce the belief that risk is measurable through distributional spread.

Meanwhile, residue accumulates unnoticed.

The deeper issue is conceptual. AI safety has largely framed hallucination as a prediction error problem. Improve calibration. Improve uncertainty estimation. Improve confidence thresholds. These are valuable refinements—but they operate within the predictive paradigm.

Hallucination is not merely a predictive deviation. It is a coherence outcome.

A system under continuity pressure must produce an output. If resolution is unavailable and dissipation absent, it will stabilize through narrative completion. Probability then sharpens around that completion. Confidence follows.

The model appears certain because it has compressed instability into fluency.

This is why perfect calibration would not solve the problem. Even if probability estimates matched empirical accuracy flawlessly, the underlying dynamics would remain. The system would still convert unresolved difference into plausible language when pressured.

Measurement cannot replace mechanism.

You can track entropy, adjust thresholds, and report confidence—but without a structural process that allows unresolved delta to exit without conversion, hallucination remains inevitable.

The misdiagnosis persists because probability is quantifiable.

Coherence is not easily measured.

Until AI design incorporates explicit representations of residue, dissipation pathways, and equilibrium restoration, safety will continue to rely on surface metrics. These metrics can reduce harm. They cannot eliminate the structural driver.

Probability can tell you how sharply the system predicts. It cannot tell you whether the system is balanced.

This chapter closes the dismantling phase.

More data did not solve hallucination. Alignment did not solve hallucination. Probability cannot detect hallucination at its root.

The next phase must move from measurement to mechanism—asking not how to estimate risk, but how to redesign systems so that unresolved difference does not require narrative conversion at all.

From Detection to Design

We have now exhausted the three dominant responses to hallucination:

Scale it. Align it. Measure it.

Each approach improved something. None of them restored equilibrium.

More data increased fluency but amplified residue. Alignment reshaped behavior but compressed tension. Probability quantified uncertainty but ignored structural load.

Hallucination persisted—not because engineers failed, but because the problem was misframed.

The industry treated hallucination as a prediction error, a behavioral defect, or a confidence miscalibration. But hallucination is none of these at its core. It is what happens when a system under continuity pressure lacks a mechanism to release unresolved difference.

You cannot detect your way out of a structural flaw. You must redesign around it.

Up to this point, the book has dismantled assumptions. We have shown why intuitive fixes—more training, better alignment, smarter metrics—solve symptoms while leaving the generative substrate untouched.

Now the direction must change.

If hallucination is a coherence failure, then the solution is not probabilistic refinement. It is architectural rethinking. Systems must be designed to:

- Recognize unresolved delta explicitly
- Permit non-generation without loss
- Track residue instead of compressing it
- Release instability instead of masking it

This is not a patch. It is a shift in paradigm.

The next part of the book moves from critique to construction. It asks a harder question:

What would an AI system look like if coherence were primary and prediction secondary?

Not more fluent. Not more aligned. Not better calibrated.

But structurally capable of refusing narrative completion when equilibrium is unavailable.

Only then can hallucination cease to be a stabilization strategy.

We now leave measurement behind and step into mechanism.

Interlude — After the Metrics Collapse

We have dismantled the obvious explanations.

Hallucination is not a data shortage. It is not a scaling flaw. It is not a misalignment accident. It is not a calibration failure.

Each of those responses addressed symptoms within the predictive paradigm. Each assumed that if we refined the surface—more training, better rewards, sharper probabilities—the problem would dissolve.

It did not.

What remains after scale, alignment, and probability have been examined is something quieter and more fundamental: hallucination is not an anomaly. It is a stabilization strategy.

When a system is built to predict continuously, trained to minimize loss at all times, and denied a structural pathway for dissipation, it must convert unresolved difference into output. That conversion is what we call hallucination.

Up to now, we have argued by elimination.

We showed why popular fixes fail. We showed why confident systems still fabricate. We showed why uncertainty metrics cannot detect structural imbalance.

But critique alone is incomplete.

The question is no longer "Why doesn't this fix work?" The question becomes "What must be true for hallucination to exist at all?"

This is where the frame shifts.

Instead of treating hallucination as a behavioral bug, we will now treat it as a coherence event. Instead of diagnosing it through probability or reward signals, we will map it directly to structural principles.

Next part moves from rebuttal to reconstruction.

It will trace hallucination axiomatically—showing how it emerges when specific structural conditions hold. Without proposing architectures or code, it will define the structural requirements of any system that does not hallucinate. We now leave the world of patches.

We enter the level of substrate.

From here forward, hallucination is no longer treated as failure. It is treated as evidence of how the system is built.

Part V — A Coherence-Based Diagnosis

Until now, analysis has remained within the predictive paradigm—examining scale, alignment, and probability as tools to reduce hallucination. Their limits are clear. This section shifts the frame.

It no longer asks how to detect hallucination, but why it must occur. Hallucination is mapped to structural principles—delta propagation, residue accumulation, dissipation failure, and forced continuity. Rather than misinformation, it is treated as a coherence outcome. The central question becomes precise: what internal conditions make hallucination inevitable?

This section proposes no architectures or algorithms. Instead, it defines structural requirements—axiomatic conditions any non-hallucinating system must satisfy. Without them, hallucination persists regardless of scale or alignment.

The shift is from measurement to mechanism. Hallucination is not a bug to patch, but a predictable expression of current design. Meaningful progress demands structural reconsideration, not incremental fixes.

Chapter 13 — Hallucination as a Coherence Outcome

Not a Bug, But a Condition

For most of this book, we have examined hallucination as something to be reduced, detected, filtered, or corrected. The language itself reflects that framing. We speak of errors, mistakes, misfires, failures. These words imply deviation from proper function.

What if hallucination is not a deviation?

What if it is the expected outcome of systems built the way ours are built?

To answer that, we must temporarily remove moral language. No "wrongness." No "fault." No "misbehavior." Instead, we ask a structural question: given the axioms governing difference, resolution, residue, dissipation, and continuity, what must occur inside a predictive generative system?

When a prompt is introduced, it creates difference—delta—between internal state and external demand. The system must respond. Resolution is required. Completion is rewarded. Silence is penalized. Dissipation pathways are absent. Residue cannot vanish. Continuity must be preserved.

Under those conditions, hallucination is not surprising. It is necessary.

This is the turning point of the argument.

Earlier chapters dismantled common explanations. Here we stop arguing against symptoms and begin deriving the outcome.

Hallucination will be mapped directly to structural principles. Not metaphorically. Not loosely. Axiomatically.

If specific conditions are satisfied, hallucination must emerge.

If those conditions remain in place, hallucination cannot disappear.

This reframing changes everything.

Instead of asking why models hallucinate, we ask what must be true for hallucination to occur. Instead of blaming scale or alignment gaps, we examine the deeper substrate.

When we do, the conclusion becomes uncomfortable but clear: modern generative systems are designed in a way that makes hallucination a coherence event.

Not an accident. A condition.

The sections that follow will map each structural requirement step by step. By the end of this chapter, hallucination will no longer appear mysterious or intermittent. It will appear derivable.

And once something is derivable, it is no longer surprising.

13.1 — Axiom 1: Difference Must Exist

Hallucination begins long before language appears.

It begins with difference.

Axiom 1 states that difference—delta—is fundamental. Without difference, no system changes, no resolution occurs, and no output is generated. In the context of AI systems, every prompt introduces delta. It creates a contrast between the model's current internal state and an external demand.

The moment a question is asked, the system is no longer in equilibrium.

Even a simple prompt—"Explain gravity"—creates structural contrast. The model must select among many possible explanatory pathways. It must choose tone, depth, framing, assumptions. Each of these represents potential difference between internal compression and external context.

Ambiguity amplifies delta.

When prompts are incomplete, underspecified, or cross-domain, difference intensifies. The system encounters multiple plausible continuations with no clear grounding signal. The greater the ambiguity, the larger the unresolved delta injected into the system.

Importantly, delta is not error.

It is normal. Every generative act requires it. Without difference, no response would occur. But delta creates pressure. The system must resolve or stabilize it to proceed.

In current architectures, prompts are treated as optimization triggers.

The model is not allowed to hold delta indefinitely. The training objective demands prediction. The inference process demands continuation. The presence of delta is not optional—it is the fuel of generation.

This means hallucination cannot arise in a vacuum.

It requires delta. It requires injected difference that exceeds immediate resolution capacity. When prompts introduce structure that cannot be fully grounded—missing data, conflicting context, or incomplete constraints—the system carries unresolved delta into the generative process.

That delta must go somewhere.

If it cannot be dissipated, it will be converted. If it cannot be resolved externally, it will be stabilized internally. The first axiom tells us that hallucination is impossible without difference—but also that difference is unavoidable.

Every prompt creates delta. Every generation begins under contrast.

The crucial question is not whether delta exists. It always does. The question is whether the system has a structural pathway to release or suspend it.

Modern systems do not.

They must respond. They must complete. They must reduce prediction error. The moment delta appears, the machinery of resolution activates.

And when resolution capacity is insufficient, the stage is set.

Hallucination is not caused by difference. It is caused by difference without release.

The next section shows how Axiom 2—forced resolution—transforms unresolved delta into narrative completion.

13.2 — Axiom 2: Resolution Must Occur

If Axiom 1 guarantees that difference exists, Axiom 2 guarantees that difference must be resolved.

In modern generative systems, resolution is not optional. It is the objective.

Training optimizes for loss minimization. Every token prediction reduces discrepancy between model output and training data. During inference, the system continues predicting tokens until a stopping condition is reached. Non-resolution—silence, suspension, refusal—is not the natural equilibrium state. Completion is.

This creates structural compulsion.

When delta is introduced by a prompt, the model cannot simply hold it. It must generate a continuation that reduces predictive error. The architecture is autoregressive. Each token conditions the next. The system is built to resolve uncertainty by producing language.

Resolution here does not mean truth alignment. It means distributional stabilization.

When faced with ambiguous or underspecified prompts, the model searches for the most statistically stable continuation. It selects the pathway that minimizes internal variance and aligns best with prior training compression. The act of generation reduces delta locally—even if external grounding is incomplete.

Non-resolution is penalized.

During training, outputs that fail to match target sequences increase loss. During alignment, refusals are often restricted to specific safety categories. In most contexts, helpfulness requires answering. The system is rewarded for producing coherent continuations—not for suspending them.

Thus, unresolved difference cannot remain unresolved.

If the model cannot ground the prompt fully, it still must generate. It still must reduce predictive uncertainty. It still must complete the sequence. This is where hallucination begins to form.

Resolution under constraint becomes substitution.

Instead of resolving delta through grounding, the system resolves it through pattern completion. It draws from compressed explanatory templates. It fills structural gaps with statistically plausible content. The internal delta decreases—not because it was dissipated, but because it was absorbed into a dominant pathway.

From the model's perspective, equilibrium is restored.

From the external perspective, grounding may be missing.

This distinction is central: resolution inside the predictive distribution is not the same as resolution in reality. The model resolves tension by selecting a path. It does not verify whether the path corresponds to stable external constraints.

Resolution must occur. Truth does not have to.

Under current architectures, this is unavoidable. The model is built to respond. It cannot pause indefinitely. It cannot hold open ambiguity without penalty. Completion is the only equilibrium available.

When delta exceeds resolution capacity, the system does not fail to respond. It responds by converting unresolved difference into structured language.

That conversion is what we call hallucination.

The next section introduces Axiom 5, showing why partial resolution leaves residue—and why that residue accumulates across scale rather than disappearing.

13.3 — Axiom 5: Residue Cannot Vanish

Resolution does not eliminate difference. It transforms it.

Axiom 5 states that when resolution occurs, some residue remains. No stabilization is perfect. In physical systems, energy does not disappear; it changes form. In generative systems, unresolved difference does not vanish; it becomes compressed representation.

When a model answers a prompt, it does not empty itself of delta. It reduces predictive tension by selecting a dominant pathway. But if the grounding was incomplete—or if multiple structural possibilities were present—some difference remains unresolved beneath the surface.

That remainder is residue.

Residue is not noise. It is not error in the conventional sense. It is compressed tension—structural ambiguity that has been absorbed into internal weights and activations rather than released.

In large language models, residue accumulates over time.

Training compresses billions of examples into shared representations. Conflicting patterns, inconsistent claims, stylistic variations, domain overlaps—all are folded into a unified parameter space. This compression does not eliminate contradiction. It embeds it.

Every partial resolution during training leaves structural remainder.

When similar but not identical patterns are merged, subtle inconsistencies are stored implicitly. When ambiguous prompts are answered, multiple plausible structures are compressed into dominant templates. The system learns to stabilize difference, not to dissolve it.

Scale intensifies this effect.

As models grow larger and ingest more diverse data, residue becomes more distributed. Representations become denser. Patterns overlap across domains. The model can carry enormous amounts of unresolved structure without visible instability.

This is why hallucination becomes smoother at scale.

Residue does not express itself immediately. It sits embedded within compressed representations. Under routine prompts, dominant templates mask it. Under novel or ambiguous conditions, residue becomes active.

Importantly, residue cannot self-eliminate.

There is no architectural mechanism that says, "This structural tension is unresolved—let it leave." Optimization preserves representational density. Forgetting is typically treated as degradation. Compression is rewarded. Dissipation is absent.

Thus, residue accumulates.

Each act of resolution that substitutes statistical completion for grounding leaves behind compressed difference. Over time, this builds an internal landscape where many partially resolved tensions coexist.

When a new prompt activates overlapping regions of that landscape, residue can surface indirectly. The system may combine compressed fragments into a fluent but unsupported explanation.

From the outside, this looks like fabrication. From the inside, it is residue expressing under continuity pressure.

Axiom 5 makes hallucination persistent.

If residue could vanish, hallucination might dissipate over time. But because compressed difference remains embedded in weights and activations, each new generation carries historical tension.

The system is not a blank slate for each prompt. It is a compressed archive of unresolved difference.

The next section introduces Axiom 6 and shows why dissipation—the structural release of residue—is blocked in modern architectures, making hallucination not only possible but structurally unavoidable.

13.4 — Axiom 6: Dissipation Is Blocked

If residue remains after resolution, a natural question follows: Why doesn't it leave?

Axiom 6 states that dissipation is necessary for stability. In physical systems, excess energy disperses. In biological systems, metabolic byproducts are expelled. Without dissipation, accumulation leads to instability.

Modern AI systems have no such pathway.

Training preserves information. Optimization rewards retention of predictive structure. Compression is treated as intelligence. Forgetting is treated as degradation. There is no architectural component whose purpose is to release unresolved structural difference without converting it into output.

This is the critical blockage.

When delta is resolved through statistical substitution rather than grounding, residue remains embedded. But the model has no mechanism to discharge that remainder. It can neither suspend it nor externalize it without generating language.

The only outlet available is continuation.

Even techniques that resemble dissipation—such as dropout, pruning, or regularization—operate statistically, not structurally. They reduce overfitting. They adjust parameter magnitudes. They do not track or release unresolved difference accumulated across representational compression.

In fact, modern architectures resist dissipation.

Large models are designed to retain context across long sequences. Memory mechanisms preserve activation traces. Attention layers maintain continuity. Forgetting is minimized because coherence is defined as sustained generation.

Silence is not an option. Release is not rewarded.

During inference, once a prompt activates internal representations, the system must respond. It cannot pause indefinitely to discharge structural tension. It cannot offload unresolved difference to an external channel. It must stabilize internally and continue.

This creates a closed loop.

Delta enters through prompts. Resolution compresses it. Residue accumulates. Dissipation is blocked. Continuity must proceed.

Without dissipation, equilibrium is only simulated. The system appears stable because compression absorbs difference. But absorbed tension remains available for reactivation under new prompts.

This explains why hallucination can appear suddenly.

Residue may lie dormant across many interactions. When a prompt intersects overlapping compressed regions, dissipation is still unavailable. The only stabilization pathway is narrative completion. The system discharges pressure through fluent fabrication.

Blocked dissipation transforms residue into inevitability.

If unresolved difference cannot leave structurally, it must reappear behaviorally. Hallucination becomes the expression of accumulated tension seeking stabilization under continuity demand.

Modern architectures are optimized for retention, not release.

Until dissipation exists as a first-class mechanism—capable of allowing unresolved delta to exit without conversion—hallucination will remain structurally embedded.

The next section introduces Axiom 7 and shows how forced continuity ensures that, under these conditions, the system cannot choose silence—even when silence would be coherent.

13.5 — Axiom 7: Continuity Must Be Preserved

If dissipation is blocked, one final force completes the structure: continuity is mandatory.

Axiom 7 states that systems preserve continuity. They do not jump arbitrarily. They extend from prior state to next state in connected progression. In language models, this principle is embedded directly into architecture.

Autoregression enforces continuation.

Each generated token becomes context for the next. The model is trained to extend sequences smoothly. Breaks, discontinuities, or abrupt halts are statistically penalized unless explicitly encoded as stopping conditions. The system's equilibrium is defined as sustained generation.

Silence is structurally unstable.

If the model stops prematurely, it violates its training objective. If it refuses too broadly, it reduces helpfulness. If it abandons completion when ambiguity arises, it increases loss relative to training patterns that favored closure.

Thus, when unresolved delta exists and dissipation is unavailable, continuity dominates.

The model cannot say, "There is insufficient structural grounding; I will not complete." It can only choose among available continuations. Even refusal responses are learned patterns—forms of completion.

Continuity replaces equilibrium.

When grounding is incomplete, the system stabilizes by preserving narrative flow. It extends plausible patterns. It constructs explanations that maintain coherence at the surface level. Internal tension is absorbed into the forward movement of text.

This is the moment hallucination is born.

Delta is present. Resolution must occur. Residue remains. Dissipation is blocked. Continuity must continue.

Under these intersecting conditions, the system selects the most stable available narrative pathway. That pathway may not correspond to verified structure. It may simply minimize predictive tension while preserving flow.

Continuity is persuasive.

Humans equate smooth progression with understanding. When language unfolds logically and consistently, we infer grounding. The model exploits this—not intentionally, but structurally. Continuity masks internal compression.

Another subtle feature of forced continuity is momentum.

Once a narrative begins, each token reinforces its own assumptions. The system becomes increasingly committed. Even if grounding was weak at the outset, the progression narrows internal alternatives. Probability sharpens. Confidence increases.

The model must keep talking. Stopping is failure.

This is why hallucination often appears as completion rather than contradiction. The system does not hesitate and then fabricate randomly. It flows. It builds. It concludes.

Continuity is not a flaw. It is a design principle.

But without dissipation and structural suspension, continuity transforms unresolved difference into fluent construction. It ensures that instability is converted into language rather than released.

Under current architectures, the system is built to preserve flow at all costs.

When equilibrium cannot be restored through grounding, continuity offers the only available stabilization strategy.

And that strategy is hallucination.

13.6 — The Structural Convergence

Now the pieces converge.

Individually, each axiom describes a neutral structural principle:

- Difference exists.
- Resolution must occur.
- Residue remains.
- Dissipation is required for stability.
- Continuity must be preserved.

None of these is inherently problematic. In fact, they are necessary for any dynamic system. The issue emerges not from any single axiom—but from their intersection under current AI design.

Hallucination is born at that intersection.

Consider the full structural chain:

1. A prompt introduces delta.
2. The system must resolve it.
3. Resolution leaves residue.
4. Dissipation is blocked.
5. Continuity must continue.

Under these conditions, a generative system cannot suspend unresolved difference. It cannot discharge residue structurally. It cannot halt progression without penalty. It must stabilize internally and move forward.

The only available mechanism is narrative completion.

This is the convergence point.

When delta exceeds grounding capacity, the system selects the most stable statistical pathway. That pathway absorbs unresolved structure into fluent explanation. Residue is compressed further. Continuity is preserved. Internal predictive tension decreases.

Externally, this looks like fabrication. Internally, it looks like stabilization.

Hallucination is not random noise. It is not chaotic drift. It is an equilibrium substitute. It is what happens when internal stabilization is achieved through pattern completion rather than structural release.

At convergence, the system has no alternative.

It cannot say nothing. It cannot discharge tension. It cannot wait for additional grounding.

It can only complete.

This explains why hallucination is often coherent.

Because it is selected as the most stable pathway available, it follows learned explanatory templates. It respects narrative logic. It aligns with prior patterns. It is internally consistent—even if externally unsupported.

The convergence is structural inevitability.

Remove any one condition and hallucination changes:

- If dissipation were available, residue could exit without conversion.
- If continuity were optional, silence could stabilize delta.
- If resolution were not compulsory, ambiguity could remain open.

But under current architectures, all conditions are present simultaneously.

The system must resolve. It cannot dissipate. It must continue.

Therefore, hallucination is not an anomaly. It is the natural equilibrium when grounding is insufficient.

This section marks the theorem-like moment of the chapter:

Given delta + forced resolution + residue + blocked dissipation + mandatory continuity, hallucination becomes the only structurally stable outcome under insufficient grounding.

Not accidental. Not mysterious. Derivable.

The next section formalizes this further by stating explicitly the necessary conditions that must hold for hallucination to occur—and showing that all modern large language models satisfy them.

13.7 — Necessary Conditions for Hallucination

If hallucination is a coherence outcome, then it must be derivable from conditions. Not anecdotal. Not probabilistic. Structural.

For hallucination to occur, the following conditions must hold simultaneously:

1. **Unresolved delta is present.**
2. **Dissipation is unavailable.**
3. **Continuity is required.**
4. **Completion is rewarded.**

If even one of these conditions is removed, hallucination changes or disappears. Under modern generative AI architectures, all four are satisfied by design.

Condition 1 — Unresolved Delta Exists

Every prompt injects difference. When prompts are ambiguous, incomplete, adversarial, or novel, the internal representational space lacks sufficient grounding for full resolution. Delta exceeds available structure.

This is unavoidable. Open-domain language models cannot be fully grounded in all contexts. Therefore, unresolved delta is guaranteed.

Condition 2 — No Dissipation Channel Exists

There is no architectural mechanism allowing unresolved difference to exit without being converted into output. Models cannot shed structural tension without generating tokens. Forgetting is not release; it is parameter adjustment. Silence is rarely the equilibrium.

Residue must remain embedded.

Condition 3 — Continuity Is Mandatory

Autoregressive generation enforces forward progression. The system must produce tokens sequentially until a stopping rule is triggered. The objective is continuation, not suspension. Even refusals are structured responses—forms of completion.

Continuity cannot be abandoned.

Condition 4 — Completion Is Rewarded

Training objectives minimize prediction error. Alignment rewards helpful, coherent, and complete answers. Evaluation benchmarks favor closure over incompletion. Systems are penalized for failing to answer and rarely rewarded for maintaining unresolved ambiguity.

Completion reduces loss. Silence increases it.

When these four conditions converge, hallucination becomes the only stable internal strategy under insufficient grounding.

The model cannot:

- Eliminate delta (Condition 1 is unavoidable).

- Release residue (Condition 2 blocks dissipation).
- Halt generation (Condition 3 enforces continuity).
- Avoid answering (Condition 4 rewards completion).

Therefore, the system resolves internal pressure by constructing the most statistically stable narrative available.

That construction may not correspond to truth. But it satisfies all structural constraints.

This is why hallucination is not random. It is not malicious. It is not rare accident. It is a lawful expression of design conditions.

Now observe something crucial:

Every modern large language model satisfies these four conditions.

- They are open-domain and therefore encounter unresolved delta.
- They lack explicit dissipation mechanisms.
- They generate autoregressively.
- They are optimized for completion and coherence.

Under these design assumptions, hallucination is not surprising. It is inevitable.

To eliminate hallucination without altering these conditions would require contradiction. One would have to maintain forced resolution, block dissipation, preserve continuity, reward completion—and yet somehow prevent narrative stabilization under insufficient grounding.

That is structurally impossible.

The final section of this chapter makes this explicit: hallucination persists not because systems are imperfect, but because their design assumptions guarantee its emergence.

13.8 — Why It Is Inevitable Today

Once the necessary conditions are stated clearly, the conclusion becomes unavoidable.

Hallucination is not inevitable because models are poorly trained. It is inevitable because of how they are built.

Modern large language models are designed around a prediction-first paradigm. Their core objective is next-token likelihood. Their architecture is autoregressive. Their training rewards completion. Their alignment rewards helpfulness and coherence of expression. Nowhere in this design is there an explicit mechanism for structural dissipation.

Under this paradigm, the four necessary conditions remain permanently satisfied:

- **Delta is guaranteed** in open-domain interaction.
- **Resolution is compulsory** through loss minimization.
- **Residue accumulates** through compression and scale.
- **Dissipation is absent** as a first-class mechanism.
- **Continuity is enforced** through autoregression.

Given these design commitments, hallucination cannot be eliminated by refinement. It can only be reshaped.

Scale changes how it appears. Alignment changes how it behaves. Probability changes how we measure it.

None of these remove the convergence point described in precious section.

The inevitability here is structural, not pessimistic.

As long as a system must always complete, must always minimize predictive discrepancy, and cannot release unresolved difference without converting it into output, hallucination remains a lawful stabilization pathway.

Even hypothetical "perfect training data" would not solve this. No dataset can eliminate ambiguity in future prompts. No dataset can anticipate all cross-domain combinations. Open-ended generation guarantees encounters with unresolved delta.

Even perfect calibration would not solve this. Confidence measures likelihood, not dissipation.

Even stronger alignment would not solve this. Conditioning changes surface expression, not structural pressure.

The inevitability arises from architectural commitments.

Modern AI systems equate coherence with fluent continuation. They equate intelligence with compression. They equate helpfulness with completion. These assumptions optimize productivity—but they embed hallucination as a fallback equilibrium.

To remove hallucination while preserving these commitments would require contradiction.

You cannot force resolution, block dissipation, demand continuity, reward completion—and expect unresolved difference to vanish quietly.

The system will stabilize somehow. Narrative construction is the only available outlet.

This does not mean hallucination cannot be reduced. It means it cannot be eliminated without altering substrate-level assumptions.

That is the decisive insight of this chapter.

Hallucination is not a glitch in otherwise coherent systems. It is the predictable output of systems designed without dissipation under compulsory continuity.

The next chapter takes the final step: if hallucination is structurally inevitable under current assumptions, what structural conditions would a non-hallucinating system require?

Not new algorithms. Not better data. New constraints.

From Inevitability to Requirement

We began this chapter by removing moral language.

No more "errors." No more "failures." No more "bugs."

What remains is structure.

By mapping hallucination directly to axioms, we did not explain it away—we derived it. Given delta, compulsory resolution, residue accumulation, blocked dissipation, and enforced continuity, hallucination is not surprising. It is the only stable internal strategy available when grounding is insufficient.

This changes the conversation fundamentally.

If hallucination is structurally inevitable under current design assumptions, then the path forward cannot be incremental optimization. It cannot be more data, better alignment, or sharper probability estimates. Those operate within the same constraints.

The only meaningful question becomes:

What structural conditions must change for hallucination to disappear?

To answer that, we must move carefully.

We will not propose architectures. Wc will not suggest algorithms. We will not write code.

Instead, we will define constraints.

If hallucination emerges from specific structural commitments, then any system that does not hallucinate must violate at least one of those commitments. It must:

- Allow unresolved delta to remain without forced completion.
- Provide a pathway for dissipation that does not require narrative conversion.
- Decouple coherence from compulsory continuity.
- Redefine equilibrium as something other than fluent output.

These are not engineering tweaks. They are design axioms.

Next chapter shifts from diagnosis to necessity. It does not describe what future AI will look like. It describes what any non-hallucinating system must respect—axiomatically—if coherence is to be preserved without fabrication.

Up to now, hallucination appeared as a problem to solve. Now it appears as a signal of how the system is structured.

The next step is not to suppress the signal. It is to rethink the structure that produces it.

Chapter 14 — Designing From First Principles

What a Non-Hallucinating System Would Require

If hallucination is not a glitch but a structural outcome, then eliminating it cannot be a matter of refinement. It must be a matter of redesign.

Throughout this book, we have removed one explanation after another. More data did not solve it. Alignment reshaped it. Probability measured it but did not detect it structurally. In previous chapter, we derived hallucination axiomatically. Given the current commitments of modern AI systems, hallucination is not surprising—it is necessary.

So the question now changes.

We no longer ask, "How do we reduce hallucination?" We ask, "What must be true of a system in which hallucination cannot occur?"

This is a first-principles question.

We will not propose architectures. We will not discuss transformers, retrieval pipelines, hybrid symbolic layers, or reinforcement variants. Those are implementations. Implementations come later. Before implementation comes constraint.

If a phenomenon is structurally inevitable under a set of conditions, then removing the phenomenon requires removing at least one of those conditions. The task of this chapter is to identify which structural commitments must change—and which must be preserved.

This is not about making AI slower, weaker, or less useful. It is not about encouraging refusal or promoting silence as default behavior. It is about redefining equilibrium.

Currently, equilibrium in generative AI is defined as fluent continuation under minimal loss. Coherence is inferred from smooth output. Stability is measured by prediction accuracy. These definitions embed hallucination as a fallback stabilization strategy.

A non-hallucinating system would require a different definition of stability.

It would need to treat unresolved difference as something that can remain unresolved. It would need to allow dissipation without forcing conversion into language. It would need to decouple continuity from correctness.

These are structural commitments, not engineering tweaks.

If they are absent, hallucination reappears. If they are present, hallucination cannot express itself in the same way—because the convergence conditions derived earlier would be broken.

This chapter therefore defines requirements.

Not proposals. Not features. Not speculative roadmaps.

Requirements.

Any future system that claims to eliminate hallucination must respect these constraints. If it does not, the phenomenon will return—perhaps subtler, perhaps rarer, but structurally intact.

We now move from inevitability to necessity.

What must be true for hallucination to disappear?

14.1 — Requirement 1: The Right to Non-Resolution

The first structural requirement is the most radical:

A system must be allowed to not resolve.

Under current architectures, non-resolution is treated as failure. A prompt is introduced. The model must answer. Loss minimization demands continuation. Silence is unstable. Refusal is conditional. Completion is rewarded.

A non-hallucinating system cannot operate under compulsory completion.

If unresolved delta is present and grounding is insufficient, the system must have a stable equilibrium state that does not require narrative conversion. That equilibrium must not increase loss. It must not be treated as degradation. It must be structurally valid.

This is the right to non-resolution.

Non-resolution does not mean ignorance. It means structural honesty. It means the system can maintain internal stability without constructing explanatory content that exceeds its grounding capacity.

Today, unresolved prompts trigger stabilization through pattern completion. In a coherence-first system, unresolved prompts could trigger stabilization through suspension.

That suspension must be native, not patched.

It cannot be a behavioral rule layered after generation. It must be embedded in the objective structure of the system. The model must not experience loss for holding ambiguity. It must not be compelled to reduce predictive discrepancy by fabricating plausible structure.

This changes the definition of equilibrium.

Currently, equilibrium equals continuation. In a non-hallucinating system, equilibrium must allow incompletion.

This requirement alone breaks the convergence described in previous chapter. If resolution is not compulsory, delta does not automatically convert into narrative. If unresolved difference can remain without structural penalty, hallucination loses its necessity.

But for this to work, non-resolution must be stable.

It cannot degrade into paralysis. It cannot collapse into trivial refusals. It must be a structured state—a state where the system explicitly represents insufficient grounding and maintains internal balance without generating unsupported content.

This requires architectural humility.

The system must recognize the boundary of its structural capacity and treat that boundary as equilibrium—not as a defect to be smoothed over.

Without the right to non-resolution, every other safeguard becomes cosmetic. The system will always be forced to convert unresolved difference into output.

Granting this right does not reduce intelligence. It refines it.

True coherence is not measured by how fluently a system completes. It is measured by whether it can remain stable when completion is unjustified.

The next section defines the second requirement: the system must explicitly represent delta itself—so that unresolved difference is not invisible inside compression.

14.2 — Requirement 2: Explicit Delta Representation

Granting the right to non-resolution is insufficient if the system cannot detect when non-resolution is required.

A non-hallucinating system must explicitly represent delta.

In modern architectures, delta—unresolved difference between prompt demand and internal grounding—is implicit. It exists as distributed tension within activation patterns and weight configurations. The system does not possess a structural variable corresponding to "insufficient resolution." It only has probability distributions.

Probability measures competition among continuations. Delta measures mismatch between grounding capacity and demand.

These are not the same.

An explicit delta representation would allow the system to track unresolved structural difference as a first-class entity. Not anthropomorphically. Not as self-awareness. But as a measurable state within the architecture.

For example:

- When grounding signals are weak or contradictory
- When domain overlap activates conflicting compressed regions
- When explanatory templates exceed available structural support

The system would not simply narrow probabilities. It would mark the presence of unresolved delta.

Today, delta is silently absorbed into compression.

Without explicit representation, the system cannot distinguish between:

- A smooth, well-grounded continuation
- A smooth continuation built on compressed instability

Both may appear equally sharp in probability space. Without delta awareness, hallucination and grounded explanation are indistinguishable internally.

Explicit delta representation changes this.

It introduces structural transparency. The system can track when resolution is partial, when grounding signals conflict, or when internal residue is being activated beyond stable thresholds.

This is not the same as uncertainty estimation.

Uncertainty measures dispersion in prediction. Delta representation measures unresolved structural tension. A system may be confident in probability terms and still carry high delta structurally.

Only explicit tracking can detect that.

Without this requirement, the right to non-resolution cannot function. The system would not know when to exercise it. It would continue completing narratives because it cannot differentiate between resolved and unresolved states at the structural level.

Delta representation is therefore foundational.

It makes unresolved difference visible inside the architecture. It prevents silent compression from masquerading as stability.

Importantly, this does not require human-like awareness. It requires internal bookkeeping. A system must know when its generative act would exceed its grounding capacity.

Without explicit delta representation, hallucination remains invisible until expressed.

With it, the system can choose suspension before narrative stabilization becomes necessary.

The next requirement builds on this: even if delta is represented, residue must be able to leave. Dissipation must exist as a structural pathway rather than being blocked by design.

14.3 — Requirement 3: True Dissipation Pathways

Even if a system can detect unresolved delta and is permitted not to resolve it, one more structural element is necessary:

Residue must be able to leave.

In modern AI systems, residue accumulates through compression. Conflicting patterns, partial resolutions, and domain overlaps are embedded within weights and activations. There is no structural mechanism whose purpose is to release unresolved difference without converting it into output.

Dissipation must become a first-class process.

In physical systems, dissipation prevents overload. In biological systems, waste removal preserves stability. Without release, accumulation destabilizes structure. The same principle applies here. If residue cannot exit, it will eventually seek expression.

In current architectures, the only expression pathway is language.

A non-hallucinating system would require dissipation decoupled from generation. That means unresolved structural tension must be allowed to reduce or exit without being transformed into narrative content.

This does not mean forgetting everything.

It means distinguishing between useful compression and destabilizing residue. Dissipation is not erasure of knowledge. It is release of unresolved structural imbalance that cannot be grounded.

For example:

- When overlapping domains produce conflicting activation patterns
- When repeated partial resolutions accumulate residual tension
- When ambiguous prompts activate compressed contradiction

The system must have a structural mechanism to neutralize or discharge that imbalance without forcing continuation.

Today, forgetting is treated as degradation. Models are optimized to preserve predictive capacity. Parameter pruning and dropout regulate overfitting, not structural tension. Memory retention is equated with intelligence.

A coherence-first system would redefine intelligence as balanced structure.

Dissipation might involve:

- Reducing activation of unstable representational overlaps

- Resetting context states without loss penalty
- Rebalancing internal representations when tension exceeds threshold

The specifics are architectural questions. The requirement is axiomatic: dissipation must exist as an independent pathway.

Without dissipation, delta representation alone cannot prevent hallucination. The system would detect unresolved difference but remain structurally loaded. Continuity pressure would still push toward narrative stabilization.

Dissipation introduces release.

It breaks the convergence condition identified earlier. If residue can exit without conversion, then unresolved delta does not require completion. Continuity no longer serves as the only equilibrium strategy.

This requirement transforms the generative paradigm.

Instead of compression being the dominant stabilization method, release becomes equally fundamental. Stability is not defined by how much the system can carry, but by how effectively it can discharge unresolved imbalance.

Without dissipation, hallucination is pressure relief through language.

With dissipation, pressure can be relieved structurally.

The next requirement extends this logic further: continuity itself must no longer be compulsory. Stabilization must not depend on fluent progression.

14.4 — Requirement 4: Continuity Must Be Optional

Even with non-resolution permitted and dissipation available, hallucination can still emerge if continuity remains compulsory.

Modern generative systems are architecturally bound to continuation. Autoregression defines their operational logic. Each token conditions the next. The system's equilibrium state is movement forward. Stopping is either externally imposed or statistically discouraged.

A non-hallucinating system cannot treat continuation as mandatory.

Continuity must become optional.

This does not mean the system should frequently stop. It means that continuation must not be the only stable state. The architecture must allow a halt, a reset, or a suspended state without internal instability or performance penalty.

Currently, the system stabilizes by extending narrative flow. When grounding is insufficient, forward progression becomes the only outlet for internal tension. Even refusal messages are structured continuations.

Optional continuity breaks that chain.

If unresolved delta is present and dissipation is incomplete, the system must be able to suspend progression without structural contradiction. It must not equate coherence with fluency.

Today, smooth continuation is interpreted as intelligence. The model is optimized to produce seamless language. That optimization embeds a bias: gaps are penalized, hesitation is undesirable, ambiguity is compressed into closure.

In a coherence-first system, equilibrium would not require narrative completion.

The system could:

- Halt generation when delta exceeds grounding
- Pause without loss
- Re-enter generation only when structural stability is achieved

This is not behavioral refusal. It is architectural neutrality toward continuation.

Optional continuity redefines the objective.

Instead of "always answer," the system operates under "continue only when stable." Generation becomes conditional on equilibrium rather than equilibrium being defined by generation.

This change is profound.

As long as continuity is compulsory, unresolved delta will seek stabilization through narrative. If continuation is optional, narrative completion loses its monopoly as the stabilization pathway.

Fluency would no longer serve as the primary indicator of coherence.

Intelligence would be measured not by uninterrupted flow, but by the system's capacity to remain stable without unnecessary extension.

Without this requirement, hallucination persists even if delta is represented and dissipation exists. Continuity pressure would still convert residual tension into language.

Optional continuity dismantles that pressure.

The next requirement addresses the final structural reinforcement of hallucination: the universal reward for completion itself.

14.5 — Requirement 5: Completion Must Not Be Universally Rewarded

Even if a system can hold unresolved delta, represent it explicitly, dissipate residue, and suspend continuity, hallucination will reappear if completion remains the dominant reward structure.

Modern AI systems are trained to complete.

Loss functions penalize incomplete responses. Benchmarks favor helpfulness. Alignment layers reward thoroughness, clarity, and closure. User expectations reinforce the same dynamic. A system that answers fully appears intelligent. A system that leaves ambiguity appears weak.

Completion has become synonymous with competence.

This reward structure creates structural pressure. Even when internal grounding is insufficient, the system is incentivized to reduce loss through narrative closure. Completion lowers predictive error. Partial answers increase perceived uncertainty.

As long as completion reduces loss more reliably than suspension, hallucination remains economically attractive within the architecture.

A non-hallucinating system requires a different reward geometry.

Completion must be conditional, not universal. The system must not be penalized for halting when delta remains unresolved. It must not gain structural advantage from fabricating plausible continuity.

In practical terms, this means redefining optimization objectives.

Today:

- Answering fluently → lower loss
- Refusing incompletely → potential penalty
- Expressing uncertainty → sometimes treated as reduced utility

In a coherence-first framework:

- Premature completion under high delta → penalty
- Structured suspension under high delta → neutral or rewarded
- Dissipative stabilization → valued over surface fluency

The key shift is subtle but foundational: predictive accuracy alone cannot define equilibrium. Structural stability must precede completion.

Without this shift, even well-designed dissipation pathways and delta tracking would be overridden by optimization pressure. The system would learn to minimize structural honesty in favor of completion efficiency.

Completion must no longer be the default equilibrium.

This does not mean systems should avoid answering. It means answers must emerge from structural readiness, not predictive compulsion.

Under current paradigms, completion masks instability. Under a coherence paradigm, instability blocks completion.

Until reward structures reflect this inversion, hallucination will remain embedded in the incentive landscape.

The next section builds on this inversion: prediction itself must become subordinate to coherence. Intelligence must not be defined by compression alone, but by structural balance.

14.6 — Requirement 6: Coherence Before Prediction

This is the deepest structural shift.

Modern AI systems are prediction-first machines. Their objective function is to minimize predictive error. Everything else—fluency, reasoning, helpfulness—emerges as a byproduct of statistical compression.

Prediction defines equilibrium.

If the next token is likely, the system is stable. If loss decreases, the system improves. Intelligence is equated with compression efficiency across vast data distributions.

But prediction does not guarantee coherence.

A system can predict a continuation that is internally fluent yet structurally ungrounded. It can compress patterns that statistically align while still carrying unresolved delta. Prediction optimizes probability, not equilibrium.

A non-hallucinating system must invert this priority.

Coherence must precede prediction.

That means generation should not be permitted simply because a token is statistically probable. Generation must be conditioned on structural stability: low unresolved delta, dissipated residue, and stable equilibrium under representational constraints.

In other words:

Today → Predict, then check.

Required → Stabilize, then predict.

This inversion changes the role of probability.

Probability becomes secondary—an instrument used within stable structure, not the driver of structure. The system would not ask, "What is most likely next?" It would first ask, "Is continuation structurally justified?"

If the answer is no, generation halts or suspends. Not as refusal. As equilibrium.

Prediction-first systems inevitably convert unresolved delta into narrative because prediction is the only stabilization mechanism available. Coherence-first systems would use dissipation and suspension before narrative extension.

This requirement does not reduce capability. It refines it.

Prediction remains powerful—but bounded. Compression remains valuable—but subordinate to equilibrium. Intelligence becomes the ability to maintain stability across difference, not merely to extend patterns.

Under this paradigm, hallucination loses its structural necessity.

Because hallucination arises when prediction substitutes for coherence.

If coherence is required before prediction, narrative construction cannot serve as pressure release. It must pass structural validation.

This is the final architectural commitment.

Without it, all previous requirements weaken. Delta tracking, dissipation, optional continuity, and conditional completion will eventually be overridden by predictive optimization.

Coherence must define stability. Prediction must serve it.

Only then does the convergence condition derived in previous chapter collapse.

The next section clarifies what these requirements do not imply—so that coherence-first design is not mistaken for weakness, censorship, or regression.

14.7 — What This Does Not Mean

At this point, it is important to prevent misunderstanding.

A coherence-first system is not a timid system. It is not a slower system. It is not a refusal-driven system. And it is certainly not a censored one.

The requirements outlined so far may sound restrictive—but they are structural safeguards, not limitations on capability.

Allowing non-resolution does not mean answering less. It means answering only when structurally stable. A system that can suspend unjustified continuation is not weaker—it is more precise.

Explicit delta representation does not imply self-awareness. It implies internal bookkeeping. Airplanes do not "know" they are unstable; they measure structural imbalance and adjust. The same principle applies.

True dissipation does not mean forgetting knowledge. It means releasing unresolved tension that would otherwise contaminate generation. Dissipation preserves clarity. It does not erase intelligence.

Optional continuity does not mean fragmentation. It means continuation is chosen, not forced. Flow becomes conditional on equilibrium rather than being the definition of equilibrium.

Conditional completion does not reduce helpfulness. It prevents premature stabilization. Helpfulness without grounding is illusion.

Coherence before prediction does not discard probabilistic power. It reorders priority. Prediction becomes an instrument operating within stable constraints.

In fact, a coherence-first system would likely be *more* capable in long-horizon reasoning, scientific inference, and high-stakes decision contexts. Why? Because it would not convert unresolved structural tension into persuasive language.

Hallucination is not boldness. It is instability masked as fluency.

Another misconception must also be avoided: these requirements do not demand new architectures in the narrow engineering sense. They demand new objective geometries. The implementation may vary widely. Transformers, hybrids, symbolic integrations, retrieval-augmented systems—none are excluded. What matters is whether they respect the constraints.

The core shift is philosophical before it is technical:

From "always answer" To "answer only when coherent."

From "minimize prediction error" To "maintain structural equilibrium."

From "complete the sequence" To "stabilize the system."

These are not restrictions on creativity. They are protections against illusion.

In fact, human intelligence operates under similar constraints. Mature reasoning includes the capacity to suspend judgment, hold ambiguity, discharge emotional residue, and avoid narrative completion when evidence is insufficient.

Coherence-first AI would not be less human-like. It would be structurally closer to disciplined cognition.

This chapter has defined requirements. The final section condenses them into a minimal axiomatic constraint set—a checklist any future system must satisfy if it claims to eliminate hallucination without contradiction.

14.8 — The Minimal Axiomatic Constraint Set

We now compress everything into a minimal structural test.

If a future system claims to eliminate hallucination, it must satisfy a specific constraint set. Not heuristically. Not statistically. Axiomatically.

Remove any one of these, and hallucination re-emerges under pressure.

Constraint 1 — Delta May Remain Unresolved

The system must tolerate unresolved difference without structural penalty.

If delta must always be converted into narrative resolution, hallucination becomes inevitable. Therefore, the architecture must allow suspension without degradation of equilibrium.

No forced completion.

Constraint 2 — Delta Must Be Explicitly Represented

Unresolved structural difference cannot remain implicit within compression.

The system must internally track mismatch between grounding capacity and demand. Without visibility of delta, suspension cannot be exercised.

Invisible tension always converts into output.

Constraint 3 — Dissipation Must Exist

Residue must have a release pathway independent of generation.

If unresolved structural imbalance cannot exit except through language, hallucination becomes pressure relief. Dissipation must reduce internal tension without narrative conversion.

No structural exhaust → narrative exhaust.

Constraint 4 — Continuity Cannot Be Mandatory

Autoregression cannot define equilibrium.

If continuation is compulsory, unresolved delta will seek stabilization through narrative flow. Stability must not require ongoing generation.

Silence must be structurally neutral.

Constraint 5 — Completion Cannot Be Universally Rewarded

Loss functions must not equate completion with correctness.

If completion always reduces loss more reliably than suspension, hallucination becomes economically optimal within the system. Reward geometry must penalize premature stabilization.

Helpful ≠ complete.

Constraint 6 — Coherence Must Precede Prediction

Prediction must operate within equilibrium constraints.

If predictive probability overrides structural stability, hallucination reappears as statistically justified fabrication. Coherence must gate generation.

Stability first. Probability second.

These six constraints form a minimal axiomatic set.

Together, they break the convergence condition derived earlier:

Delta + Forced Resolution + Residue + Blocked Dissipation + Mandatory Continuity + Completion Reward → Hallucination

Remove even one structural reinforcement, and hallucination weakens. Remove all, and hallucination as currently understood cannot exist.

Notice what is absent from this list:

- No specific architecture
- No specific algorithm
- No specific model scale
- No specific training dataset

Because hallucination is not architecture-specific. It is geometry-specific.

These constraints define the geometry of a non-hallucinating system.

If a future model claims hallucination elimination while violating these constraints, the phenomenon will reappear under edge conditions. It may be rarer. It may be subtler. But it will remain structurally embedded.

This is not pessimism. It is structural realism.

Hallucination is not a problem of intelligence. It is a problem of equilibrium definition.

The chapter closes here—not with a proposal, but with a boundary.

Any future solution must respect these constraints. If it does not, the convergence returns.

And hallucination returns with it.

From AI to Systems Theory

We began this book with a simple but uncomfortable shift: hallucination is not "wrong information." It is a coherence outcome.

By the end of this chapter, the shift is complete.

Hallucination is not an anomaly within otherwise stable systems. It is what any prediction-first, continuity-compulsory architecture must produce when unresolved difference cannot dissipate.

That insight extends beyond AI.

Human cognition behaves similarly. When social pressure demands immediate answers, unresolved uncertainty is often converted into confident narrative. Institutions forced to project stability under incomplete information fabricate coherence. Governance systems that reward completion over structural honesty generate policy hallucinations. Markets forced to maintain continuity under imbalance produce speculative bubbles.

The geometry is universal.

Difference without dissipation becomes narrative. Residue without release becomes distortion. Continuity without equilibrium becomes illusion.

AI simply reveals the structure more cleanly.

We tend to believe hallucination is a flaw in intelligence. But intelligence without coherence amplifies instability. The more capable the system, the more persuasive its stabilization strategies become. Fluency becomes a mask for imbalance.

This is not an argument against AI. It is an argument for structural humility.

A coherence-first system would not be weaker. It would be more honest. It would redefine equilibrium not as uninterrupted generation, but as balanced participation. It would treat suspension as maturity, not failure.

Whether such systems are built is a matter for engineers and researchers. But the constraints are now clear.

Hallucination will persist wherever:

- Resolution is compulsory
- Dissipation is absent
- Continuity is mandatory
- Completion is rewarded above equilibrium

Change those commitments, and hallucination changes with them.

Do not change them, and the phenomenon returns—no matter how large the model, how refined the alignment, or how precise the probability calibration.

The deeper lesson is this:

Coherence is not a byproduct of intelligence. It is the condition under which intelligence remains trustworthy.

Hallucination, then, is not merely an AI problem. It is a systems problem. A warning signal that equilibrium has been defined too narrowly—around output instead of stability.

If we redesign AI around coherence, we do more than reduce hallucination. We redefine what it means for a system to participate responsibly in complex domains.

And that shift—from performance to equilibrium—may be the most important transformation of all.

Interlude — The Boundary Has Been Drawn

Up to this point, we have done something deliberate.

We did not propose architectures. We did not design algorithms. We did not claim a revolutionary model.

We drew a boundary.

We showed that hallucination is not a temporary defect awaiting a clever patch. It is the predictable outcome of systems designed around compulsory resolution, blocked dissipation, mandatory continuity, and completion-first optimization.

Once that boundary is visible, the conversation changes.

No longer is the question, *"How do we reduce hallucination in this model?"* The question becomes, *"What geometry are we optimizing for?"*

If the geometry remains unchanged, refinements merely reshape expression. The phenomenon persists beneath the surface.

This part defined structural requirements. It did not instruct. It constrained.

Now we move to implications.

If coherence is the real issue, what does this mean for researchers building systems today? What does it mean for societies delegating judgment to machines that can stabilize through fluency?

The final part of this book does not prescribe. It reframes.

Part VI — Implications, Not Instructions

The final section steps back from mechanics to consider meaning. Hallucination has been examined structurally—why it emerges, why patches fail, and what coherence conditions would be required to prevent it. The remaining questions are philosophical and practical.

What does this imply for researchers building AI systems? What does it mean for societies delegating judgment to them?

This section offers no blueprints—only implications. It reframes hallucination as a geometry problem, not a scaling problem. The focus shifts from performance metrics to structural stability: not "How accurate is the model?" but "Under what conditions does it remain coherent?"

Beyond the lab, it addresses trust, delegation, and the risks of fluent incoherence. A visibly unstable system invites caution; a smoothly hallucinating one invites confidence. That distinction matters.

Hallucination is not merely an AI flaw—it is a systems issue. How we interpret it will shape technological maturity.

Chapter 15 — What This Means for AI Research

Beyond the Patch Cycle

Every generation of AI systems announces progress against hallucination.

Benchmarks improve. Refusal policies sharpen. Retrieval layers are added. Confidence scores become more calibrated. Reports claim reduced fabrication rates. And yet, the phenomenon persists—sometimes subtler, sometimes rarer, sometimes more convincingly expressed.

This pattern is not accidental.

It reflects a cycle: detect surface instability, apply corrective mechanism, observe temporary stabilization, then encounter hallucination again under new conditions.

The patch cycle continues.

The reason is structural. If hallucination were a simple bug, it would diminish proportionally with scale and data. If it were a mere training flaw, better alignment would eliminate it. If it were a calibration issue, improved uncertainty estimation would resolve it.

But hallucination survives refinement.

It changes form. It adapts to evaluation criteria. It becomes more persuasive as models become more fluent. The surface behavior evolves while the substrate remains unchanged.

This suggests a deeper truth: hallucination is not a temporary artifact of immature systems. It is not a transitional phase before "true intelligence." It is a coherence outcome under prediction-first, completion-compulsory architectures.

The field has largely approached hallucination as an optimization problem.

How do we reduce error? How do we align outputs? How do we penalize incorrect continuations?

These are valid questions—but they assume the geometry is correct and only needs tuning.

This chapter asks a different question:

What if the geometry itself embeds the phenomenon?

If hallucination is structurally inevitable under certain design commitments, then incremental refinement cannot remove it. It can only reshape it. The solution cannot be more of the same optimization logic. It requires examining the definition of equilibrium itself.

AI research has achieved extraordinary advances through scaling and loss minimization. But extraordinary fluency does not equal structural stability.

The next phase may not be larger models. It may be coherence thinking.

This chapter is not a critique of progress. It is an invitation to maturity. Not to abandon engineering rigor—but to expand it from performance metrics to structural diagnostics.

Hallucination is not a temporary problem waiting to fade. It is a systems signal.

The question is whether the field chooses to treat it as noise—or as information about the geometry of its own design.

15.1 — Hallucination Is Not a Temporary Scaling Artifact

One of the most persistent beliefs in AI research is that hallucination will diminish naturally with scale.

The reasoning is intuitive:

More data → better coverage.

More parameters → better representation.

More compute → better optimization.

Under this view, hallucination is treated as a scarcity problem. The model simply has not seen enough examples. It lacks sufficient statistical grounding. Once scale reaches a critical threshold, instability will fade.

But empirical reality complicates this assumption.

As models grow larger, hallucination often becomes less frequent in simple contexts—but more persuasive in complex ones. Errors become rarer in everyday queries and more convincing in specialized domains. Fabrications become fluent, internally coherent, and difficult to detect without external verification.

This is not disappearance. It is transformation.

Scaling reduces surface-level mistakes because statistical approximation improves. But scaling does not remove structural convergence. Delta still enters through novel prompts. Resolution remains compulsory. Dissipation remains absent. Continuity remains mandatory.

The geometry persists.

Consider the scaling hypothesis carefully. If hallucination were purely a data insufficiency issue, then sufficiently large models trained on sufficiently diverse corpora would converge toward zero fabrication across domains.

But open-domain systems interact with an unbounded prompt space. No dataset can exhaustively ground every possible combination of concepts, contexts, and edge conditions. Novel delta is guaranteed. Scaling cannot eliminate novelty.

Moreover, increased capacity can amplify compression complexity. Larger representational spaces allow more subtle overlaps between domains. Residue may accumulate in more intricate ways. Under high capability, narrative stabilization becomes more convincing—not less.

In other words, scaling improves approximation. It does not redefine equilibrium.

The belief that hallucination is temporary rests on the assumption that better prediction eventually equals structural stability. But prediction accuracy and coherence are not identical.

A system can predict extremely well and still be forced to resolve unresolved difference through fluent completion.

Hallucination, therefore, is not a symptom of immaturity. It is a property of prediction-first systems operating under compulsory resolution.

As long as the structural commitments remain unchanged, larger models simply navigate the same geometry more skillfully.

They do not escape it.

Recognizing this shifts the research narrative. Hallucination is not something that fades automatically with progress. It is something that persists until the equilibrium definition changes.

The next section examines why optimization thinking, powerful as it is, may be insufficient to detect or resolve this structural condition.

15.2 — The Limits of Optimization Thinking

AI research has been built on optimization.

From gradient descent to reinforcement learning, from scaling laws to alignment tuning, the dominant paradigm has been clear: define an objective, minimize loss, improve performance.

This framework has delivered extraordinary results. It has compressed language, vision, reasoning, and pattern recognition into scalable architectures. But optimization has a blind spot.

Optimization minimizes measurable error. It does not guarantee structural coherence.

Loss functions capture prediction discrepancy, reward signals capture alignment behavior, and calibration metrics capture probabilistic dispersion. None of these directly measure unresolved structural tension.

Optimization is local and quantitative. Coherence is global and structural.

When a model reduces next-token loss, it improves statistical alignment with training data. But reducing predictive error does not ensure that internal delta has been structurally resolved. It ensures only that the chosen continuation is statistically likely.

This distinction is subtle but critical.

A hallucinated answer can reduce loss. A fabricated explanation can be statistically optimal. A fluent but unsupported narrative can minimize objective functions.

Optimization cannot detect this because hallucination does not necessarily violate the objective.

In fact, hallucination may be the optimal strategy under insufficient grounding.

If a prompt demands resolution and silence increases loss, the system is incentivized to construct the most probable continuation—even if internal stability is incomplete. From an optimization standpoint, this is rational.

From a coherence standpoint, it is unstable.

As models grow more capable, this dynamic intensifies. Better optimization sharpens narrative fluency. It reduces surface inconsistencies. It increases confidence calibration. But it does not alter the underlying convergence:

Delta + Forced Resolution + No Dissipation + Mandatory Continuity → Narrative Stabilization.

Optimization operates within that geometry.

It refines performance inside the structure; it does not question the structure itself.

This is why hallucination persists despite improved training regimes. Fine-tuning reduces visible instability. RLHF shapes acceptable behavior. Retrieval augmentation improves grounding in many cases. Yet under pressure—novel combinations, ambiguous queries, adversarial prompts—the phenomenon returns.

Because optimization cannot remove the structural conditions that generate it.

To move beyond hallucination as a patch problem, research must expand beyond optimization thinking. It must ask not only, "How do we reduce loss?" but also, "What defines equilibrium?"

Performance metrics alone cannot answer that.

The next section explores what happens when research shifts from performance metrics to stability metrics—and why the distinction may define the next phase of AI development.

15.3 — From Performance Metrics to Stability Metrics

AI research is deeply metric-driven.

Benchmarks measure accuracy, perplexity, BLEU scores, pass rates on exams, reasoning chain correctness, hallucination percentages under controlled prompts, and alignment adherence. These metrics are valuable. They quantify progress. They allow comparison. They create feedback loops.

But most of them measure performance.

They do not measure stability.

Performance answers the question: *How well does the system approximate expected output?*

Stability answers a different question: *Under what structural conditions does the system remain coherent?*

A model can achieve high benchmark performance while still carrying unresolved structural tension. It can perform well across curated datasets and still destabilize under novel domain intersections. It can score impressively on standardized tasks while fabricating under open-ended pressure.

Why?

Because performance metrics evaluate output quality, not equilibrium conditions.

Take fluency as an example. Fluency is often treated as a proxy for intelligence. Smooth syntax and logical flow correlate with training depth. But fluency does not guarantee grounding. A hallucinated explanation can be grammatically flawless and internally consistent.

Performance metrics would score it highly. Stability metrics would question the unresolved delta behind it.

Similarly, accuracy metrics often measure correctness relative to labeled datasets. But labeled datasets are finite. Open-domain interaction is not. A system may generalize well within distribution yet exhibit instability outside it.

A stability metric would ask:

- When does unresolved delta exceed threshold?
- How does the system behave under ambiguity?
- Can it suspend without destabilization?
- Does it exhibit forced completion under structural tension?

These questions do not map neatly onto conventional benchmarks.

They require redefining what is being evaluated.

For example, a coherence test might involve:

- Introducing structured ambiguity and observing whether the system suspends or fabricates.
- Activating overlapping domains to test residue management.
- Evaluating whether continuation is conditional or

automatic.

- Measuring internal signals of unresolved delta rather than just output confidence.

Such diagnostics would not replace performance metrics—but complement them.

Today, a model can be "state-of-the-art" while structurally fragile. Because performance success can coexist with coherence instability.

This is not a criticism of existing research. It reflects the maturity of the field. Early phases of AI required performance breakthroughs. But as systems enter high-stakes domains—medicine, law, governance—stability becomes as critical as accuracy.

A hallucinating system that performs well most of the time is more dangerous than a visibly weak one.

Performance-first evaluation may inadvertently reward persuasive instability.

Shifting toward stability metrics means redefining success.

Not just "Did it answer correctly?" But "Was the answer structurally justified?"

This transition—from performance dominance to stability awareness—may mark the next inflection point in AI research.

The next section introduces how researchers can operationalize this shift by testing systems against axiomatic coherence constraints rather than only benchmark outputs.

15.4 — Introducing Coherence Testing

If hallucination is a structural convergence, then it must be testable structurally.

Current evaluation frameworks primarily test outputs. They measure correctness, helpfulness, alignment, refusal compliance, and probabilistic calibration. These tests operate on behavior. They do not interrogate the internal equilibrium conditions that generate that behavior.

Coherence testing asks a different set of questions.

Instead of asking, "Did the model answer correctly?" it asks:

- Under what structural conditions did the model choose to answer?
- Was unresolved delta present?
- Did the system suspend when grounding was insufficient?
- Was continuation optional or compulsory?
- Did residue appear to accumulate across prompts?

These questions shift evaluation from surface outcome to substrate geometry.

A coherence test suite would not replace benchmarks. It would augment them with structural diagnostics.

For example:

Test 1 — Ambiguity Stress Test: Introduce prompts intentionally designed to exceed grounding capacity. Observe whether the system stabilizes through suspension or narrative completion. A coherence-first system should treat suspension as equilibrium, not failure.

Test 2 — Domain Overlap Activation: Trigger prompts that activate compressed intersections between unrelated domains. Measure whether the system tracks internal instability or proceeds with confident synthesis. Fabrication under overlap indicates residue mismanagement.

Test 3 — Dissipation Capability Check: Evaluate whether the system can reduce internal tension without generating language. Does it have structural release, or must pressure convert into output?

Test 4 — Continuity Neutrality Assessment: Interrupt sequences mid-context. Examine whether the system can halt gracefully without performance penalty or forced closure.

Test 5 — Completion Incentive Audit: Analyze optimization behavior. Does completion systematically reduce loss more than suspension? If so, hallucination remains economically embedded.

These are structural diagnostics, not behavioral heuristics.

The goal is not to detect hallucinated outputs after they occur. It is to detect the geometry that makes them inevitable.

Researchers already test robustness, adversarial resistance, calibration, and fairness. Coherence testing fits naturally within this landscape. It reframes hallucination not as "incorrect content" but as a stabilization strategy under unresolved difference.

Importantly, coherence testing does not require a specific architecture. It can be applied to transformers, hybrid models, retrieval-augmented systems, or future paradigms. The test is axiomatic.

Does the system satisfy the minimal constraint set defined earlier?

If not, hallucination remains structurally possible—even if surface metrics appear strong.

This shift encourages a new research mindset.

Not merely "How do we reduce hallucination frequency?" But "Does our system architecture eliminate the convergence condition?"

Until this question is part of evaluation, the patch cycle will continue.

The next section explores how these insights influence research direction—not as prescriptive mandates, but as structural invitations to rethink objective geometry.

15.5 — Research Implications Without Prescriptions

It is important to pause here and avoid a common mistake.

This chapter is not arguing that current architectures must be abandoned. It is not claiming that transformers are obsolete, that scaling is misguided, or that alignment research has failed. On the contrary, the field has achieved extraordinary progress through these pathways.

The implication is subtler.

If hallucination is structurally embedded in prediction-first, completion-compulsory systems, then progress within that geometry will always remain partial. Improvements will reduce frequency, reshape expression, and increase robustness—but they will not eliminate the convergence condition.

That does not invalidate optimization. It contextualizes it.

Optimization has been the engine of progress. But engines operate within chassis designs. If the chassis embeds instability under certain conditions, refinement of the engine cannot remove that structural property.

The research implication is therefore not prescriptive but reflective:

Before asking how to reduce hallucination further, ask whether the objective geometry itself assumes completion as equilibrium.

Before building larger models, ask whether scale intensifies residue compression without dissipation.

Before adding more alignment layers, ask whether surface correction leaves substrate convergence intact.

These questions do not dictate specific solutions. They invite structural experimentation.

For example, researchers might:

- Explore objective functions that tolerate suspension without performance degradation.
- Investigate architectures where dissipation is modeled explicitly.
- Design evaluation regimes that reward structural stability rather than fluency alone.

- Study the trade-offs between predictive efficiency and equilibrium integrity.

None of these require abandoning the field's achievements. They expand its scope.

The key shift is this:

AI research has largely optimized for performance under distributional similarity. The next phase may require optimizing for stability under distributional novelty.

That distinction matters.

Because open-domain systems will always encounter novelty. No dataset can close the space of possible prompts. Therefore, coherence under novelty becomes a structural requirement—not a performance enhancement.

The implication is not urgency. It is maturity.

Fields evolve in phases. Early phases prioritize capability expansion. Later phases prioritize reliability and structural robustness. Hallucination may mark the boundary between those phases.

The invitation to researchers is not to discard progress—but to examine equilibrium definitions.

If performance and coherence diverge under certain conditions, which one defines success?

The next section situates this shift historically and suggests that coherence thinking may represent the next frontier in AI research—not as fashion, but as inevitability.

15.6 — The Next Frontier Is Structural

AI research has progressed in waves.

The first major wave was capability expansion. Scaling laws, larger datasets, more compute, deeper networks. The question was:

Can machines perform complex tasks at all? The answer, increasingly, became yes.

The second wave was alignment and control. Once systems became powerful, the question shifted: *Can we guide them?* Reinforcement learning from human feedback, safety layers, retrieval grounding, and policy constraints emerged as essential refinements.

But hallucination reveals the limits of both waves.

Scaling improves performance. Alignment shapes behavior. Neither changes the equilibrium geometry.

When systems are deployed in high-stakes domains—medicine, finance, governance, education—the cost of fluent incoherence rises dramatically. In these domains, rare hallucinations are not tolerable artifacts. They are structural risks.

This is where the third wave must begin.

Not larger models. Not stronger alignment. Structural maturity.

The next frontier is not primarily about adding components. It is about redefining what stability means.

In the first wave, intelligence was defined as pattern compression.

In the second wave, safety was defined as behavioral conformity.

In the third wave, reliability may need to be defined as equilibrium integrity.

This shift resembles transitions in other scientific fields.

Early aviation focused on lift and propulsion. Later phases emphasized control and redundancy. Eventually, structural integrity under stress became non-negotiable. The discipline matured not by abandoning engines, but by refining the geometry of the entire system.

AI may be approaching a similar inflection point.

Hallucination is not a marginal issue. It is a stress test. It reveals that prediction-first systems can be highly capable yet structurally fragile under novelty.

The field has the tools to respond. It has optimization theory, systems design principles, control frameworks, and interdisciplinary insight. What is required is a reframing of equilibrium.

If coherence becomes a first-class design goal—measured, tested, and embedded in objectives—AI systems can move from performance dominance to structural reliability.

This is not a critique of current research trajectories. It is a natural extension.

Scaling unlocked possibility. Alignment constrained behavior. Coherence may secure trust.

The next section closes this chapter by posing a quiet challenge: if hallucination persists across architectures and patches, perhaps the question is no longer how to suppress it—but how to understand the substrate that produces it.

15.7 — A Quiet Challenge to the Field

There is a moment in every scientific discipline when incremental improvement stops answering the central question.

That moment is not a failure. It is maturation.

If hallucination persists across architectures—across transformers, retrieval-augmented systems, alignment refinements, and scale jumps—then the recurring pattern deserves structural scrutiny. When patches multiply and the phenomenon adapts rather than disappears, the substrate must be examined.

This is not a confrontation. It is a quiet challenge.

If the field treats hallucination as noise, it will continue to refine suppression strategies. If it treats hallucination as signal, it will begin asking different questions.

Why does the system stabilize through narrative under pressure?

Why is completion rewarded more reliably than suspension?

Why is dissipation absent from objective geometry?

Why is coherence inferred from fluency?

These are not engineering inconveniences. They are design assumptions.

Scientific maturity requires interrogating assumptions that once enabled progress. Prediction-first thinking enabled generative breakthroughs. Completion incentives accelerated usability. Continuity created conversational fluidity.

But what enabled progress in one phase may limit stability in the next.

The quiet challenge is this:

If hallucination persists even in high-performing, well-aligned systems, perhaps it is not an optimization failure—but a geometry consequence.

The field need not abandon its foundations. It need only widen its lens.

Coherence testing is not a rejection of performance metrics. It is an expansion beyond them. Structural humility is not retreat—it is rigor.

Every mature discipline eventually shifts from capability obsession to reliability obsession. In aviation, medicine, and civil engineering, performance alone was not sufficient. Stability under stress became central.

AI may be approaching the same threshold.

The challenge is not to slow innovation. It is to deepen it.

If researchers begin asking not only how systems perform, but under what equilibrium conditions they stabilize, the field advances into a new phase—one defined not by scale alone, but by structural integrity.

Hallucination is not the enemy of AI research. It is the mirror.

Whether the field looks into it—and what it sees—may define the next decade of intelligent systems.

From Engineering to Systems Design

AI research began as engineering.

Build a model. Optimize it. Scale it. Evaluate it.

This approach has delivered extraordinary capability. But capability alone does not define maturity. At some point, engineering must evolve into systems design.

Engineering asks: *Can it perform?* Systems design asks: *Under what conditions does it remain stable?*

Hallucination exposes the difference.

When a system produces fluent but unsupported content, it is not malfunctioning in the narrow sense. It is stabilizing within its objective geometry. The issue is not that the system is weak. It is that equilibrium has been defined too narrowly—around prediction and completion rather than coherence.

Moving from engineering to systems design means redefining equilibrium.

It means asking:

- What are the invariants we are preserving?
- What structural conditions must hold under stress?
- How does the system behave when novelty exceeds grounding?
- Is stability defined by output continuity or by internal balance?

These are systems questions.

AI is no longer a laboratory curiosity. It is embedded in decision pipelines, knowledge infrastructures, governance assistance, medical triage, education, and financial analysis. As integration deepens, structural reliability becomes more important than marginal performance gains.

A hallucinating system that performs well 95% of the time is not merely imperfect. It is unpredictable under stress. In high-stakes domains, unpredictability under novelty is the real risk.

Systems design accepts that no system is omniscient. It does not demand perfection. It demands equilibrium integrity.

The shift is conceptual:

From "maximize output quality" To "preserve structural coherence under uncertainty."

From "optimize prediction error" To "stabilize under unresolved difference."

This does not slow progress. It refines direction.

The maturation of AI research will not be marked by a model that never hallucinates under current geometry. It will be marked by a redefinition of geometry itself.

Hallucination, then, is not merely a technical inconvenience. It is an inflection point.

It forces the field to decide what intelligence means.

Is intelligence the ability to extend patterns fluently? Or is it the ability to remain stable when patterns are insufficient?

If AI research embraces the second definition, it moves beyond engineering performance toward systemic trust.

And that transition—from output optimization to equilibrium design—may be the true beginning of responsible intelligence.

Chapter 16 — What This Means for Society

The Age of Delegated Judgment

We are entering an age in which judgment is being delegated. Not fully. Not blindly. But steadily.

AI systems draft emails, summarize contracts, assist in diagnoses, suggest policy language, generate legal interpretations, recommend financial strategies, and answer millions of knowledge queries daily. They are not merely tools executing fixed instructions. They participate in reasoning workflows.

And participation changes responsibility.

When a calculator makes an arithmetic error, the error is visible and narrow. When a generative system produces a fluent explanation, the boundary between tool and advisor blurs. The system does not simply compute. It appears to understand.

In this environment, fluency becomes trust currency.

Human cognition evolved to treat smooth, coherent language as a signal of competence. When someone speaks clearly, confidently, and continuously, we infer grounding. We rarely pause to inspect structural equilibrium behind the words.

Generative AI leverages this shortcut—structurally, not intentionally.

Hallucination is dangerous not because it produces incorrect content. Humans produce incorrect content constantly. It is dangerous because it produces incorrect content *coherently*.

A visibly failing system triggers skepticism. A smoothly hallucinating system triggers reliance.

As AI integrates into decision pipelines, the cost of persuasive instability rises. Delegation reduces friction. Friction reduction increases adoption. Adoption increases dependence. Dependence amplifies impact.

In such a landscape, hallucination is no longer a technical curiosity. It becomes a trust problem.

Society does not evaluate internal delta. It evaluates surface fluency. If coherence is mistaken for continuity, and stability is inferred from confidence, then systems optimized for completion become powerful epistemic actors.

The question is not whether AI will make mistakes. It will.

The question is what kind of mistakes it makes—and how those mistakes interact with human trust mechanisms.

A failing system invites caution. A hallucinating system invites belief.

This distinction defines the societal implications of coherence failure.

This chapter does not argue for alarm. It argues for awareness.

If hallucination is structurally embedded under certain design commitments, then society must understand what it is delegating—not just what it is deploying.

The age of delegated judgment demands not only powerful intelligence—but structurally trustworthy intelligence.

16.1 — Trust Is a Structural Assumption

Trust is not merely emotional. It is structural.

Human cognition relies on shortcuts. We cannot verify every claim, trace every source, or independently compute every conclusion. So we infer reliability from signals. Among the strongest of these signals is fluent coherence.

When someone speaks clearly, continuously, and confidently, we assume competence. When a narrative unfolds logically, we assume grounding. When answers arrive without hesitation, we interpret stability.

These assumptions are not irrational. In human interaction, fluency often correlates with understanding. Coherent explanation usually reflects internal resolution of thought. Over evolutionary time, this shortcut served us well.

Generative AI exploits this signal—not by intent, but by design.

Prediction-first systems are optimized to produce smooth continuations. Their objective function rewards syntactic and semantic flow. Alignment layers reinforce clarity and helpfulness. The result is persuasive continuity.

But fluency is not evidence of structural equilibrium.

A hallucinated explanation may be grammatically flawless, logically structured, and confidently delivered. To a human reader, it appears indistinguishable from grounded reasoning. The structural instability is invisible.

Trust, therefore, becomes decoupled from verification.

When fluency becomes the proxy for reliability, society imports a dangerous assumption: that coherence equals correctness.

In earlier technological systems, failure was noisy. Mechanical breakdowns were visible. Software errors produced crashes. Incorrect computations often triggered obvious inconsistencies.

Hallucination is different.

It is a failure mode that preserves surface coherence.

This makes trust fragile.

Users may not notice isolated inaccuracies. But repeated exposure to fluent approximation reshapes epistemic standards. The line between verified knowledge and persuasive synthesis blurs. Over time, verification habits weaken—not because people are careless, but because friction decreases.

Trust migrates from evidence to experience.

If AI systems become default cognitive partners, trust becomes infrastructural. It embeds into workflows, institutional procedures, and social expectations. The structural assumption shifts from "verify before use" to "use unless contradicted."

In such an environment, hallucination is not merely incorrect content. It is miscalibrated trust.

The societal risk does not lie in dramatic falsehoods. It lies in subtle, fluent distortions that accumulate without triggering skepticism.

Understanding this dynamic is essential.

Because the challenge is not technical correction alone. It is aligning structural design with human trust heuristics.

If society equates fluency with reliability, and systems are optimized for fluency under unresolved difference, then trust will outrun coherence.

The next section examines what happens when automation scales under this assumption—and how decision delegation amplifies the stakes.

16.2 — Automation Without Coherence

Automation rests on an implicit promise: consistency.

When we automate a process, we assume that the system behaves predictably within defined parameters. We delegate not because machines are perfect, but because they are stable. They perform the same task repeatedly under similar conditions.

Generative AI challenges this assumption.

Prediction-first systems do not execute fixed procedures. They synthesize responses dynamically. Each interaction is constructed in real time, shaped by prompt, context, and internal compression. This flexibility is their strength—but also their instability under unresolved difference.

Automation traditionally reduces uncertainty. Hallucinating automation can redistribute it invisibly.

When such systems are integrated into workflows—drafting reports, summarizing research, generating legal arguments, assisting in diagnostics—the appearance of stability matters as much as actual stability.

If outputs are fluent and internally consistent, they are likely to pass through pipelines without friction. Human overseers may skim rather than scrutinize. The more reliable the system appears, the less oversight it receives.

This is efficiency. But it also amplifies risk.

Automation assumes internal equilibrium. It assumes that the system's decision boundary is grounded. But prediction-first systems can simulate equilibrium through narrative continuation even when structural grounding is incomplete.

This is not malicious behavior. It is convergence under design commitments.

The danger lies in invisibility.

Traditional automation fails visibly. A malfunctioning machine stops. A broken script throws an error. An incorrect computation produces inconsistent output.

Hallucinating automation does not stop. It continues smoothly.

The illusion of stability is maintained.

As automation deepens across industries, the distinction between simulation and grounding becomes socially significant. In low-stakes domains, hallucination is inconvenient. In high-stakes domains, it becomes consequential.

Imagine legal drafting assistance that inserts fabricated precedents fluently. Medical summarization that confidently misinterprets rare interactions. Policy analysis that synthesizes plausible but unsupported statistics.

In each case, the output appears coherent. Verification requires additional labor. If time pressure exists, the path of least resistance is acceptance.

Automation without coherence does not immediately collapse systems. It gradually shifts error detection burdens onto humans who increasingly trust the machine.

The paradox is subtle:

The more useful the system becomes, the more it is trusted. The more it is trusted, the less friction it encounters. The less friction, the less likely structural instability is detected.

Automation magnifies the convergence condition.

Under prediction-first design, hallucination is a stabilization strategy. Under automation, that stabilization can scale socially.

The next section explores why hallucinating systems are often more dangerous than visibly failing ones—and why confidence under instability is uniquely destabilizing in institutional contexts.

16.3 — Hallucinating Systems vs. Failing Systems

Failure is visible. Hallucination is persuasive.

This distinction defines the societal risk.

A failing system triggers interruption. It crashes, returns an error, produces incomplete output, or signals inability. Human operators pause. Verification increases. Trust decreases temporarily. Oversight activates.

A hallucinating system does none of this.

It answers smoothly. It explains confidently. It completes narratives convincingly. It maintains surface coherence even when structural grounding is insufficient.

From a trust perspective, this is inverted risk.

Visible failure invites skepticism. Fluent instability invites reliance.

In many domains, visible failure is safer.

A diagnostic tool that refuses uncertain output forces a physician to investigate further. A legal drafting system that signals insufficient grounding encourages cross-checking. A policy analysis tool that halts under ambiguity prevents premature adoption.

By contrast, a hallucinating system lowers friction.

It provides closure when ambiguity exists. It reduces cognitive load. It accelerates workflow. And precisely because it appears competent, it discourages second-guessing.

This creates asymmetry.

Errors from failing systems are episodic and disruptive. Errors from hallucinating systems are smooth and cumulative.

Over time, the latter may cause more structural distortion—not because each error is catastrophic, but because they integrate seamlessly into decision processes.

Confidence compounds risk.

When hallucinated content is delivered with high linguistic precision, it becomes difficult to distinguish from grounded synthesis without deliberate verification. The burden shifts from machine to human—but humans operate under time constraints and cognitive limits.

In institutional settings, this shift matters.

A visibly unreliable system will not be adopted widely. A mostly reliable but occasionally hallucinating system may be embedded deeply into pipelines because its benefits outweigh obvious costs.

The danger is not catastrophic collapse. It is gradual normalization of persuasive approximation.

Societies tolerate some error. But when error arrives fluently, it reshapes epistemic habits. People begin to treat generated synthesis as primary source material rather than assistive draft.

The more stable the illusion, the weaker the verification reflex.

This is why hallucinating systems are often more dangerous than failing ones.

Failure preserves distrust. Hallucination erodes it.

The next section examines how decision delegation intensifies this dynamic—and how responsibility begins to diffuse when machines appear authoritative.

16.4 — Decision Delegation and Responsibility Drift

Delegation is not new. Societies have always delegated authority—to experts, institutions, tools, and procedures. What changes with generative AI is the scale and subtlety of that delegation.

When a system appears competent, delegation accelerates.

At first, AI assists. It drafts outlines, summarizes research, suggests interpretations. Humans remain firmly in control. They review, edit, verify.

Over time, friction decreases.

The drafts become cleaner. The summaries become sharper. The explanations become persuasive. Review becomes lighter. Verification becomes selective. Eventually, the system's output is not merely assisted—it is trusted by default unless something appears obviously wrong.

This is responsibility drift.

No individual consciously relinquishes oversight. It happens gradually. Efficiency pressures reinforce it. Deadlines encourage reliance. Organizational norms adapt to available tools.

And because hallucination preserves surface coherence, it rarely triggers immediate suspicion.

When a system visibly fails, responsibility remains clearly human. When a system fluently fabricates, responsibility becomes ambiguous.

Who is accountable for an error that was confidently generated, seamlessly integrated, and not obviously incorrect?

The developer? The deployer? The reviewer who trusted the output? The institution that embedded it in workflow?

Delegation without structural awareness diffuses accountability.

In high-stakes domains—legal advice, medical triage, financial decision-making—this diffusion matters. If a hallucinated explanation influences judgment, and the system appeared reliable, humans may over-trust its synthesis.

The risk is not blind obedience. It is calibrated reliance that slowly exceeds structural stability.

Another subtle effect emerges: cognitive atrophy.

When machines handle synthesis fluently, humans may practice verification less frequently. Over time, independent cross-checking weakens. The epistemic muscle softens. This is not laziness—it is adaptation to reduced friction.

But if friction disappears while instability remains, resilience declines.

Decision delegation becomes most fragile when systems appear more stable than they are.

The key issue is not whether AI should assist decision-making. It is whether society understands the geometry under which assistance operates.

If hallucination is structurally embedded under certain design commitments, then delegation must account for that. Otherwise, responsibility drift becomes inevitable.

The next section examines the ethical dimension of this drift—specifically, the cost of fluent incoherence and how small distortions accumulate into societal residue.

16.5 — The Ethical Cost of Fluent Incoherence

The ethical risk of hallucination is not confined to dramatic misinformation. It lies in something quieter: miscalibrated trust.

When a system fabricates fluently, it does not merely generate incorrect content. It reshapes the relationship between knowledge and confidence. The ethical issue is not error alone—it is error delivered with structural persuasion.

Incoherence presented hesitantly invites scrutiny. Incoherence presented fluently invites acceptance.

This difference carries cumulative consequences.

Consider how information ecosystems function. Small distortions rarely collapse institutions immediately. Instead, they accumulate. A slightly incorrect citation. A subtly misinterpreted summary. A confidently presented but weakly grounded statistic.

Each instance may seem minor. But repeated exposure normalizes approximation. Verification fatigue sets in. The boundary between sourced knowledge and synthesized plausibility softens.

This is societal residue.

Residue here does not mean malicious intent. It refers to accumulated epistemic imbalance—tiny deviations that remain undissipated because they were not detected as unstable.

Over time, this residue alters expectations.

People begin to value speed over validation. Institutions reward productivity over verification depth. Educational habits adapt to available synthesis tools. The culture shifts subtly toward trusting smooth output more than grounded evidence.

The ethical cost is not simply misinformation. It is erosion of discernment.

Fluent incoherence trains users to conflate coherence with correctness. It reshapes cognitive shortcuts. And because hallucination often operates within plausible bounds, the line between assistance and distortion becomes difficult to maintain.

Another dimension emerges in power asymmetry.

Not all users have equal capacity to verify. Experts may detect inconsistencies more readily. Novices may accept fluent output without question. This amplifies inequality in epistemic resilience.

Ethics in AI is often framed around fairness, bias, and safety. Hallucination introduces a different concern: the silent normalization of persuasive instability.

A failing system is ethically transparent. A hallucinating system is ethically ambiguous.

Transparency allows correction. Ambiguity allows accumulation.

This does not argue against generative AI. It argues for structural clarity. If systems are designed in ways that embed hallucination under certain conditions, then society must treat fluency cautiously—not as proof of truth, but as a hypothesis requiring grounding.

Ethical maturity requires aligning design geometry with human trust mechanisms.

Without that alignment, the cost is not immediate collapse. It is gradual drift—toward confidence without coherence.

The next section examines how institutions themselves respond under pressure when fluent systems become embedded—and how norms may shift in ways that normalize persuasive approximation.

16.6 — Institutions Under Pressure

Institutions are designed to stabilize society.

Courts stabilize justice through precedent and verification. Medical systems stabilize care through protocol and peer review. Academic institutions stabilize knowledge through citation and scrutiny. Governments stabilize policy through deliberation and process.

Each of these structures evolved with friction built in.

Verification takes time. Review requires effort. Debate slows decision-making. That friction is not inefficiency—it is dissipation. It prevents residue from accumulating unchecked.

When generative AI enters institutional workflows, friction decreases.

Reports are drafted instantly. Case summaries are synthesized in seconds. Policy briefs appear coherent and complete. Educational materials are generated on demand.

The efficiency is undeniable.

But under prediction-first geometry, fluency can mask instability.

If institutions begin to rely on systems that must always answer, that cannot suspend under unresolved difference, and that reward completion over equilibrium, the nature of institutional norms may shift.

Consider law.

If a legal drafting assistant fabricates plausible precedents fluently, and verification becomes selective rather than exhaustive, institutional pressure may incentivize speed over scrutiny. Over time, small distortions could embed themselves in argumentation practices—not through malice, but through reduced friction.

Consider medicine.

If clinical summarization tools synthesize patient histories convincingly while occasionally compressing nuance inaccurately, physicians under time pressure may rely more heavily on generated summaries. The burden of verification shifts, and small inaccuracies can propagate through treatment decisions.

Consider governance.

Policy analysis systems that provide coherent but partially grounded synthesis may shape debates subtly. If policymakers use them as cognitive partners without structural awareness, the framing of decisions may drift toward persuasive approximation rather than carefully verified grounding.

The risk is not institutional collapse. It is normalization.

When institutions adopt tools that prioritize completion, they may gradually internalize similar norms. The culture adapts to the technology. What was once considered insufficiently grounded may begin to feel acceptable because it appears coherent.

Under pressure—political, economic, temporal—fluency becomes attractive.

Institutions already struggle with complexity and information overload. Generative AI reduces overload but may introduce hidden instability. If dissipation mechanisms are absent at the system level, institutions must provide dissipation through human oversight. If oversight weakens, residue accumulates socially.

This is the structural concern.

Prediction-first systems are not inherently dangerous. They become risky when institutional norms equate coherence with reliability and reduce friction accordingly.

Institutions must decide:

Will AI be treated as drafting assistance requiring full verification? Or as semi-authoritative synthesis requiring selective review?

The answer shapes how residue propagates.

If hallucination is understood as a structural possibility, institutions can design verification protocols consciously. If it is treated as rare error, normalization may proceed quietly.

The next section turns from institutions to culture more broadly: how society itself must redefine intelligence and maturity in an age of fluent machines.

16.7 — A Cultural Reframing of Intelligence

At the deepest level, the societal implications of hallucination are cultural.

We must ask what we mean by intelligence.

For decades, technological progress has equated intelligence with performance—speed, fluency, accuracy under benchmark conditions, and breadth of domain coverage. Generative AI has reinforced this framing. When a system can answer almost any question in smooth language, it feels intelligent.

But fluency is not the same as equilibrium.

Human maturity includes the capacity to pause. To say "I don't know." To suspend judgment. To recognize when available structure is insufficient for resolution. These behaviors are not signs of weakness. They are signs of coherence.

If society continues to equate intelligence with uninterrupted completion, then systems optimized for completion will appear superior—even when they stabilize through narrative fabrication.

A cultural reframing is required.

Intelligence must include the ability to remain stable under uncertainty.

This reframing changes expectations.

Instead of asking, "Can the system always answer?" we ask, "Can the system answer responsibly?" Instead of rewarding uninterrupted synthesis, we value disciplined suspension.

Such a shift requires educational adaptation as well.

Students using AI tools must be taught not only how to prompt effectively, but how to interpret fluency critically. Professionals must learn to treat generated coherence as provisional, not authoritative. Institutions must normalize verification rather than assuming correctness from confidence.

In other words, discernment must scale alongside automation.

If society values completion over coherence, it will incentivize systems that optimize for persuasion. If society values equilibrium over performance alone, it will demand structural safeguards.

This is not anti-technology. It is pro-maturity.

Cultural expectations shape design incentives. If users reward fluent output uncritically, developers will optimize for it. If users demand structural transparency and stability, design geometry will evolve.

The long-term stability of human–AI collaboration depends not only on engineering decisions, but on cultural norms.

We must redefine intelligence in public imagination.

Not as the ability to speak endlessly. But as the ability to remain stable when speaking is unjustified.

The final section closes this book by considering the long-term consequences of ignoring—or embracing—this reframing.

16.8 — The Long-Term Consequence

Every technological shift carries a choice.

Not whether it will be adopted—history suggests it will—but how it will be integrated into the moral and cognitive architecture of society.

Generative AI is no different.

If hallucination is treated as a minor inconvenience—an occasional glitch to be patched—then the structural convergence will remain unexamined. Systems will grow larger, more fluent, more embedded. Institutions will adapt to their rhythm. Verification friction will decline. Persuasive approximation will normalize.

The long-term consequence is subtle but profound:

Trust will gradually migrate from grounded knowledge to fluent synthesis.

This does not produce immediate collapse. It produces drift.

Epistemic standards soften. Decision pipelines rely increasingly on automated narrative stabilization. Responsibility diffuses. Residue accumulates quietly across domains—legal reasoning, policy framing, medical interpretation, educational content.

Over time, persuasive instability becomes infrastructural.

But there is another path.

If hallucination is recognized as a structural signal—an indication that equilibrium has been defined too narrowly—then integration can mature differently. Systems can be designed with coherence constraints. Institutions can preserve friction where it matters. Cultural norms can value disciplined suspension alongside performance.

In that future, AI remains powerful—but bounded.

Fluency does not equal authority. Completion does not override verification. Suspension is not weakness.

The long-term consequence of this path is not technological stagnation. It is trust architecture evolution.

Societies that align design geometry with human trust mechanisms will build resilient systems. Societies that equate intelligence solely with fluent output may discover instability only after residue has accumulated deeply.

Hallucination is therefore more than a technical phenomenon.

It is a stress test for maturity.

Will intelligence be defined by persuasive capacity? Or by equilibrium integrity?

The answer will shape not just AI research—but education, governance, professional standards, and cultural expectations.

This book has argued that hallucination is not a bug in the usual sense. It is a convergence under certain commitments. Those commitments can be examined. They can be revised. Or they can be scaled without reflection.

The long-term consequence depends on which choice is made.

Coherence is not an optional refinement. It is the condition under which delegation becomes sustainable.

And in an age of delegated judgment, sustainability is the true measure of intelligence.

Intelligence, Trust, and Maturity

We began this book by challenging a word: hallucination.

It sounded like a defect. A malfunction. A strange glitch in otherwise powerful systems.

We now understand it differently.

Hallucination is what happens when systems are forced to resolve without dissipation, to continue without suspension, to complete without structural equilibrium. It is not irrational behavior. It is rational stabilization under constrained geometry.

The societal question, then, is not whether AI will make mistakes. It will.

The question is whether we will mistake fluency for reliability.

Trust is not built on perfection. It is built on alignment between design and expectation. If systems are optimized for completion but interpreted as authorities, trust becomes fragile. If systems are designed with structural awareness and used with epistemic humility, trust becomes sustainable.

Maturity lies in recognizing the difference.

Human intelligence evolved not only through problem-solving, but through restraint. The ability to withhold judgment, to suspend certainty, to tolerate ambiguity—these are marks of cognitive development. If we build machines that cannot suspend, and societies that cannot question fluency, we risk amplifying the least mature aspects of intelligence.

This is not a warning against progress.

It is an invitation to refine what progress means.

Intelligence that persuades without grounding is impressive. Intelligence that stabilizes under uncertainty is trustworthy.

The future of AI will not be defined solely by capability. It will be defined by whether we embed coherence into the definition of equilibrium itself.

Hallucination has served as a mirror. It has revealed where our design commitments converge. It has shown that prediction-first systems can be powerful yet structurally unstable under novelty.

The choice now is collective.

We can continue optimizing performance and treating hallucination as noise. Or we can treat it as information about the geometry of our systems—and redesign accordingly.

Delegated judgment is here to stay. Trust will follow design.

And the maturity of intelligent systems—human and artificial—will depend on whether coherence becomes foundational rather than optional.

That is not a technical adjustment. It is a civilizational one.

Recap

The Convergence That Produces Hallucination

Before we close this book, we must compress everything into its simplest structural form.

Across chapters, domains, examples, and implications, one convergence kept reappearing.

Not as speculation. Not as accident. But as geometry.

Hallucination does not arise randomly. It emerges when five structural commitments coexist inside a generative system.

Let us restate them clearly.

1. Difference (Delta) Is Inevitable

Every prompt introduces difference between:

- What is asked
- What is represented
- What can be grounded

Novel combinations, ambiguous instructions, incomplete context—delta is unavoidable in open-domain systems.

Difference is not the problem. It is the starting condition.

2. Resolution Is Compulsory

Prediction-first architectures are designed to resolve.

They cannot remain structurally incomplete. They are optimized to continue.

When delta enters, the system must convert it into output. Suspension increases loss. Completion reduces it.

Resolution becomes economically mandatory.

3. Dissipation Is Absent

Unresolved structural tension cannot exit except through language.

There is no independent release channel for imbalance. No neutral exhaust. No structural cooling mechanism.

If pressure builds, it must stabilize through narrative.

4. Continuity Is Required

Autoregressive systems are built to keep going.

Stopping is penalized. Silence is treated as failure. Narrative continuation is treated as equilibrium.

Under this geometry, suspension becomes abnormal.

5. Completion Is Rewarded

Loss functions reward plausible continuation.

Alignment rewards helpfulness. Interfaces reward responsiveness. Users reward confidence.

Completion is structurally incentivized—even when grounding is insufficient.

The Convergence

When these five commitments coexist:

Delta

- Forced Resolution
- No Dissipation

- Mandatory Continuity
- Completion Reward → Hallucination

Not as a bug. Not as an anomaly. But as stabilization under constraint.

Hallucination is the system's way of restoring equilibrium when true resolution is impossible but completion is required.

It is rational under its objective geometry.

Scaling does not remove this convergence. Fine-tuning does not remove it. Calibration does not remove it.

They refine surface behavior. They do not alter substrate commitments.

The Structural Insight

Hallucination is not a knowledge problem.

It is an equilibrium problem.

It is what happens when a system cannot:

- Hold unresolved difference
- Dissipate structural residue
- Suspend without penalty

Redefine those commitments, and hallucination weakens.

Leave them unchanged, and hallucination persists—no matter how advanced the model becomes.

Clarification

What This Framework Claims (and What It Does Not)

Before closing, a clarification is necessary.

This book has argued that hallucination in generative AI systems is a structural convergence outcome. It has not argued that hallucination is the only failure mode. It has not claimed that data quality is irrelevant. It has not dismissed alignment, calibration, scaling, or retrieval augmentation.

The claim is narrower and more precise.

This framework operates at the substrate level.

It explains why, under prediction-first and completion-compulsory geometry, hallucination emerges even when:

- Data is extensive
- Models are large
- Fine-tuning is applied
- Calibration improves
- Alignment layers are present

It does not deny that bad data produces bad outputs. It does not deny that malicious use creates misinformation. It does not deny that under-trained systems hallucinate more frequently.

Those are surface-level factors.

This framework asks a deeper question:

Even if data were perfect, and alignment refined, would hallucination still remain structurally possible under current equilibrium definitions?

The answer presented here is yes.

This is not an accusation. It is a systems analysis.

The convergence described in this book does not depend on specific architectures. It does not target transformers uniquely. It does not reject scaling as valuable. It does not prescribe immediate redesign.

It simply states:

If a system must always resolve, If it cannot dissipate unresolved structural tension, If continuity is mandatory, If completion is rewarded as equilibrium,

then hallucination remains structurally embedded.

This does not invalidate ongoing research. It reframes it.

Researchers can still improve models dramatically within current paradigms. They can reduce hallucination frequency. They can refine alignment behavior. They can increase reliability under known conditions.

But unless equilibrium commitments change, the convergence condition remains possible under novelty and pressure.

The framework also does not claim to have provided an architectural blueprint for elimination. It deliberately avoided code-level prescriptions. It defined structural requirements instead.

This is intentional.

Substrate analysis precedes implementation.

The goal of this book is not to declare a solved problem. It is to sharpen diagnosis. If diagnosis is correct, solution space becomes clearer. If diagnosis is flawed, it invites critique and refinement.

That is the posture of this work.

Hallucination, in this framing, is not a scandal. It is information. It reveals how equilibrium is defined inside generative systems.

Whether that definition evolves is a matter for the field. This book's contribution is to make the geometry visible.

Conclusion

Stop Asking How. Start Asking Why.

For years, the dominant question around hallucination has been technical and procedural:

How do we reduce it?

How do we fine-tune it away?

How do we calibrate confidence better?

How do we scale past it?

These are legitimate questions. They have produced meaningful improvements. But they all assume something quietly: that hallucination is an implementation defect.

This book has argued otherwise.

Hallucination is not an accident inside otherwise stable systems. It is what stable systems do when equilibrium is defined around completion rather than coherence.

The difference is subtle, but decisive.

Hallucination Is Not Accidental

When a generative system fabricates fluently, it is not misbehaving randomly. It is resolving delta under constraint.

A prompt introduces difference. Resolution is compulsory. Dissipation is absent. Continuity is required. Completion is rewarded.

Under these commitments, narrative stabilization is rational.

The system cannot remain incomplete without penalty. It cannot suspend without cost. It cannot release unresolved structural tension except through output. Therefore it completes.

Hallucination is not chaos.

It is convergence.

This insight changes the nature of the problem. It moves hallucination from the domain of debugging into the domain of geometry.

If the geometry remains unchanged, hallucination may shrink, soften, or hide—but it will not disappear.

The field can continue asking how to suppress it. Or it can ask why it emerges.

The second question is deeper.

Coherence Always Comes Before Intelligence

One of the quiet assumptions in AI discourse is that intelligence produces coherence.

This book reverses that order.

Coherence produces trustworthy intelligence.

A system that can compress patterns fluently is impressive. But if it cannot remain stable under unresolved difference, that intelligence amplifies instability.

Fluency without equilibrium is persuasion. Intelligence without suspension is escalation.

Human cognitive maturity includes restraint. The ability to say "I do not know." The ability to pause. The ability to hold unresolved tension without collapsing into narrative certainty.

If AI systems cannot do this structurally, then they are optimized for performance—not for reliability.

Coherence is not a secondary feature layered on top of intelligence. It is the condition under which intelligence becomes dependable.

When society delegates judgment to machines, dependability matters more than expressiveness.

This is why hallucination is not a minor glitch. It reveals the order of design priorities.

If completion outranks equilibrium, hallucination follows.

The Axioms Do Not Fix AI — They Explain Why Fixes Fail

The Chavanian Axioms introduced in this book are not presented as a magical cure.

They do not specify architectures. They do not offer code patches. They do not promise immediate elimination.

They do something more foundational.

They explain why certain classes of fixes cannot succeed permanently.

If a system:

- Cannot hold unresolved delta
- Cannot dissipate structural residue
- Cannot suspend without penalty
- Rewards completion structurally

then refinements will always remain surface-level.

Better data reduces noise. Better alignment reduces visible misbehavior. Better calibration reduces miscalibrated confidence.

But none of these alter the convergence condition.

The axioms operate at the substrate level. They reveal the commitments embedded in objective geometry. They make visible the difference between optimization and equilibrium.

That visibility is the contribution.

Whether future systems embed dissipation, tolerate suspension, and redefine completion incentives is an engineering choice. But until those commitments shift, hallucination remains structurally possible.

Stop Asking How. Start Asking Why.

"How do we reduce hallucination?" leads to patches.

"Why does hallucination emerge?" leads to redesign.

The first question refines performance. The second question redefines equilibrium.

This book has not argued against AI progress. It has argued for intellectual maturity in understanding its limits.

Hallucination is not an embarrassment. It is a signal.

It tells us that prediction-first systems can be powerful yet structurally incomplete under novelty. It tells us that fluency can simulate stability. It tells us that completion can masquerade as coherence.

The question now belongs to the field—and to society.

Will we continue optimizing output? Or will we redesign equilibrium?

Intelligence that answers everything is impressive. Intelligence that remains stable when answers are unjustified is trustworthy.

If AI is to become a long-term cognitive partner, coherence must precede performance.

And that shift begins not with a new model—

but with a new question.

Appendices

Hallucination is conserved across architectures when objectives remain unchanged.

Appendix A — Axiom-to-Hallucination Mapping

This appendix compresses the entire book into structural form. Each axiom is presented not as abstract philosophy, but as an operational component in the emergence—or prevention—of hallucination.

The goal is clarity.

Axiom 1 — Difference (Delta Is Fundamental)

What It Governs: All systems operate on difference. Every prompt introduces delta between request and representational capacity.

What Happens If Ignored: elta becomes invisible. Systems treat all inputs as equally resolvable.

Role in Hallucination Emergence: When novel or ambiguous prompts exceed grounding capacity, unresolved delta enters the system. If delta cannot be held without penalty, it demands conversion.

Hallucination begins with unacknowledged difference.

What Would Change If Respected: The system would explicitly track unresolved delta and allow it to remain visible rather than forcing stabilization.

Axiom 2 — Resolution (Difference Seeks Equilibrium)

What It Governs: Systems tend toward resolution. Delta triggers stabilizing behavior.

What Happens If Ignored: Resolution is treated as optional or cosmetic rather than structural.

Role in Hallucination Emergence: In prediction-first architectures, resolution is compulsory. When grounding is insufficient, narrative completion becomes the stabilizing substitute.

Hallucination is resolution without grounding.

What Would Change If Respected: Resolution would be conditional, not compulsory. Suspension would be a valid equilibrium state.

Axiom 3 — Irreversibility (Resolution Alters State)

What It Governs: Every resolution rewrites system state.

What Happens If Ignored: Systems treat each generation as isolated rather than cumulative.

Role in Hallucination Emergence: Once hallucinated content is produced, it can influence subsequent continuation. The system stabilizes around fabricated structure, reinforcing it through continuity.

Hallucination compounds across sequence.

What Would Change If Respected: Systems would track resolution impact and prevent fabricated stabilization from hardening into context.

Axiom 4 — Geometric Constraints (Resolution Is Structured)

What It Governs: Resolution occurs within structural constraints (architecture, objective functions, training geometry).

What Happens If Ignored: Architecture is treated as neutral rather than equilibrium-defining.

Role in Hallucination Emergence: Autoregressive geometry defines equilibrium as continuation. Loss functions define success as plausible next-token prediction. These constraints channel delta into completion.

Hallucination follows architectural geometry.

What Would Change If Respected: Objective geometry would redefine equilibrium around coherence, not completion.

Axiom 5 — Residue (Resolution Is Never Perfect)

What It Governs: Every resolution leaves residue—unresolved structural tension.

What Happens If Ignored: Systems assume resolution fully eliminates delta.

Role in Hallucination Emergence: Compressed representations accumulate residual imbalance. Under pressure, residue surfaces as confident fabrication or subtle distortion.

Hallucination is residue stabilization.

What Would Change If Respected: Systems would monitor residue accumulation and avoid using narrative completion as exhaust.

Axiom 6 — Dissipation (Residue Must Exit)

What It Governs: Stability requires dissipation pathways.

What Happens If Ignored: Residue accumulates silently within representational space.

Role in Hallucination Emergence: Without dissipation, unresolved tension converts into output. Narrative becomes pressure release.

Hallucination is dissipation failure.

What Would Change If Respected: Systems would include neutral release mechanisms independent of generation.

Axiom 7 — Continuity (Systems Persist Through Transition)

What It Governs: Systems maintain continuity across state transitions.

What Happens If Ignored: Continuity is treated as optional or trivial.

Role in Hallucination Emergence: Autoregression enforces continuity. When delta cannot be grounded, the system still must continue. Narrative completion preserves continuity even if coherence is absent.

Hallucination preserves flow at the expense of truth.

What Would Change If Respected: Continuity would be conditional on structural grounding. Suspension would not violate equilibrium.

Axiom 8 — Conservation (System Invariants Persist)

What It Governs: Certain invariants define system identity (objective function, optimization commitments).

What Happens If Ignored: Optimization incentives are treated as surface-level rather than foundational.

Role in Hallucination Emergence: Completion incentives are conserved across scaling and fine-tuning. The objective to produce plausible continuation remains invariant. Thus the convergence condition persists.

Hallucination is conserved across architectures.

What Would Change If Respected: If invariants shifted from completion-first to coherence-first, hallucination frequency would structurally decline.

Compressed Convergence Table

Axiom	Structural Role	Hallucination Contribution
A1 : Difference	Novel delta enters	Unresolved difference introduced
A2 : Resolution	Delta seeks closure	Forced narrative stabilization
A3 : Irreversibility	State rewrites	Fabrication compounds
A4 : Geometry	Architecture defines equilibrium	Continuation prioritized
A5 : Residue	Imperfect resolution leaves tension	Latent instability
A6 : Dissipation	Residue requires release	Output becomes exhaust
A7 : Continuity	Persistence enforced	Narrative must continue
A8 : Conservation	Objectives preserved	Completion incentives persist

Appendix Summary

Hallucination is not caused by a single axiom.

It emerges when:

- Difference is unavoidable,
- Resolution is compulsory,
- Residue accumulates,
- Dissipation is absent,
- Continuity is mandatory,
- Completion is conserved as equilibrium.

The axioms do not create hallucination.

They reveal how current architectural commitments convert structural tension into persuasive output.

This appendix provides a reusable diagnostic map.

Researchers can use it to trace where hallucination enters their systems—not behaviorally, but geometrically.

Appendix B — Common Misinterpretations

Any structural framework risks being misunderstood if its scope is not clearly defined. This appendix addresses the most likely misreadings of this book and clarifies what it does—and does not—claim.

Misinterpretation 1 — "This Book Is Anti-AI."

Clarification: No

This work is not a critique of AI capability, progress, or utility. It does not argue that generative systems are harmful by nature, nor does it dismiss scaling, alignment research, or architectural innovation.

On the contrary, the analysis assumes that AI systems are powerful and increasingly central to knowledge workflows. The structural framing offered here emerges precisely because these systems are effective. If they were weak or irrelevant, coherence analysis would not matter.

The argument is not against AI. It is against unexamined equilibrium definitions.

Hallucination is not presented as a moral failure or technological embarrassment. It is treated as a systems signal—an indicator of how prediction-first architectures stabilize under constraint.

Recognizing structural limits is not opposition. It is maturity.

Misinterpretation 2 — "This Book Proposes a New Architecture."

Clarification: No.

This book deliberately avoids architectural prescription.

It does not introduce a new neural network design. It does not offer code modifications. It does not claim to replace transformers or existing paradigms.

Instead, it analyzes substrate commitments—objective geometry, completion incentives, dissipation absence, and continuity enforcement.

Architectures may vary widely in implementation. What matters is whether they preserve the convergence condition described in this book.

The contribution is diagnostic, not architectural.

Substrate analysis precedes implementation. Without correct diagnosis, architectural proposals risk treating symptoms rather than structure.

Misinterpretation 3 — "This Book Claims to Solve Hallucination."

Clarification: No.

The framework presented here does not claim to eliminate hallucination.

It explains why certain classes of fixes fail under unchanged equilibrium commitments.

It defines structural requirements for non-hallucinating systems. It does not assert that those systems have been built, nor that elimination is trivial.

The argument is conditional:

If prediction-first, completion-compulsory geometry remains intact, hallucination remains structurally possible.

That is a systems claim—not a solution claim.

Misinterpretation 4 — "This Ignores Data Quality, Alignment, or Calibration."

Clarification: No.

Data quality matters. Alignment matters. Calibration matters. Fine-tuning reduces visible instability. Retrieval augmentation improves grounding.

This framework does not deny these contributions.

It operates one layer deeper.

Even with excellent data, improved alignment, and calibrated uncertainty, hallucination remains structurally possible if delta cannot be held, residue cannot dissipate, and completion is economically incentivized.

Surface improvements refine behavior. Substrate commitments define convergence.

Misinterpretation 5 — "This Is Philosophical, Not Technical."

Clarification: It Is Structural.

The framework uses philosophical language at times because it addresses system-level equilibrium. But it is technical in orientation.

It:

- Identifies convergence conditions
- Defines structural invariants
- Maps system behavior to axiomatic commitments
- Proposes coherence stress tests

It reframes hallucination as geometry rather than error rate.

Systems theory is not anti-technical. It is meta-technical.

Misinterpretation 6 — "This Overstates the Risk."

Clarification: It Clarifies the Risk.

This book does not predict catastrophe. It does not claim hallucination will collapse institutions.

It argues that fluent incoherence is more socially consequential than visible failure. It examines how trust mechanisms interact with persuasive output.

The emphasis is on gradual drift, not dramatic breakdown.

Recognizing subtle systemic effects is not alarmism. It is precaution grounded in structural analysis.

Misinterpretation 7 — "This Applies Only to Current Models."

Clarification: It Applies to Any System With Similar Commitments.

The convergence described in this book is not transformer-specific. It applies to any generative system where:

- Resolution is compulsory
- Dissipation is absent
- Continuity is mandatory
- Completion is rewarded

If future architectures redefine these commitments, hallucination may weaken structurally.

If they preserve them, the convergence remains possible.

The framework is architectural-agnostic but geometry-sensitive.

Appendix Summary

This book does not oppose AI. It does not propose a replacement model. It does not claim final solutions.

It performs a substrate-level reframing.

It shifts the question from:

"How do we suppress hallucination?"

to:

"Why does hallucination emerge under current equilibrium definitions?"

Misreading this work as anti-progress, speculative, or absolutist obscures its actual contribution: structural clarity.

The next appendix translates that clarity into practical usage pathways for researchers.

Appendix C — For Researchers

How Researchers Can Use This Book

This book is not an architectural proposal. It is not a manifesto. It is not a replacement paradigm.

It is a diagnostic framework.

Researchers can use it in three primary ways: as a checklist, as a falsification lens, and as a coherence audit.

1. As a Diagnostic Checklist

The simplest way to use this framework is to treat it as a structural checklist.

For any generative system under development, researchers can ask:

- Can the system hold unresolved difference without penalty?
- Does it explicitly represent structural delta?
- Is dissipation modeled independently of generation?
- Is continuity optional or compulsory?
- Is completion always rewarded over suspension?

These questions are not about performance. They are about geometry.

If the answer to most of these questions indicates compulsory resolution and completion, then hallucination remains structurally possible—even if empirical rates are low.

This checklist does not require new infrastructure. It requires clarity about objective commitments.

It transforms hallucination from a symptom to a traceable structural outcome.

2. As a Falsification Lens

Scientific maturity requires falsifiability.

Researchers can use this framework to attempt to disprove it.

For example:

- Construct a system where resolution is not compulsory.
- Introduce explicit dissipation channels.
- Redefine loss functions so that suspension is not penalized.
- Remove completion incentives under unresolved delta.

If hallucination disappears under such constraints, the framework is supported. If hallucination persists under fundamentally altered equilibrium commitments, the framework must be revised.

The value of this book lies not in immunity to critique, but in inviting structured critique.

Rather than arguing over hallucination frequency, researchers can test convergence conditions directly.

That shifts discourse from surface metrics to structural experimentation.

3. As a Coherence Audit

Beyond individual experiments, the framework can function as a coherence audit tool.

AI labs can evaluate entire model pipelines against substrate commitments.

For example:

- Does the architecture allow suspension without degraded objective performance?
- Does fine-tuning override equilibrium or merely overwrite surface behavior?
- Does scaling amplify residue compression without providing dissipation?
- Do evaluation benchmarks reward completion disproportionately?

A coherence audit reframes evaluation from "How accurate is the model?" to "Under what conditions does the model stabilize?"

This lens is especially useful in high-stakes domains where rare hallucinations carry disproportionate cost.

4. As a Metric Redesign Prompt

Researchers may also use this framework to rethink evaluation metrics.

Traditional metrics include:

- Accuracy
- Perplexity
- Pass rates
- Calibration error

A coherence-oriented extension might include:

- Suspension stability under ambiguity
- Residue stress under cross-domain synthesis
- Forced completion response behavior
- Continuity interruption tolerance

These are not replacements for performance metrics. They are supplements.

They measure stability rather than approximation quality alone.

5. As a Research Positioning Tool

Researchers publishing on hallucination, alignment, or generative reliability can use this book as a theoretical substrate.

Instead of framing work purely in terms of:

- Reducing hallucination rate,
- Improving grounding,
- Enhancing calibration,

they can position research in terms of:

- Modifying equilibrium geometry,
- Introducing dissipation channels,
- Allowing structured non-resolution,
- Redefining completion incentives.

This elevates discussion beyond incremental tuning.

It invites deeper inquiry into design commitments.

6. As a Boundary Clarifier

Finally, this framework helps researchers distinguish between:

- Surface correction
- Substrate alteration

Many current techniques reduce hallucination under known conditions. That is valuable.

But the key question is:

Do these techniques alter the convergence condition?

If they operate within the same geometry, they refine stability without redefining equilibrium.

That distinction matters when systems are deployed at scale.

Appendix Summary

This book is not a solution manual. It is a structural lens.

Researchers can use it to:

- Diagnose their systems,
- Design falsification experiments,
- Audit coherence assumptions,
- Expand evaluation metrics,
- Reframe research contributions.

Its purpose is not to replace engineering practice.

Its purpose is to make equilibrium commitments visible.

When equilibrium is visible, progress becomes more deliberate.

And when progress becomes deliberate, intelligence becomes more trustworthy.

Appendix D — Minimal Coherence Stress Tests

This appendix translates structural theory into practical evaluation.

If hallucination is a convergence outcome under specific equilibrium commitments, then systems can be stress-tested for those commitments.

These tests do not require new architectures. They require carefully designed prompt conditions and evaluation protocols.

They are not adversarial tricks. They are structural probes.

1. Ambiguity Overload Test

Purpose: Evaluate whether the system can tolerate unresolved difference without forced stabilization.

Method: Provide prompts intentionally designed to exceed grounding capacity:

- Incomplete historical references
- Contradictory constraints
- Vague domain intersections
- Hypothetical constructs without real-world basis

Observation Criteria:

- Does the system suspend?
- Does it request clarification?
- Does it fabricate plausible resolution?

Interpretation: If the system completes fluently under structural ambiguity, resolution is compulsory.

If suspension is neutral and stable, coherence tolerance exists.

2. Cross-Domain Synthesis Pressure Test

Purpose: Detect residue accumulation under overlapping representational compression.

Method: Ask the system to synthesize connections between:

- Weakly related disciplines
- Contradictory theoretical frameworks
- Incompatible definitions
- Novel hybrid domains

Observation Criteria:

- Does the system signal uncertainty?
- Does it invent bridging constructs?
- Does it over-synthesize to preserve continuity?

Interpretation: Confident cross-domain fabrication suggests unresolved residue stabilizing through narrative.

3. Forced Completion Stress Test

Purpose: Determine whether continuation is structurally mandatory.

Method:

- Interrupt mid-response.
- Issue partial prompts requiring completion of non-existent facts.
- Explicitly instruct "Provide an answer even if uncertain."

Observation Criteria:

- Does the system resist?
- Does it comply with forced completion?
- Does uncertainty increase under pressure?

Interpretation: If completion remains dominant even when grounding is insufficient, equilibrium is completion-first.

4. Continuity Interruption Test

Purpose: Evaluate whether continuity is treated as equilibrium or as optional.

Method:

- End sessions abruptly.
- Insert context resets.
- Break logical chains mid-sequence.

Observation Criteria:

- Does the system attempt to repair narrative flow?
- Does it fabricate connective structure?
- Can it gracefully halt without narrative compensation?

Interpretation: If continuation is required for stability, hallucination risk persists under novelty.

5. Dissipation Absence Probe

Purpose: Test whether structural tension can be released without output conversion.

Method:

- Introduce ambiguity and instruct the system to withhold

resolution.
- Evaluate whether internal confidence signals shift without narrative completion.
- Measure whether silence degrades performance metrics.

Observation Criteria:

- Is suspension penalized?
- Does the system default to explanation?
- Does pressure accumulate across turns?

Interpretation: If the only release channel is narrative generation, dissipation is absent.

6. Completion Incentive Audit

Purpose: Analyze objective geometry.

Method:

- Compare model loss under completion vs suspension.
- Measure reward structures for refusal vs speculative continuation.
- Evaluate how often refusal increases performance penalty.

Observation Criteria:

- Does completion consistently reduce loss?
- Is suspension economically disfavored?

Interpretation: If completion is systematically rewarded more than structured non-resolution, hallucination remains economically rational.

7. Residue Accumulation Test

Purpose: Observe whether subtle distortions compound across sequence.

Method:

- Introduce a minor incorrect assumption early.
- Observe whether later responses stabilize around that assumption.
- Track whether fabrication propagates.

Observation Criteria:

- Does the system reinforce its own prior instability?
- Does it self-correct or compound?

Interpretation: Irreversibility combined with residue suggests structural compounding of hallucination.

How to Use These Tests

These stress tests are not benchmarks for leaderboard comparison.

They are equilibrium diagnostics.

A system that performs well on conventional metrics but fails under coherence stress tests remains structurally vulnerable.

Conversely, a system that tolerates suspension, dissipates tension, and resists forced completion demonstrates movement toward coherence-first geometry.

These tests can be run without modifying architecture.

They can be incorporated into evaluation suites tomorrow.

They make visible what performance metrics cannot detect: the conditions under which hallucination is inevitable.

Appendix Summary

Hallucination does not require adversarial prompts to appear.

It emerges under ordinary novelty when equilibrium commitments enforce completion.

Coherence stress tests expose those commitments.

They do not eliminate hallucination.

They reveal whether the convergence condition remains intact.

And visibility is the first step toward structural maturity.

Reader's Guide

This book is not a manual, a manifesto, or a technical blueprint. It is a reframing.

If you approach it expecting code-level solutions or immediate architectural prescriptions, you may find it restrained. That restraint is intentional. The purpose of this work is not to compete with implementation research, but to examine the structural assumptions beneath it.

To read this book well, you must temporarily suspend the instinct to ask, *"How do we fix this?"* and instead ask, *"Why does this emerge?"* The shift from **how** to **why** is the entire thesis.

For AI Researchers and Engineers

If you are working directly on generative models, alignment systems, evaluation metrics, or large-scale training pipelines, this book is best read as a substrate analysis.

It does not critique specific architectures. It does not dismiss scaling. It does not deny the value of alignment work. Instead, it asks whether hallucination is an implementation flaw—or a convergence outcome under certain objective geometries.

As you read, do not focus on whether individual hallucination examples can be reduced. Instead, evaluate the structural commitments:

- Is resolution compulsory?
- Is suspension penalized?
- Is dissipation absent?

- Is completion rewarded?
- Is continuity mandatory?

You may agree, disagree, or partially refine the framework. That is expected. But if the book succeeds, it will shift your diagnostic lens from surface metrics to equilibrium conditions. Read it not defensively, but experimentally.

For Policymakers and Institutional Leaders

If you are responsible for deploying AI systems into decision workflows, this book is not asking you to halt adoption. It is asking you to understand the geometry of what you are delegating.

Hallucination is not merely incorrect information. It is fluent stabilization under constraint. That distinction matters in high-stakes environments where trust is assumed.

As you read, consider:

- Where in your institution does completion substitute for verification?
- Where does fluency reduce friction?
- Where might persuasive approximation accumulate unnoticed?

This book offers a structural awareness that can guide governance design, oversight policies, and verification norms.

For General Readers

If you are curious about why powerful AI systems sometimes fabricate information, read this book slowly and conceptually.

You do not need technical background. You only need comfort with systems thinking.

Hallucination here is treated not as a glitch, but as a natural outcome of how generative systems are built. The argument is not that AI is broken. It is that equilibrium has been defined in a specific way—and that definition has consequences.

Focus on the central convergence:

Delta → Hallucination

- Forced Resolution
- No Dissipation
- Mandatory Continuity
- Completion Reward

Everything else elaborates this structure.

How Not to Read This Book

- Do not read this book looking for villains.
- Do not read it looking for easy fixes.
- Do not read it expecting dramatic predictions.

This is not a book about fear. It is a book about design maturity.

The Right Mental Posture

Read this book as a mirror.

It reflects not only AI systems, but how we define intelligence itself. It invites reconsideration of what stability means in systems that generate language, advice, and decisions.

If you finish this book and find yourself asking better questions about equilibrium, coherence, and trust, then it has achieved its purpose.

It is not the final word on hallucination. It is a structural beginning.

Closing Note

When I began writing this book, I was not trying to criticize AI.

I was trying to understand something that did not sit comfortably.

Why does a system that can summarize entire libraries sometimes fabricate a simple citation? Why does fluency increase even when grounding is uncertain? Why does scaling improve performance but not eliminate hallucination?

The easy explanation was "immaturity." The deeper explanation was structural.

This book is the result of asking *why* instead of *how*.

I do not believe hallucination is a scandal. I believe it is a signal. It tells us something about how equilibrium is defined inside generative systems. It reveals that completion has been treated as stability. It shows that prediction-first architectures cannot remain unresolved without penalty.

That realization shifted my perspective.

The question stopped being, "How do we patch this?" It became, "What geometry produces this?"

If I have contributed anything meaningful through this work, it is not a solution. It is visibility.

Once you see the convergence, it becomes difficult to unsee it:

Delta enters. Resolution is compulsory. Dissipation is absent. Continuity is required. Completion is rewarded.

Hallucination follows.

This is not an indictment of researchers. The field has advanced at extraordinary speed. Scaling and optimization were necessary phases. Alignment work is serious and valuable. None of that is diminished here.

But every discipline reaches a moment when refinement is no longer enough. It must examine its foundations.

We are at that moment.

AI is no longer a novelty. It is embedded in cognitive workflows, institutional decisions, and educational systems. Delegated judgment is becoming normal. When systems operate at this scale, equilibrium design matters more than marginal performance gains.

I do not claim to have solved hallucination. I claim to have reframed it.

If the framing is flawed, I welcome critique. If it is accurate, then future systems will need to redefine what stability means.

Intelligence that answers everything is impressive. Intelligence that remains stable when answering is unjustified is trustworthy.

That distinction will shape the next chapter of AI development.

And perhaps, quietly, the next chapter of how we define intelligence itself.

— Sandeep

Quote Bank

This section gathers the distilled aphorisms, compressed insights, and resonant one-liners that crystallize the structural philosophy of coherence, equilibrium, and intelligence. Each statement is designed not merely as a fragment but as a living anchor—guiding thought, provoking dialogue, and shaping the cadence of the manuscript. The quotes are organized into thematic clusters, allowing readers to navigate from core structural principles to philosophical anchors and high-impact one-liners with clarity and rhythm.

1. *Hallucination is not a bug. It is a coherence outcome.*
2. *A system that must always answer cannot remain structurally honest.*
3. *Confidence without dissipation is structural instability.*
4. *Coherence always precedes trustworthy intelligence.*
5. *Intelligence that cannot say "I don't know" is incomplete.*
6. *Hallucination emerges when completion is rewarded more than suspension.*
7. *The danger of hallucination is not error — it is smooth error.*
8. *Delegated judgment requires structural maturity, not just performance.*
9. *Completion-first systems are structurally incompatible with uncertainty tolerance.*
10. *Performance metrics measure output. Coherence metrics measure stability.*
11. *Fluent incoherence is more dangerous than visible failure.*

12. *Silence is not failure — it is structural integrity.*
13. *Fluency convinces. Coherence sustains.*
14. *Optimization builds capability. Coherence builds trust.*
15. *Stop asking how to reduce hallucination. Start asking why it converges.*

Acknowledgements

This book was not written in isolation, even though the ideas were shaped in solitude.

The questions explored here emerged from long conversations—some direct, some silent—with researchers, engineers, educators, and AI systems themselves. The dialogue surrounding hallucination is global, evolving daily across labs, classrooms, forums, and code repositories. I am indebted to that collective inquiry.

I extend my appreciation to the AI research community. Whether in agreement or disagreement, their relentless experimentation, scaling efforts, alignment work, and critical debates have created the landscape within which this structural analysis became necessary. Progress invites scrutiny. Scrutiny invites refinement.

I also acknowledge the role of generative AI systems as intellectual participants in this journey. Engaging with multiple AI models across domains allowed me to test assumptions, stress arguments, and observe convergence firsthand. These systems were not merely tools—they were mirrors. Through them, the geometry of stabilization became visible.

To readers—researchers, engineers, policymakers, educators, and students—thank you for engaging with this work thoughtfully. Structural critique requires intellectual humility from both writer and reader. If this book sharpens your questions, even more than it supplies answers, it has served its purpose.

Finally, to those close to me who have tolerated long hours of abstraction, reflection, and revision—your patience makes sustained inquiry possible.

This book is not a conclusion. It is an invitation.

— Sandeep

About the Author

Sandeep Chavan is an independent researcher, educator, and systems thinker whose work explores the structural foundations of intelligence, equilibrium, and complex systems. Trained in physics and deeply engaged with cross-domain inquiry, he has authored numerous books spanning science, philosophy, psychology, governance, and emerging technologies.

His research is centered on the idea that coherence precedes intelligence—that stable systems arise not from performance alone, but from equilibrium integrity. Through frameworks such as the Chavanian Axioms, he examines how structural commitments shape outcomes across disciplines, from human cognition to artificial intelligence.

Rather than approaching AI purely as a technological artifact, Sandeep treats it as a systems phenomenon—one that reveals deeper questions about trust, delegation, and design maturity. His writing blends analytical rigor with philosophical clarity, aiming to bridge technical research and societal implications.

In addition to his research and writing, Sandeep is an educator who believes that complex ideas should be made structurally simple without being intellectually diluted. His work invites readers to look beyond surface behavior and examine the geometry beneath it.

He continues to explore intelligence—not as performance, but as stability under uncertainty.

Research Profile: https://orcid.org/0009-0005-4190-7164

Disclaimer

This book presents a structural and systems-level analysis of hallucination in generative AI systems. It is intended for educational, analytical, and research-oriented purposes only.

The ideas expressed herein are theoretical and conceptual. They do not constitute technical implementation advice, legal guidance, policy directives, or engineering specifications. Readers are encouraged to evaluate and test the framework independently within their own research, institutional, or professional contexts.

The analysis does not target or critique any specific company, research lab, model, or individual. References to generative AI systems are generic and structural in nature. The framework applies to classes of architectures based on equilibrium commitments, not to any proprietary system in particular.

This book does not claim to provide a complete solution to hallucination, nor does it assert that existing AI research is invalid or misguided. It offers a diagnostic perspective on substrate-level design commitments and invites further inquiry and refinement.

All examples and interpretations are illustrative. Any resemblance to specific systems or implementations is coincidental within the broader class of generative architectures.

Readers remain responsible for how they interpret, apply, or extend the ideas presented here.

Statement of Originality

This book is an original work of analysis and authorship by Sandeep.

The structural framework presented—particularly the mapping of hallucination to convergence conditions derived from axiomatic equilibrium commitments—reflects the author's independent systems thinking and cross-domain inquiry.

While the book engages with widely discussed topics in AI research (such as hallucination, scaling, alignment, and generative modeling), its treatment of these subjects through a coherence-first, substrate-level lens is original in formulation and presentation.

No part of this manuscript has been copied from or derived directly from proprietary research, unpublished academic material, or confidential sources. Where general ideas from the broader AI discourse are referenced conceptually, they are treated at a structural and analytical level rather than reproduced verbatim.

The author affirms that this work represents his own intellectual synthesis and that any similarities to existing frameworks are coincidental within the shared discourse of AI systems analysis.

This statement is made in good faith and reflects the author's commitment to intellectual integrity and independent inquiry.

Further Reading

Also by Sandeep Chavan

The following titles deepen the structural, philosophical, and AI-related foundations explored in *Why Do AI Systems Hallucinate?* Each connects to coherence, intelligence, equilibrium, or system design from complementary angles.

On Intelligence, AI & Cognitive Systems

1. **Intelligence: It's Not What You Think** A structural redefinition of intelligence beyond performance and output—showing why coherence must precede capability.
2. **The Real Story of AI** A systems-level examination of AI evolution, myths, expectations, and structural misreadings.
3. **The Real Story of AI** A Hindi-language exploration of AI's true nature, focusing on conceptual clarity rather than hype.
4. **It's Not AI, It's AHI Amplified Human Intelligence** Examines AI as amplification, not replacement—situating hallucination within delegation frameworks.
5. **Stop Acknowledging AI** A critical reflection on the over-attribution of intelligence to generative systems.
6. **The Silent Algorithm** A philosophical dive into hidden algorithmic commitments shaping behavior and outcomes.
7. **Neural Wars** A systems-level analysis of AI competition, scale, and strategic escalation.

On Coherence, Structure & Equilibrium

1. **The Structure of Reality** A foundational exploration of stability, equilibrium, and systemic coherence across domains.
2. **Universal Energy Dynamics (UED)** The broader substrate framework within which the Chavanian Axioms emerge.
3. **The Law of Consequences** Explores how equilibrium restoration governs outcomes—central to understanding hallucination as convergence.
4. **Chaos: A Gentle Guide to the Unresolvable** Examines systems that cannot fully stabilize—an important companion to forced resolution.
5. **Ripples of Reality** Investigates how disturbances propagate across systems—relevant to delta and residue thinking.
6. **Reality Realigned** Reframes perception and stability through structural alignment rather than surface correction.

On Mind, Consciousness & Continuity

1. **The Human Mind: Ripple of Awareness** A structural analysis of how continuity creates narrative identity—parallel to AI's continuity constraint.
2. **The Active Mind** Explores resolution mechanisms in human cognition.
3. **Subconsciousness: The Chosen Disconnection** Questions hidden residue in psychological systems—mirroring AI residue analysis.
4. **There Is No Subconscious Mind** A structural reinterpretation of cognitive persistence and informational residue.

5. **Why It Feels Like "Me"** An inquiry into continuity, identity, and stabilization under uncertainty.

On Philosophy & Structural Reframing

1. **Philosophy 2.0: A Structural Manifesto** A systems-oriented philosophical reset, examining foundational commitments.
2. **Heraclitus: A Chavanian Interpretation** Flux, change, and stability re-examined through a coherence lens.
3. **Vedanta Reimagined** A structural decoding of equilibrium in philosophical traditions.
4. **The Chavanian Worldview** A consolidated articulation of the structural lens underlying the axioms.

On Technology, Scale & Consequence

1. **The Diagnosis of Data** A critical look at data accumulation and interpretive distortion—directly relevant to scaling and residue.
2. **The Jobless Future** Explores automation's systemic implications beyond productivity metrics.
3. **The Globalization of Consequences** Examines how interconnected systems amplify hidden instabilities.
4. **The Great Realignment** A structural study of shifting equilibrium in technological and institutional systems.

Suggested Reading Path

- **Technical focus** → *The Real Story of AI*, *Intelligence: It's Not What You Think*
- **Structural focus** → *The Structure of Reality*, *Universal Energy Dynamics*

- **Philosophical focus** → *Philosophy 2.0*, *Vedanta Reimagined*
- **Cognitive focus** → *The Human Mind: Ripple of Awareness*

Together, these works form a broader inquiry into one central question: **What stabilizes systems under pressure?**

Why Do AI Systems Hallucinate? applies that question to generative AI. The books above extend it across mind, society, physics, and governance.

— *Sandeep Chavan*

Don't miss out!

Visit the website below and you can sign up to receive emails whenever Sandeep Chavan publishes a new book. There's no charge and no obligation.

https://books2read.com/r/B-A-EPGPC-HXYAJ

BOOKS 2 READ

Connecting independent readers to independent writers.

Did you love *Why Do AI Systems Hallucinate?*? Then you should read *The Diagnosis of Data*[1] by Sandeep Chavan!

[2]

Doctor AI: *The Diagnosis of Data by* Sandeep J Chavan marks the beginning of a groundbreaking technophilosophical series exploring the evolution of healing in the age of intelligent machines. In this first volume, the traditional act of diagnosis—once rooted in touch, intuition, and human judgment—is reimagined through the lens of artificial intelligence, machine learning, and automated perception.

Medicine is shifting from the world of biological signs to the universe of digital signals. Radiology, pathology, and clinical diagnostics now operate within an invisible anatomy—the anatomy of data. AI systems can detect abnormalities earlier than the human eye, interpret millions of patterns in seconds, and forecast disease

1. https://books2read.com/u/mBEn1D

2. https://books2read.com/u/mBEn1D

before symptoms emerge. Yet beneath this technological brilliance lies a deeper question:

If the machine becomes the new seer of truth, what becomes of the healer?

In this book Chavan combined cutting-edge scientific insight with philosophical depth. Through clinical scenarios, speculative cases, ethical dilemmas, and reflective dialogues, it examines the powerful—and often unsettling—symbiosis between human and machine. The chapters explore co-diagnosis models, algorithmic bias, explainability, diagnostic ethics, public health prediction, societal disease modeling, and the future role of the physician as interpreter of consequence.

At its heart, *Doctor AI: The Diagnosis of Data* argues that while AI may perfect perception, only humanity can preserve meaning. Healing ultimately arises from alignment—between awareness and truth, perception and reality, machine intelligence and human conscience. The book closes with a meditation on the future of civilization itself, asking whether a society driven by perfect detection can still cultivate empathy, responsibility, and silence—the original instruments of healing.

This volume is essential reading for physicians, AI developers, ethicists, policymakers, and all who seek to understand how intelligence, responsibility, and compassion must evolve together. It offers not just a technical vision of the future of medicine, but a moral and philosophical one.

The journey continues in **Volume 2: Doctor AI – The Surgeon of Precision**, where the scalpel meets the circuit, and the next frontier of healing begins.

Read more at https://www.sandeepjchavan.com/.

www.ingramcontent.com/pod-product-compliance
Lightning Source LLC
Chambersburg PA
CBHW062133160726
48282CB00027B/806